Reinventing Schools, Reforming Teaching

'This is a terrif   It asks the question: how can bad policy be formulated by so many, for so long, ov   sive governments? If we are ever to learn how to improve schools and enhance the pr   of teaching we must look at the mistakes of the past, so well documented here, a   ssons from them.'

David Berliner, Professor Emeritus, Arizona State University, USA

'A ripping g   enefitting from extensive research amongst the main actors responsible for shaping   landscape over the last twenty years. The authors have constructed a compellin   r   ailing with the tortuous and sometimes convoluted route pursued by education p   and civil servants over the last two decades. The book provides both original insig   ligent commentary.'

Sir William Atkinson, Headteacher Phoenix High School,
Hammersmith and Fulham, UK

'Those now   th shaping education policy should read this book! I love the well-docume   gives to the importance of teachers. It is teachers who deliver and determ   ucation, and it is to them politicians must turn as they look for a way to rai   pu

Baroness Pauline Perry, Conservative politician and former
Her Majesty's Chief Inspector, UK

'F   anyone in   n how government really works and the myriad of factors that go into making policy,   ook offers a treasure trove of insights based on candid commentary from those who were r   ly there. It should be read by everyone who wants to understand education policy, whether i   England or beyond.'

Be   Levin, Professor and Canada Research Chair in Education Leadership and
Policy Deputy Minister of Education for Ontario, Canada

'A must read for anyone who is interested in an empirical look at the long-term effects of educational policy at a national level. The nuanced reflections of those who participated in policy and those who experienced the consequences of policy make this book timely not only for England, but also for every other country that is struggling to improve education.'

Karen Seashore, University of Minnesota, US

D0235135

What lessons can we learn from the relationship between policy makers and schools over the life of the 'New' Labour and its predecessor Conservative government? What happened to 'Education, Education, Education' as it travelled from political vision to classroom practice? What are the lasting legacies of 13 years of a reforming Labour government? And what are the key messages for the coalition government?

These are the questions addressed to the architects of educational reform, their critics and the prophets of better things to come. The 37 interviewees include ministers past and present, journalists, union officials, members of lobby groups and think tanks. *Reinventing Schools, Reforming Teaching* considers the impact of educational policies on those who have to translate political priorities into the day-to-day work of schools and classrooms. The authors argue that an evidence-informed view of policy making has yet to be realised, graphically illustrating how many recent political decisions in education can be explained by the personal experiences, predilections and short-term needs of key decision makers.

The interviews, which explore the dynamics behind the creation of education policies, cover a wide range of themes and issues, including:

- policy makers' attitudes to schools, the staff who work in them and the communities they serve
- the drivers of politicians' reform agendas and the constraints on radical reform
- the shaping and reshaping of curriculum and assessment
- the search for a more effective marriage between inspection and school self-evaluation
- the relationship of academic research to policy making
- how a vision for teaching and teachers might be constructed for the twenty-first century.

Contributions from leading figures including David Puttnam, Kenneth Baker, Estelle Morris, Gillian Shephard, Jim Knight, Pauline Perry, Michael Barber, Peter Mortimore, Judy Sebba, Paul Black, Mary James, Kevan Collins, David Hargreaves, Mike Tomlinson, David Berliner, Andreas Schleicher, Tim Brighouse, Conor Ryan, Keith Bartley, Michael Gove and Philippa Cordingley are woven in with the insights of teachers and headteachers such as Alasdair MacDonald and William Atkinson.

The book's findings and proposals will be of interest not only to professional educators and those with an interest in the current and future state of education but to those interested in the process of policy making itself.

John Bangs was, until 2010, Assistant Secretary in Education, Equality and Professional Development for the National Union of Teachers and is now working with the University of Cambridge, the Institute of Education in London and Education International.

John MacBeath, formerly Director of the Quality in Education Centre at the University of Strathclyde, is Emeritus Professor and Projects Director for the Commonwealth Centre for Education at the University of Cambridge.

Maurice Galton, formerly Dean at Leicester University, is Emeritus Professor and Senior Research Fellow for the Commonwealth Centre for Education at the University of Cambridge.

Reinventing Schools, Reforming Teaching

From political visions to
classroom reality

John Bangs, John MacBeath and
Maurice Galton

LONDON AND NEW YORK

First edition published 2011
by Routledge
2 Park Square, Milton Park, Abingdon, Oxon OX14 4RN

Simultaneously published in the USA and Canada
by Routledge
270 Madison Avenue, New York, NY 10016

Routledge is an imprint of the Taylor & Francis Group, an informa business

Typeset in Garamond by Swales & Willis, Ltd, Exeter, Devon
Printed and bound in Great Britain by TJ International Ltd, Padstow, Cornwall

British Library Cataloguing in Publication Data
A catalogue record for this book is available from the British Library

Library of Congress Cataloging-in-Publication Data
Bangs, John, 1949–
  Reinventing our schools : principles, pedagogy, and policy imperatives /
  John Bangs, Maurice Galton, and John MacBeath.
    p. cm.
    1. Education and state—Great Britain. 2. Educational change—Great Britain.
  I. Galton, Maurice J. II. MacBeath, John E. C. III. Title.
  LC93.G7B36 2011
  379.41—dc22
  2010017599

ISBN13: 978–0–415–56133–4 (hbk)
ISBN13: 978–0–415–56134–1 (pbk)
ISBN13: 978–0–203–84034–4 (ebk)

Contents

Preface

The end of schools as we know them has been much exaggerated. Their demise was forecast as new technologies and 'convivial alternatives' brought with them the promise of a brave new deschooled world. Yet the essential architecture of schools has remained stubbornly resilient despite continuous re-invention, but it is one that never strays far from the original archetype. As the Newsom boy said, somewhat presciently in 1963, 'it could be all glass and marble, sir, it's still a bloody school'.

In the weeks running up to a general election when this book was being written, political parties were full or promise – of reform which would transform the educational landscape, portents of schools run by parents, radical curriculum change, aspirations for schools to be for all children, the 'citadels of hope', described in the Cambridge Primary Review. 'Whenever you have a new government, people start off with zeal, enthusiasm and idealism', confessed Michael Gove, then Conservative shadow minister, a few weeks before embarking on his own party's election campaign. Yet the unspoken message behind his comment is that the bold rhetoric of reform inevitably bumps up against the unpleasant realities of compromise and vested interest, although the full nature of compromise, still unimagined and unmanageable.

Nor could those who greeted the incoming Labour government in 1997 have foreseen the path it would take or foreseen the gradual attrition of its bold promise. Whatever happened to the euphoria that greeted 'New' Labour thirteen years ago? Why did disappointment among those who were directly expected to carry out Labour's reforms-the teaching profession – set in so quickly after the election? Why, despite its reforming zeal, its unprecedented investment and its signal achievements, might its final report have read – 'Tried hard but could have done better'? You can mandate 'awful' to 'adequate', but you cannot mandate 'good' to 'great', said Michael Barber, reflecting ruefully perhaps on the failure of government to fulfil its ambitious agenda.

'We should have listened much more,' said Sandy Adamson, a senior civil servant closely involved in setting the policy agenda in the early years of New Labour. While there was listening it was highly selective. Some voices clearly counted while others were marginalised or silenced, particularly by a secretary of state who combined passion for educational change with an intolerance of dissent. His judgment of the impact of the government's impact on education was characteristically blunt – 'We had a crap teaching profession. We haven't any more'. (David Blunkett, in evidence to the Parliamentary Select Committee, January 2010)

It was not a point of view designed to endear him to teachers but it is highly pertinent in raising the question of the relationship between politicians and the profession, between the political voice and the voices of teachers. During his time in ministerial office Stephen Byers wrote to Robin Alexander expressing his welcome for the co-operation of academics but attended by the caveat – only to the degree that they supported government policies.

The big question for government, as it must be for parents and their children, is whether its relationship to teachers, hinders or fosters their effectiveness. Given the expectations that society has of education, it is a question that governments should ask themselves much more than they do.

In this book the story of reinventing schools and reforming teaching is told by the architects of systemic change, by the prophets who foretold a brighter future and by the critics who have tried their best to render a balanced judgment. Each account, gathered over a ten month period from mid-2009 to early 2010, adds piece by piece to the final narrative presented here.

We interviewed a large number of 'actors', some who have occupied centre stage under successive governments, some who provided the script and the prompts, others who watched from the wings or rendered their verdict. Among those centre stage were former Conservative secretaries of state, Kenneth Baker and Gillian Shephard, two former Labour ministers, Estelle Morris and Jim Knight, Pauline Perry, the Conservative's eminence grise behind its public service reforms, Barry Sheerman, chair of the government's Select Committee on Education, and potential ministers in waiting Michael Gove and David Laws. Sandy Adamson, Michael Barber, Kevan Collins, Richard Harrison, Fiona Miller, Conor Ryan, and Mike Tomlinson, provided insights from back stage – from inside government in its many iterations, local as well as national. David Puttnam is someone who defies easy categorization but he brought with him a profound knowledge of direction, stage management and of how to tell the players from the play.

Mick Waters, recently of QCA, Graham Holley of the TDA, and Keith Bartley of the GTC(E) were among those who represented the satellite organizations providing official advice to the government. And speaking for the academics and independent consultants, Robin Alexander, Paul Black, Phillipa Cordingley, Mary James, Peter Mortimore, Bethan Marshall, and Geoff Whitty, together with three witnesses-David Hargreaves, Tim Brighouse and Judy Sebba whose dual identity in academe and the policy arena give them voice as architects, and critics and sometime prophets.

Representing headteachers were William Atkinson, Alasdair Macdonald and Richard Marshall. Viewing policy and practice from a critical distance but nonetheless well versed in the way we do things round here – David Berliner, Karen Seashore and Andreas Schleicher of the OECD, director of the PISA Programme.

For the representatives of the third estate, Richard Garner of the *Independent*, and for the unions, we have our very own co-author, John Bangs, for twenty years the NUT's head of education, Mary Bousted, ATL's general secretary and John Lloyd, in 1997, the AEEU's link with the incoming Labour government.

Their accounts provide what Andre Brink describes in his wonderful book of that title 'A Chain of Voices', each linked to one another, each taking the narrative forward but, as in that book, the story told is never quite the same from one narrator to the next. We are left, tantalizingly perhaps, as the readers of Andre Brink's book, to decide for ourselves what really happened. This book, we hope, gets as close as possible to the reality of 'the way we were' , and the sets the stage for the way we will be under the coalition politics of a new government. We are deeply indebted to all of those in our book, whether or not they were mentioned earlier, who so generously gave of their time and willingness to tell their stories, render their verdict and their hopes for the future.

Acknowledgements

We would like to thank the National Union of Teachers, including its General Secretary Christine Blower, for supporting the production of this book. Special mention should be given to Janet Friedlander, the NUT's Information Officer, who tirelessly tracked down every reference. Thanks too to NUT's Janet Theakston who made sense of much of the 'raw' text and to Katie O' Donovan at the University of Cambridge Faculty of Education who oversaw the page making of the original manuscript. Also thanks to Judith Judd who gave us invaluable help on promoting the book.

A profound thank you to all of those very busy people who gave up their time for an interview lasting often beyond the agreed hour and who were so frank, and sometimes delightfully indiscreet.

1 Architects, critics and prophets

How did schools come to assume their present form and function? How recognisable would schools for the twentieth century be to that ubiquitous time traveller? Who were the ideological architects who bequeathed us forms of curriculum and assessment which have been largely impervious to their critics and often sceptical of the prophets? Can schools be fundamentally re-designed when it is only in opposition that governments seem to offer radical solutions and visionary promise? Is there scope for something completely different in the face of public expectations and media pressures which push elected government relentlessly back to safer, shallower waters?

It is engrained in the fabric of recent history that on a momentous day in 1997 all would be different. On the first of May 1997 education came alive as the top priority for a new government. Without 'Education, Education, Education', the recent history of education policy would have been very different and the impact on the day to day lives of teachers and young people an imponderable. All through the Labour Party's 13 year tenure of office education was to remain a top priority and many of the accomplishments under Blair and Brown were not disputed by Conservatives and Liberal Democrats. However, unlike the United States, education is not a bipartisan issue so that it is often difficult to perceive where the real and enduring successes lie and what the alternatives might have been.

With media's penchant for the dramatic, one of Labour's greatest success slipped under the radar. Raising funding levels for education to the OECD average may seem too unspectacular to report or celebrate but it signalled an intent to realise the promise of the three educations. Indeed one of Gordon Brown's last acts as chancellor in his 2007 Mansion House speech was to call for the funding of each pupil in state schools to rise to £8000 a year to match the current spending for pupils in private schools. In the fragile financial climate at the time such a commitment now seems hugely ambitious, although one of the Brown government's last acts was to legislate targets for ending child poverty. As a result no future government will find it easy to compromise on the priority given by the Labour government to education.

We live in a global community in which education is widely accepted as the medium for economic success. Understanding the processes of education reform is vital in how we evaluate of the triumphs and failures of governments. Even more vital is an understanding of the relationship between those entrusted by governments to provide education – teachers and support staff on the one hand and policy makers on the other.

This book is about that relationship. At its centre are a set of interviews with key people who were, and are, responsible for education policies and educational reform. We are grateful to those interviewees for their honesty and insights, some of which unfortunately we have had to omit both in order to protect the innocent, and the guilty. For every interview, there could have been many more but we hope that those who appear in this book are a reasonably representative cross section of current opinion and historical memory. Their views are complemented by evidence from research, including four studies of primary, secondary and special schools between 2002 and 2009, carried out by two authors of this book, John MacBeath and Maurice Galton, and commissioned by John Bangs for the National Union of Teachers, the book's third author.

The evidence from our interviewees provides a complex mosaic of views, reflecting differing ideological, political and pragmatic standpoints, from inside and outside the 'big tent'. They bring into sharp relief tensions and paradoxes that connect, or fail to connect, the world of classrooms and the world of policy makers. We have sought to be faithful to the emerging narratives and what we believe they imply for school life and learning under an incoming government.

If there are areas of debate, such as governance and funding that do not figure large in this account, it reflects perhaps the issues to which our witnesses gave most emphasis, or perhaps the nature of the questions we asked. We hope that the issues to which we have given priority are those that reflect the common aspiration for 'a world class education system' and why that dream is so often frustrated.

A spring of hope

The book was written in the months running up to the general election. It was a time of reflection sharpened by the worst economic crisis since the 1930s. Our interviews took place in that climate and we were privileged to catch that moment.

The election of Margaret Thatcher as prime minister in 1979 and that of Tony Blair in 1997 had raised expectations for something completely different. Both governments, elected with substantial majorities, enough to give confidence that they would retain power at the following general election, allowed the possibility of thinking long-term and of developing policies designed to restructure the education system so as to meet the needs of the twenty-first century.

The legacy of 'first past the post' system of parliamentary democracy, and the need to seek re-election within five years of taking office, has tended to focus policy making on the short term with short life initiatives outnumbering strategic approaches. In education, as in other areas of government, the apparent lack of coherence and continuity in policy making is often attributed to a need for political parties to emphasise their differences, to be adversarial rather than consensual. The drive by parties to create clear blue political water between themselves tends therefore to be more important than embedding practical and effective education policies. However, the promise of at least a two term government, for both Thatcher and Blair, offered an opportunity to build on the best of what had gone before and think radically about the rest.

Coherence and continuity: a focus on curriculum

In 1979, Mrs Thatcher was unimpressed by the school curriculum her government had inherited. Education was not, for her, off limits. By the early 1980s incipient disquiet had grown to a serious concern about the extent to which pupils in different schools were being offered similar curriculum provision. Surveys by Bassey (1978) and Bennett *et al.* (1980) had shown, for example, that in primary schools the amount of time devoted to the teaching of English ranged from a minimum of four to a maximum of twelve hours. For mathematics the range was only slightly less. Among academic architects and critics there was an ongoing dialogue about the purposes of reforming the curriculum. Some tended to focus on learning as a social activity whereby, as argued by Bruner and Haste (1987), children attempted to reconstruct their world as social beings rather than as 'lone scientists' where a seemingly ordinary occurrence, such as an apple falling off a tree, can trigger a flight of the imagination leading to a theory of gravity. A broad and balanced curriculum was therefore required; one based on social democratic ideals which should include aspects of citizenship and community education as well as traditional academic subjects (Lawton, 1975).

These views, however, were in marked contrast to those of the 'New Right' which had set the agenda for the incoming Conservative government (Tomlinson, 1992). In their view society was merely reflected in the uncoordinated actions of its individual members and there was thus no collective responsibility of the community as a whole, to nurture its weakest individuals. A common curriculum designed to empower the underprivileged, such as argued for by Lawton (1975), was therefore no longer in step with contemporary political orthodoxy. The main rationale for curriculum reform was economic; to allow the next generation of workers to compete effectively in the marketplace of the future (Lawlor, 1988).

The coming of the National Curriculum

By 1988 the Educational Reform Act was in place with the result that a system which for the previous 35 years,

> Had been run through broad legislative objectives, convention and consensus had been replaced by one based on contract and management. . . . The aim was to make an irreversible change in the public education system to that already achieved in other aspects of economic policy, such as trade union legislation, the sale of council houses and the privatisation of the nationalised industries.
>
> (Tomlinson, 1992: 48)

In some ways the Act represented a compromise between those arguing for a free market approach and those wanting a greater degree of central control of education.

Schools were encouraged to break away from local authorities either in the form of 'grant maintained' or 'city technology colleges'. In addition more assisted places at independent schools were provided. At the same time schools remaining within the Local Authority framework were given delegated budgets and were free to enrol as many pupils as they felt able to cope with by recruiting from outside their designated catchment areas. Since the size of the budget depended on the number of enrolments, neighbouring schools were now in direct competition with each other for the available resources.

In a totally free market, however, schools would also have been permitted to design their own curriculum, as in the private sector. This would have left parents with the task of choosing a school whose offerings best matched what they judged to be their children's needs or abilities. The eventual compromise between the 'free marketers' and those wanting centralised control of the curriculum was that a testing regime should be put in place with the results made available to the general public so that parents could take an informed decision as to which school constituted the 'best buy'.

Criticisms of the pace of change were largely ignored or viewed as ideological rather than genuine expressions of practical concern. Ministers were determined not to be 'in thrall to the prejudices of academics' (Baker, 1993:198). Within two years of the Reform Act a statutory primary curriculum had been introduced in primary schools, assessment at seven plus was in place and trials at 11+ were underway. New agencies were established for determining the initial teacher training curriculum and establishing teachers' conditions of service. By 1993 it was clear that teachers were faced with a massive curriculum overload, particularly at Key Stage 1 where time for teaching reading had to be reduced in order to meet statutory requirements (Campbell, 1993). Also the testing arrangements accompanying the National Curriculum had become a nightmare. Although excessive workload created by tests was ostensibly the trigger, the 1993 boycott of the Key Stages 1–3 tests by the NUT (National Union of Teachers), NASUWT (National Association of Schoolmasters Union of Women Teachers) and ATL (Association of Teachers and Lecturers) was motivated also by the tests' high stakes nature. The National Curriculum which had been a dream at conception had according to Professor Campbell become a nightmare at delivery.

Then there were three wise men

The move of Kenneth Baker to the Home Office and his replacement by Kenneth Clarke did little to improve matters although concerns began to shift towards the quality of current classroom practice. Among a number of scare stories was the 1990 equivalent of the William Tyndale affair (Auld, 1976) at Culloden Primary School which was singled out for strong criticism in an HMI (Her Majesty's Inspectorate) report for its over-reliance on 'progressive practices,' particularly the use of 'real books' to teach reading (see Alexander, 1997: 187). The chief executive of the National Curriculum Council, Duncan Graham, came under increasing criticism from ministers for making the National Curriculum too complicated and for failing to 'sort out the way that teachers teach' (Graham, 1993: 111). On resigning, Graham was replaced by an existing member of the NCC team, Chris Woodhead, who was relatively unknown within the larger educational community but to 'insiders' was seen as a likely replacement given his willingness 'to work with increasingly right wing councils,' (Watkins, 1993: 66). There followed the setting up of the so-called team of 'three wise men' consisting of Woodhead, the chief inspector of primary education, Jim Rose, and Professor Robin Alexander charged with reviewing:

> Available evidence about the delivery of education in primary schools and to make recommendations about curriculum organisation, teaching methods and classroom practice appropriate for the successful implementation of the National Curriculum, particularly at Key Stage 2.

From the start, according to Alexander (1997), Kenneth Clarke appeared to anticipate the conclusions of the review when, announcing the membership of the team, the next day's newspaper headlines described him as backing 'the return to formal lessons' and shutting 'the door on 25 years of trendy teaching'. Indeed support for this assertion comes from Alexander's (1997: 245) account of the final drafting process where many of his original versions were changed to give a positive spin in favour of whole class teaching.

And then a reign of terror

One of Kenneth Clarke's last tasks as education secretary was to privatise the inspection process. HMI was abolished and the resources used by LEAs (Local Education Authorities) when conducting local inspections transferred to a specially created Office for Standards in Education (Ofsted). Clarke's successor, John Patten, stayed for under two years at the Department of Education. His resignation coincided with the appointment of Chris Woodhead as Her Majesty's Chief Inspector (HMCI) and the first full time and head of Ofsted on the recommendation of the then prime minister, John Major. According to Mike Tomlinson (Woodhead's eventual successor) one minister at least particularly admired the way Woodhead had 'put real grit into the mission' while head of the then School Qualifications and Curriculum Authority (SCAA) and had urged the appointment as HMCI on the grounds that he would do a similar job in sorting out schools and teachers, Woodhead's regime has been described as a 'reign of terror' by Tim Brighouse (1997:106) who later became vice chair of the New Labour Task Force on Raising Educational Standards.

This was not an isolated view. Writing in the *Guardian* (12 March 1997) the former deputy leader of the Labour Party, Roy [now Lord] Hattersley, argued that the chief inspector was 'the apostle of improvement by confrontation' and accused him of rewriting reports to exclude passages of support for struggling schools and LEAs, and of misinterpreting research in pursuit of his own point of view. According to the chief inspector himself pupils were badly taught in half of all our schools, too many teachers saw themselves as facilitators rather than moral authorities, were apt to divide classes into small groups rather than teaching them as a whole and viewed subjects such as history and English as arcane and irrelevant to today's needs.

Colin Richards, a former senior inspector provides further support for these allegations. He quotes from the original and final drafts of the Ofsted (1996) Reading Survey where in one instance, the draft version:

> the unevenness in teaching quality as pupils move from class to class seriously weakens progress in these schools.

Emerges in final form as:

> far too many children were found to be not making the progress which they should. The main reason for this was weak teaching . . .
>
> (Richards, 1997: 11–12)

Findings represented in this way easily succeeded in gaining wide press coverage with such headlines as 'Inspector Attacks Woolly Teachers' (*Daily Telegraph* 27 January 1995) or demands that the government should 'Sack these Failed Teachers Now' (*Evening Standard* 5 February 1996). Commenting on the impact of these continuing criticisms of teaching methods together with the imposition of 'high stakes' tests and ever increasing workloads one ex-deputy head teacher, then working as an independent consultant, offered the following reflection:

> However well intentioned the reforms might have been they have resulted in an essentially flawed system that is made worse by the effects of league tables and a punitive model of inspection. On a daily basis I encounter teachers driven by fear and a misplaced sense of over-commitment to work themselves into the ground. Were it not for the fact that teaching is ultimately such a fascinating profession they would have given up long ago.
>
> (Bayley, 1998: 54)

The main problem was not the heavy workloads and the stress that these caused. It could often be deeply fulfilling to work in pressurised situations providing that individuals concerned share a common belief that the tasks being undertaken are worthwhile. The problem, she argued was that the architects of these reforms seem to have naively believed that if there was a clear logic to support their actions the teaching profession would fall into line; thus ignoring a basic truth – that 'effective learning is dependent on emotional energy . . . so that, not to put too fine a point on it, it all depends on how we feel' (Bayley, 1998: 53).

Studies undertaken at the time (Galton and Fogelman, 1988; Webb and Vulliamy, 1996) all support Brighouse's (1997:106) assertion that 'headteachers and teachers had had their confidence and self-esteem challenged at every turn'. They no longer felt trusted to do a professional job and regretted the fact that there were fewer 'magic moments' when a child's face finally indicated that understanding had replaced incomprehension. Thus when the general election took place in 1997 it would have been unreasonable to surmise that the teaching profession, as a whole, eagerly awaited the anticipated change of government.

The coming of New Labour

Given the emphasis on education in its 1997 election manifesto, 'New' Labour, (an epithet that was quietly put aside as its governments matured into middle and old age) entered office with a flood of goodwill from the teaching profession as will be evident from later chapters.

While in opposition, the Labour Party had promised to review the National Curriculum. In anticipation of this process contributors, mostly teachers and academics, in a series of essays setting out views of what it was hoped the Labour Party would achieve in the field of education, expressed the hope that the promised review of the National Curriculum would be the last for a very long time (Dainton, 1998). While committed to the review, Mr Blunkett frequently reminded teachers of their statutory duty to develop a 'balanced and broadly based curriculum'. This included a responsibility to promote the 'spiritual, moral, cultural, mental and physical development of pupils' while at the same time announcing a number of measures which, it was claimed, would ensure that primary teachers continued to focus on basics in order to meet the government's challenging literacy and numeracy targets. The retention of Chris Woodhead as chief inspector was also not calculated to reassure the profession.

Despite numerous warnings that the previous decade had produced a profession suffering from 'reform fatigue' (Campbell, 1998: 96) the Labour government in their first year of office, produced seven major bills and policy statements (Tomlinson, 2005). These included the setting up of the Standard and Effectiveness Unit inside what had now become the Department for Education and Employment (DfEE), the launch of the 'New Deal' with the Summer Literacy Schools Initiative, the White Paper, *Excellence in Schools*, on which the National Literacy Strategy was based (including a decision to devote one hour a day to literacy in all primary schools) and the Schools Standards and Frameworks Bill. This was followed in the second year of office, in 1998, by the setting up of Educational Action Zones, the National Grid for Learning, the introduction of the Literacy and Numeracy Strategies, the publication of homework guidelines, the launching of Surestart programmes for the 0-to 3-year-olds in areas of deprivation and the creation of Specialist and Beacon schools for inner cities. This raft of government initiatives, new Acts, new bodies (mostly consisting of nominated quangos or task forces), new Green and White Papers have continued apace throughout successive Labour governments. By the end of their first decade in office there was little evidence to support the view that the feelings expressed by teachers towards the end of Conservative rule had been ameliorated (Galton and MacBeath, 2008; Hargreaves *et al.,* 2007). Teachers still claimed they often felt stressed, regretted the lack of 'light bulb' moments and felt their professional integrity was continually being called into question.

Some, such as Bentley (1998), then a director of the think-tank DEMOS (heavily influential in New Labour's thinking), also expressed concerns about the rigidity of these imposed structures and argued that the emphasis on qualifications in schooling should be reduced and that the skills needed for what he termed the new knowledge economy should be integrated into mainstream teaching. Out of these concerns came the publication in 2003 of *Excellence and Enjoyment: A strategy for primary schools* (DfES, 2003). At its launch the then secretary of state, Charles Clarke, said that some targets would be dropped in 2004 in response to headteachers' complaints about excessive pressures and that there would be more autonomy for teachers in the way that they managed their classrooms. However, as Alexander (2004) has also pointed out, the central dilemma of how teachers were to exercise this autonomy in a regime of targets and performance tables was left unclear.

Typical of the 'mixed messages' given to primary headteachers was the view expressed by one of Ofsted's more recent chief inspectors, David Bell, in his 2003 Annual Report. There, the chief inspector argued that pressure on primary schools to improve literacy and numeracy was producing a two-tier curriculum while at the same time continuing to express concern that the test scores at Key Stage 2 were at a standstill.

Some key questions

Attempts by successive governments to bring about curriculum and pedagogic reform, although driven from different ideological perspectives, seem to have adopted similar implementation strategies and to have resulted in similar outcomes; partial success in achieving the objectives but at the cost of teacher goodwill and enthusiasm. For anyone wishing to bring about future policy changes a number of questions arise if lessons are to be learnt from these previous attempts. Among the more important ones are the following:

- To what extent is policy making a rational process?
- Why does there appear to be no 'policy memory' involved in decision-making.
- Why did neither the Conservatives nor New Labour have a strategy for the future of the teaching profession? And why was such a strategy conspicuously absent from the Conservative and Liberal Democrats election manifestos?
- What has mandated reform felt like to school communities? New Labour claimed that unlike its predecessors, its policy was evidenced based. How were research findings factored into policy making?
- Were New Labour's education policies mainly influenced by the limitations of the parliamentary cycle or was there a more strategic long-term approach?

And finally in respect to the conclusions to be drawn from the above questions,

- What, to use Estelle Morris' famous phrase, is the direction of travel for the future?

In search of some answers

There are several ways that one can go about investigating the effects of policy changes and the perceived rationale for their implementation. The first of these relies on detailed documentary analysis which might include government White and

Green Papers, extracts of parliamentary speeches, submissions to and minutes of Parliamentary Committees and so forth. An approach of this kind can be found in the work of Tomlinson's (2005) volume, *Education in a Post-Welfare Society*. Then there are approaches based on the use *of critical theory* which tend to situate their analysis of policy within a specific ideological framework. There are also autobiographical accounts from politicians, and others caught up in policy formulation. These are most useful when they concern the same policy events such as Kenneth Baker's (1993) account of the creation of the National Curriculum, *The Turbulent Years* and Duncan Graham's (1993) book, *A Lesson for us all: The making of the National Curriculum*. Because such accounts, particularly those of politicians, tend to be strong on self-justification, contributions from other 'insiders' can act as a useful antidote. Finally there are historical accounts which make use of all the sources mentioned earlier in endeavouring to explain the rationale behind events. In education, the works of the late Brian Simon, such as his 1994 book, *The State of Educational Change: Essays in the History of Education and Pedagogy*, constitute an outstanding example of this genre.

For those wishing to take lessons from the past, the historical approach, although providing a more comprehensive and more rounded perspective, suffers an obvious disadvantage in that it requires a period of time to elapse before the analysis can be undertaken. It is therefore less likely to influence immediate events. In this book, however, we have attempted a different approach. We have dealt with contemporary themes by going to key players involved in policy deliberations over the last two decades. We have asked them to give an account of their involvement in the formulation of educational policy, to reflect on the part played by others and to indicate what they thought were the 'main drivers' in the decision-making process.

In selecting our interviewees we had in mind a distinction between the architects of policy (mainly the politicians, senior civil servants and advisers) the critics (mostly academics who had served on government advisory committees but had become disillusioned by events) and prophets (those whose ideas challenged existing orthodoxies and led to new policy initiatives). In some cases certain individuals could claim to be an amalgam of all three types of contributor.

Transcripts of interviews were returned to the interviewee for added comment or amendment. As far as possible an individual's account of any event leading to decision-making is triangulated with other participants' accounts of the same incidents. We have striven to attach names to quotes whenever this has been agreed. Generally permission was only refused when it could be the cause of embarrassment to the individual mentioned in the quotation.

In this way we hope we have provided a vivid and dynamic account of recent policy making which has lessons for all of us involved in the field of education.

One thing is clear from our interviews and the evidence we have gathered. Policy initiatives in the view of teachers are similar to waiting for a bus – if you miss one another soon comes along. Indeed, teachers and their school communities also often experience them as inconsistent and irrational. As one of those interviewed, Sir Mike Tomlinson, a former chief inspector, concluded:

There's nothing rational about decision-making and policy making at all. There's a rationale behind the headline but there is rarely a rationale behind the operationalisation of that headline. I'm known to say on many occasions, 'Please do not imagine that politicians make decisions based on logic and a broad base of evidence, because they don't.' And neither do we make our decisions in that way either. . . . I have seen policies decided or seriously influenced by the most minor of incidents; such as meetings at the weekend between the minister and members of a constituency, by political expediency or personal prejudice; all play a part in making decisions.

The following chapters set out to explore how true this was of those policies, in particular, those which have been of greatest concern to the teaching profession. When the Labour Party came to power it was said of education that they 'hit the ground running' with a raft of policy initiatives ready for immediate implementation. We begin by examining teacher morale and expectations in schools immediately following the 1977 general election and the nature of the decision-making in the first few months of Tony Blair's government leading up to the creation of the Standards and Effectiveness Unit and the launch of the Literacy and Numeracy strategies.

2   In the beginning was euphoria

The sense of euphoria, 1997, when the Blair government was elected, is embedded in public memory. It was no different in schools. A senior college lecturer recalls a visit to a comprehensive school, on the morning after the election:

> There was a party going on – the head had brought in a case of champagne and everyone in the school was there . . . A glass of champagne was thrust into my hand and a nice bagel with smoked salmon and cream cheese! The break was extended by half an hour (and) the kids had a can of Coke and a Kit-Kat each.

This sense of celebration among teachers was hardly surprising. An ICM research poll in March 1997 found that teachers' voting intentions stood at 59 per cent for Labour with only 15 per cent intending to vote for the Conservatives and 21 per cent voting for the Liberal Democrats. The triggers for this unprecedented shift in voting intentions are revealing.

Teachers cited 'constant changes', lack of support, disruptive pupils and government and political interference in that order as the main pressures and problems they had experienced in the last two years. The changes teachers wanted from the new government were sharply defined. Smaller class sizes and more funds and finance were by far the top priorities for teachers. Their next two priorities, better pay and more stability were some way behind (Galton and MacBeath, 2008).

Interestingly, the vast majority of teachers looked to the government as the organisation which could do the most to help them, with their unions coming second as a source of support.

What then did those in the incoming Labour government think was necessary for the reinvention of schools? The Labour Party in opposition had made it clear that it wanted to be seen as the party of the consumer not the party of the provider. A range of policy proposals had been agreed including the intention to introduce the Literacy and Numeracy Strategies into every primary school in England and to take action against schools it believed were failing.

It was clear that teachers expected the incoming Labour government to deliver 'producer' defined change. Indeed, the public campaigning appeared to support this expectation. One of the five credit card promises identified by Labour in its election campaign was a reduction to a maximum of thirty for the number of 7-year-olds in each class.

Quite obviously teachers were in no mood to make a coolly dispassionate analysis of Labour's pre-election policies; neither were they inclined to do so. Such was the fevered nature of teachers' (along with the majority of voters') expectations for change.

The expectations of teachers were radically different from those of the incoming government. The 'necessary corrective', to use the phrase which described the bursting of the bubble in financial markets, was not long in coming. Three weeks into office the new government 'named and shamed' in the press and media a number of secondary schools which it deemed to be failing. This action led to deep dismay among teachers and their school communities. Some felt that immense damage had been done to the support of the teaching profession for Labour's reforms.

The gap between teachers' expectations of New Labour and the approach of a reforming regime which had not sought to evaluate the impact of its policies on teachers themselves made the euphoria short lived. Why this gap between school communities and the perceptions of the policy makers was there, and whether such a gap was and is inevitable, is at the heart of this book.

Does educational reform have to be characterised by a series of sharp jolts and 'necessary correctives' to the perceptions of all those involved in education? In examining the influences, constraints and pressures on policy makers in a democratic society, we ask what lessons can be learnt from the educational reform programmes of governments since 1988?

Primary colours

> In politics, there is always the desire to paint the differences between Parties in primary colours, but, more often than not, they are in pastel shades. I think there is a difference, but not an exaggerated one.

So said Michael Gove, in his role then as shadow education minister, interviewed a few months before the 2010 general election. He added, not without a note of cautious scepticism:

> Whenever you have a new government, people start off with zeal, enthusiasm and idealism.

While in office in May 2010 zeal, enthusiasm and idealism were to be tempered by the unexpected presence of Liberal Democrats at the top table, the pastel shades of both parties left greater room for an educational coalition than in other more contentious areas of policy.

Every government has ambitions. For the incoming Blair government there were to be three priorities, 'Education, Education, Education'. While implicitly building on much of what had gone before Tony Blair wanted his government to be the government of education. His ambition was for educational reform which would raise vital questions about the nature of school education and the challenge of improving its quality. The 1997 government wanted a reform that would be owned by the teaching profession and support staff as well as by young people, parents, and the wider public.

His government had one primary and incontestable aim: that is, the achievement of high quality education for all children and young people. To achieve that teachers were seen by governments as the objects of reform. It was a view, however, that simply got policy makers into trouble.

Nevertheless it was a prescient move of the new Labour government to include teachers in the newly established Standards Task Force and to create a forum to hear their voice. It was not always one that its chair, David Blunkett wholeheartedly welcomed but it signalled an important intent. In Michael Barber's words it was an intent to 'show the breadth of the coalition'. It was recognised, although sometimes by default, that the relationship of teachers to educational reform had to be at the forefront of government thinking both now and in the future.

1997 and all that

> One of Blair's huge contributions to British politics was to take the key elements of some of those Conservative reforms and turn them into a more coherent strategy. They had the elements there, but they didn't have the investment, they didn't have the relationship with the teachers, they didn't prioritise equity enough.

In this summary of Blair's contributions, Michael Barber was clear about the pastel colours of reform while at the same placing emphasis on a fundamental change in the government's relationship with teachers. He was well aware of the tendency among Labour politicians to say that everything that the Conservative government attempted before 1997 was either irrelevant or ineffective but as he is quick to point out:

> Even though there were adversarial politics, Blair, before 1997 didn't fight any of that. In fact his first big speech on education was 'League Tables are here to Stay'.

Although Conservative reforms had, in fact, provided a basis for future Labour government policy, they were deemed to have had no impact. An example of this were the Literacy and Numeracy Projects set up by Gillian Shephard in 1996, a fact unacknowledged by the incoming government. Yet the importance of the projects for the Labour government was profound, as they provided the shape, structure and core for its Literacy and Numeracy Strategies. Michael Barber, appointed in 1997 to be responsible for the implementation of New Labour's flagship policies on school standards, described the Literacy and Numeracy Projects as;

> [A] classic piece of 80s, 90s policymaking, where a government is under pressure because it's not doing enough about literacy, so it sets up a project which at that

> rate would make no difference over decades . . . They had a small amount of money and were lacking ambition, but the content was fantastic.

This comment provides just one example of New Labour's approach. Many Conservative policies were appropriated and adopted for the Labour government's purposes.

Indeed, the Labour Party, in opposition, had chosen to work with the framework and paradigm of the 1988 Education Act. The Education Reform Act (ERA) included the National Curriculum, Local Management of Schools, Grant Maintained Status (which was subsequently converted into Foundation Status), Open Enrolment and the abolition of the Inner London Education Authority. As Kenneth Baker said in an interview, Labour chose to accept the Conservative framework, despite the opposition of some senior figures such as Jack Straw. Indeed at a recent meeting of the House of Commons Children, Schools and Families Committee he said that he was 'very grateful in 1997 that an incoming Labour government broadly accepted the changes that were in place' (CSF Select Committee, 2010).

Yet there are important and subtle differences about how the ERA framework would be viewed by both the Conservatives and Labour. Baker was very clear that despite opposition from the then prime minister, Margaret Thatcher, the National Curriculum should lead to a broad and balanced offer for every child, and also that the curriculum and test results from each school should provide a benchmark against which parents could choose schools.

Initially the first Labour government was less concerned about curriculum reform than Baker. As Fiona Millar, ex No 10 Advisor and education campaigner and journalist says, the Blair government had other concerns, which focussed on the perceived failures of comprehensive education.

> There was a real divide within Number Ten, between people they would see as old Labour like me and Alastair and Bruce Grocott, and to a certain extent Sally Morgan and the sort of thrusting young Middle-England people, who allegedly knew what parents wanted . . . Some of them had just made their minds up that Comprehensive schools were a disaster, without thinking what the term Comprehensive actually meant . . . All it means is an all abilities school, but it's become a phrase that was used to brand something else, which was failing inner city schools, basically, made up of very tough kids.

This was confirmed by Blair's ex-chief speech writer and advisor, Peter Hyman (2005), who describes the profound 'Islington' effect on Blair's views about comprehensive schools when the Blairs refused to send their children to secondary schools in their home borough, Islington.

It would be wrong, however, to ascribe solely to an anti-comprehensive group with 'barmy ideas', Tony Blair's dissatisfaction with low achievement. In his interview for this book Sir Alasdair MacDonald, the head of Morpeth Community Specialist School in Tower Hamlets, was asked whether he agreed with Barber's characterisation of the era prior to 1997 as an era of 'uninformed professionalism'. He said;

I buy into that quite a lot, actually, but not at the level necessarily of the individual teacher, but at the level of the system. I think there have been good individual teachers throughout . . . I think in the seventies, certainly, and into the eighties there was a huge, I think mistaken, belief that basically children who came from difficult backgrounds, you couldn't expect much from to achieve very much . . . I think our expectations were unbelievably low . . . I think young people were patronised and I think there's still some of that.

He even went on to describe past low expectations as a form of conspiracy:

Many of us were probably complicit in that sort of conspiracy . . . if you look at Morpeth now we've got an honours board and on that honours board in 1987, we had a sixth form then, one student went into Higher Education, in a school with an intake of over 200, one student . . . now I think we're probably closer to 100 students a year going into Higher Education.

MacDonald's reflection was from an inner city school perspective. It coincided with Millar's to the extent that both identify the issue as failing inner city schools but both, explicitly in Millar's case and implicitly in MacDonald's case, rejected the conclusion that such perceived failure meant that comprehensive education was failing. To both, the issue was, and is, one of low aspirations.

Indeed it is not clear what kind of education system the new Labour government, in 1997, thought it was facing. Michael Barber in *The Learning Game* described the Education Service in mid-1990s thus:

A sense of crisis pervades the Education Service . . . On the face of it, this is very odd because more young people are achieving more than ever before . . . Indeed, if the available indicators are to be believed, there has never been a period in British history when standards have risen so fast.

. . . In spite of the progress of recent years, international statistics reveal that, our Education Service is still relatively ineffective . . .

Finally, it is important to recognise that amid all the evidence of progress, there is also evidence of a deterioration in some specific aspects of education (including) evidence of a declining reading standard at primary level in recent years.

Thus, improbable though it may seem, it appears that we have rising standards and falling standards at the same time . . . While they are rising for the many, they are low for perhaps 40 per cent and perhaps falling for a significant minority of this group . . . In this failing group, white working-class males are predominant.

(1996: 27)

The four-point scale of 'awful', 'adequate', 'good' and 'great', which Barber applied as a benchmark to the quality of individual public services, raises a number of questions; 'Where was the education service in 1996? Was it awful? Was it adequate? Indeed, was some of it good or great or did bits of it fall into all four categories?

Certainly, the new government thought that literacy and numeracy outcomes in primary schools in 1997 were either awful or adequate since it clearly believed that primary schools themselves were unable to unleash improvement in literacy and numeracy.

> Basically, you can drive from Whitehall 'awful' to 'adequate', but you cannot drive from 'good' to 'great' in Whitehall . . . You can mandate 'awful' to 'adequate', but you cannot mandate 'good' to 'great'; you have to unleash it.

As a result Barber believed that improvements had to be mandated from the top down.

> (The strategies were) unapologetically top-down. This is the Literacy Hour and here is the training programme . . . If you are going to scale up that fast, you have to have top-down.

There was, however, another reason for government mandated improvement; one which Ben Levin described from his experiences in Canada as an education minister in Manitoba and Ontario.

> Satisfying public preferences is hard to do. The first difficulty is that it is hard to know what the 'public' wants . . . people can and do have strongly held views based on astonishingly little evidence . . . people are not generally given to the calculation of probabilities, but are strongly influenced by stories and events.
>
> Because unusual events stand out, they tend to be given greater weight. Things that are relatively unimportant in the larger scheme . . . can become all-consuming in the public mind, at least for a short time, especially when fanned by political opponents and the media.
>
> (Levin, 2005)

It was very obvious that in 1997 the government wanted to go on the front foot and establish its own stories and events; stories and events which demonstrated success. As Michael Barber put it:

> We were very conscious in our minds that you had to demonstrate you could improve the system to get permission from the tax payer to spend more of their money on the education system.

And then, of course, there were the internal political issues which occupied sections of the government. The Treasury, he said, needed convincing that money should be invested in schools. It needed to be persuaded that additional financial input would, in the language of policyspeak, 'deliver higher outcomes'.

> By achieving short-term results, we got credibility that even went beyond education but, certainly in education for the bigger investments that came later,

none of that would have been possible if we hadn't got the results out of the system . . .

(Barber, 2009)

For the government, it was, therefore, vital to achieve quick wins for political purposes, particularly in order to influence the Treasury, the tax payer and the media – to be achieved by mandating the roll-out of the Literacy and Numeracy Strategies.

The model which was developed to demonstrate such success did not necessarily need to be grounded in reality, but it had to have its own internal logic to be explicable to the public and to the Treasury. For political reasons, therefore, a conceptual model of success to demonstrate quick public wins had to be established. That model for success was constructed by setting national targets based on Key Stage 2 National Curriculum test results. The targets were then disaggregated into targets for local authorities which in turn disaggregated them into specific targets for each primary school.

Kevan Collins, who joined the National Strategies in 1997 described the importance of the targets:

> The setting of the targets . . . was a key moment . . . it kind of said, actually, we're reducing the whole thing down to a single number for each community so numbers are tabled and that's what we're all measured by and we literally progress towards them.

Thus, the target setting regime was established.

The drive to mandate the strategies was informed by political necessities which were both internal and external to the new government. It could be said that the lack of knowledge and understanding of education by the Treasury and its chancellor was the driving force for mandated improvement.

This determination highlights a not generally known but very odd characteristic of the first two Blair governments. That is, Blair's commitment to 'Education, Education, Education' had not been internalised within his own government. It almost looked like a personal campaign by Blair himself supported by his Number 10 advisers and the original DfEE team.

Fiona Millar, recalls that:

> Brown made more speeches about education in the Third World than (he) did about education in this country. Although I assume he was pretty much behind 'Sure Start' . . . I don't think he was focused on education or else he would have been focused on the spending budgets of the time.

The government's model for telling a success story worked with the press; at least initially. When asked what was the most effective action the government had taken to raise standards, Richard Garner, the education editor of *The Independent* and the longest serving national newspaper education correspondent, certainly recognised that the government had got its story through to the press:

I think focusing on the primary sector and on the core curriculum first off . . . was what generated the rise in standards.

The introduction of the strategies however, created considerable turbulence in schools. Teacher organisations considered boycotting the strategies at the time, although subsequent research on the lives of primary teachers (Galton and MacBeath, 2002) showed that teachers thought that the strategies had provided positive support for their pedagogy, with the Numeracy Strategy being rated more highly than the Literacy Strategy.

In order to drive the strategies forward the government established the Standards and Effectiveness Unit (SEU) within the DfEE with, as Michael Barber put it, 'an instruction to deliver'. Its explicit responsibilities were to deliver on the Literacy and Numeracy Strategies and to tackle the issue of failing schools.

It was a concept which Gillian Shephard, the last Conservative secretary of state for education under the Major government, did not recognise. According to Shephard:

> It's the case . . . that the (Education Department) did not run schools . . . If you were in the Treasury and someone said, 'Let's reform VAT' . . . they would say, 'Alright, we'll do that then' . . . Now, compare and contrast being secretary of state for Education . . . You could do that for the Ministry of Agriculture, Fisheries and Food (MAFF) . . . you could say, 'Right I'm going for non-food crops, such money as we have, we'll make grants for that' . . . You could do it . . . you could say, 'We will reform the benefit system with social security' . . . You could say, 'We will change the personal help for unemployed people in employ-ment' . . . All of these things you could do . . . in education, you couldn't do any of them because the local authorities were your agents.

This view, from a senior Conservative minister was that government could not run schools is, perhaps, a little simplistic. After all, the Education Reform Act alongside the 1986 Education Act, which altered fundamentally the governance of schools, ini-tiated profound and, indeed, seismic changes in the curriculum and governance of schools, as did the 1992 Act which introduced Ofsted. As a non-ministerial govern-ment department, Ofsted intervened directly and judgementally into the very nature of pedagogy itself.

Nevertheless, Shephard's point still remains partially valid. The government is not the employer of school teachers and support staff; neither does it provide the gov-ernance of schools (except now through the funding agreements for academies). It can certainly intervene directly through financial incentives, removing governing bodies and using the ultimate sanction of school closure. But, it cannot, itself, direct pedagogy.

Shephard's belief was that civil servants could not, therefore, directly order teachers to adopt a particular form of pedagogy nor could they translate the newly established National Curriculum in a particular way. The civil service, in short, could not deliver the Literacy and Numeracy Strategies because it did not run schools.

This belief was not obvious to David Blunkett as Labour's secretary of state for education in 1997 nor to Barber, as head of the new SEU. Barber's book, *Instruction to Deliver*, had no time for such distinctions between government departments which could or could not deliver directly.

> (The) crucial concept was the delivery chain . . . The best way to think about it is to imagine what is implicit when a minister makes a promise . . . supposing that a minister promises, as David Blunkett did, to improve standards of reading and writing among 11 year olds . . . implicit in this commitment is that . . . the minister can influence what happens inside the head of an 11 year old in, for example, Widnes. The delivery chain (from the SEU to the 11 year old in Widnes) makes that connection explicit . . .

Indeed, as indicated earlier, the four-point scale of 'awful', 'adequate', 'good' and 'great' and the assertion that you can mandate 'awful' to 'adequate' (from Whitehall) was confirmation that the government believed that, in its chosen areas of educational reform, the government could direct reform in schools. It is captured in its bluntest of Blunkettspeak, in his testimony to the Government Select Committee in March 2010: 'We had a crap teaching profession. We haven't any more.'

The thinking and psychology behind the idea of centrally mandated improvement of the United Kingdom's public services is set out in detail in *Instruction to Deliver* (2007). Indeed, Barber described his experience at the SEU, and its perceived success in introducing the Literacy and Numeracy Strategies, as the reason why Tony Blair asked him in 2006 to be head of the Prime Minister's Delivery Unit (PMDU).

Barber's interview for this book, however, offers an interesting insight into why an outsourced company (CfBT) was asked to deliver the Literacy and Numeracy Strategies. It had nothing to do with Blair's perception that privatisation of the delivery of public services was a good thing in itself and everything to do with the inability of the civil service to do the job for government.

> Implementation . . . wasn't really what they've done before . . . I don't regret having a relationship with CfBT (who delivered the Literacy and Numeracy Strategies) it worked; it was much easier and more flexible than it would have been if it had been in-house

Indeed, Barber conceded that there was, 'a massive advantage to not having them as civil servants'.

This raises a considerable number of questions about the issue of central government mandated reform and, indeed, as to whether government or its agents can, or should, intervene directly into the issue of pedagogy and teaching content. It is probably worth recording however, that the gamble of turning the DfEE into a delivery department, as far as government was concerned, paid off handsomely, at least initially. Indeed, it was probably the perceived success of the introduction of the strategies which provided the encouragement and benchmark for the very many mandated reforms which followed during the life of three Labour governments.

The government's 'unapologetically top-down' improvement model, as Barber puts it, was based on the idea of 'removing all excuses for not doing it from the table'; the excuses being not enough books and the lack of high quality training.

Yet, even Barber recognised that, despite having 370 conferences for head teachers, there was 'some negative feeling' about the strategy. Indeed, there is a strong argument that the kind of pressure the government exerted alienated many primary head teachers who felt initially challenged by the accusation that, 'primary teachers think they know about how to teach reading even when they don't'.

There is a very real debate about the long-term impact of a mandated initiative like the Literacy and Numeracy Strategies where, as Barber says, 'If you're going to go to scale-up that fast, you have to have top-down'.

The government at the time was anxious about the impact of a mandated policy introduced at the speed of the strategies. Conor Ryan, Blunkett's ex special adviser, confirmed that the DfEE, at the time, considered legislation which would require primary schools to adopt the strategies. In the end, the government concluded that in Ofsted, there was, to use Conor Ryan's words, 'a fairly persuasive mechanism', and that, 'the sharp edge of Ofsted inspection was part of that strategy, and (Chris Woodhead) gave it a sharp edge'.

So powerful were the government's intentions that the National Union of Teachers, in order to protect their members from excessive workload created by the strategies, persuaded Estelle Morris to introduce temporary regulations to allow primary schools to solely 'have regard' to the Foundation Subjects, which, in effect, suspended the statutory requirement to teach them. Also concerned about the narrowing impact on the curriculum, was Robin Alexander, who together with four other members of the board, met with Estelle Morris and Michael Barber and, as he recalled it;

> We said, this is a bad move and curriculum breadth must be protected, not least because of the two Ofsted reports which showed a clear relationship between high test scores and the quality of the rest of the curriculum. . . . And why is it anyway, that you have just set up a body called QCA but what you regard as the two most important aspects of the curriculum – numeracy and literacy-have been taken out of our hands and are controlled directly by the department? And Michael Barber, then chief adviser on standards, lent smoothly across and said, before Estelle Morris could say anything, 'Ah, but minister numeracy and literacy are standards, not curriculum. Standards are the responsibility of the department, curriculum is the responsibility of the QCA'.

Kevan Collins, who joined the Standards and Effective Unit in 1998, said he was 'shocked by how passive people were and how quickly people took to the strategies'. It is worth recording that the government's action in taking, 'a bit of policy straight out to the system without mediating it through a number of channels', stood in stark contrast to anything that the previous Conservative government would have considered.

I never attempted to tell teachers how they should teach. I think that's quite wrong. No more should a health secretary tell a surgeon how to operate . . . but I think it's quite right for the secretary of state and the government to decide the nature of the curriculum and really define the basic knowledge that children should have to acquire over the 11 years of compulsory education.

Kenneth Baker's view expressed in interview was endorsed by Gillian Shephard who was firm in her belief that it was not the job of ministers to tell teachers how to teach. Neither Shephard nor Baker envisaged that the architecture of the Education Reform Act would be used to intervene directly so as to shape pedagogy in the classroom. For Baker, National Curriculum tests were about providing parents with, 'information so they could make an effective choice'. The tests, against the benchmark of the National Curriculum, were to introduce, as he said, 'certain market mechanisms'. For Shephard, the predecessor to the National Strategies, the Literacy and Numeracy projects which she introduced in 1996, were about building 'on what teachers thought was right'.

The trigger for the introduction of Ofsted, in 1992, was primarily as a result of the then Conservative government's dissatisfaction with local authorities. As Shephard ruefully admits:

I could have done without Kenneth Clarke being entirely ranged to the depths of his being against local government. I used to say that he had perhaps been bitten by an Alderman when he was in his pram.

Baroness Pauline Perry, ex Her Majesty's Inspector and author with Stephen Dorrell, of the Conservative Party's *Review of Public Services* (2007), gave a more specific reason why Ofsted was introduced:

What we would really like is some control over the local inspectorate because the local inspectorate . . . didn't inspect . . . they'd almost become social workers . . . (they would say) this is my favourite school so I give them this and this . . . It had become very corrupt.

The final post ERA architecture developed by the Conservative Party was neatly summarised by Shephard.

I wanted to simplify things for teachers . . . by saying . . . here is a curriculum, here are some tests, here are the inspections, sort of get on with it really.

In that phrase, the contrast between the previous Conservative government and the incoming 1997 Labour government could not be starker. While taking a decision not to substantively amend the ERA, the one thing the incoming Labour government was not going to do was to allow teachers to 'get on with it'.

Sandy Adamson, a senior civil servant at the time and the first head of the School Effectiveness Division, was witness to what he described as an irretrievable mistake of incoming New Labour. He makes two points. He blames the civil servants, not excusing himself, for underestimating the distrust the new ministers were bound to have for a group who had worked for a Conservative government for 18 years and adds, 'We should have listened much more, not immediately presented them with our plans, even if the latter were intended to implement New Labour policy'. He also criticises the politicians:

> Despite pouring money into the system, sadly, they lost the confidence of the teaching profession in the first twelve to eighteen months, tragically lost their confidence. Talked, talked, talked at them. Command and control. Told them what had to be done and the way it was going to be done. Some of that was necessary, but velvet glove and all that.

There is a certain irony in the fact that Estelle Morris, whose understanding and empathy with teachers was a singular attribute among education ministers, should adopt such a strong stance against 'the producer interest'. Describing the approach the Labour Party took to public services on taking office, she said:

> Labour had to shift in the opposition years from being seen to be the party of the provider or to the party of the producer to the party of the consumer. It has done that throughout its relationship with the trade union movements. It wanted to become citizen focused.

This policy thrust was not hidden from schools. Morris' views simply reflected common policy adopted by the entire Labour front bench. Indeed, as then professor at the Institute of Education in London, Michael Barber had set out a range of proposals in his 1996 book, *The Learning Game* which was self evidently influential on Tony Blair since he himself described the proposals as 'provocative and timely, illuminating and optimistic' on the book's front cover.

Conor Ryan, education adviser to David Blunkett when he was secretary of state, described the series of policy documents which the Labour Party had developed in opposition.

> We had *Diversity and Excellence*, which was on structures, we had *Excellence for Everyone* which was on standards (and) . . . what was a template to a fair degree . . . the document Michael Barber's team produced on literacy which was published about seven months before the general election and. . . . was ready-made when we went into the department.

It was a government determined to hit the ground running, determined to be tough and, not to be diverted from its ideological mission. As Sandy Adamson, a key player and close observer of the incoming administration commented:

> I was staggered by the uncompromising culture of the Labour government when they came in. But the civil servants didn't help themselves by talking rather than listening.

While it came as a shock to many of their most ardent supporters, 'naming and sham-ing' was perfectly congruent with a deep antipathy to compromise. Mary Bousted (General Secretary, Association of Teachers and Lecturers) recalled the depth of disillusion she and others felt.

> Everybody was just delighted (with Labour's election but) within six months, Blunkett had just destroyed that through naming and shaming (and) through a phrase which I'll never forget; kids in inner city schools fail because teachers have no expectations.

In fact the interviewees for this book do not ascribe to Number 10 responsibility for the naming and shaming strategy. Both Michael Barber, and then Estelle Morris, par-liamentary under secretary at the time, recalled that the 'naming and shaming' strat-egy was a collective decision of the whole ministerial team in the DfEE. In Michael Barber's words:

> It wasn't driven from Number 10 . . . Steve (Stephen Byers), David Blunkett and I were all quite committed to it and we had known before the election that we would do something serious about school failure. . . . Remember the Greenwich Lecture?
> (Michael Barber,1998)

It certainly wasn't driven by Ofsted. According to Mike Tomlinson:

> The first 14 schools named and shamed were not checked with Ofsted before the announcement . . . we didn't think they were the right schools anyway, if we'd have been asked. Naming and shaming was essentially a political action designed to give a political message.

Yet Estelle Morris justified the strategy on political grounds:

> I think naming and shaming of schools gave two clear messages; in the eyes of the public politically it put it on the side of the users of the services, not the pro-ducers of the services; and secondly it gave the message to the teaching profes-sion that we weren't the same Labour Party as last time we came into power but we would have a different focus.

There is some evidence that a lack of understanding about teachers' expectations and the nature of teaching itself contributed to the government's public promotion of naming and shaming. Peter Hyman, ex adviser to Tony Blair, who went on to take a teaching assistant's post at Islington Green School is remarkably frank about the unique nature of the art of teaching itself.

> We all think we know what teaching is like . . . but observing teachers close up . . . brings a fresh perspective . . . at a school like this, with a lot of difficult chil-dren, the sheer will-power of teachers is extraordinary. . . . To do this five lessons

a day, five days a week must require huge stamina!! . . . Teaching seems to me physically demanding, you are on your feet the entire time . . . I have never seen a teacher sit down. . . . The need to control, animate, enthuse, whilst dealing with constant provocation makes teaching also emotionally draining.

(Hyman, 2005: 118)

It was, of course, 'schools like this', schools with a large number of pupils from socially deprived backgrounds, that were named and shamed.

Despite Estelle Morris' description of the political reasons behind the naming and shaming strategy, she too recognises the unique pressures on teachers; pressures which in the early years of government, Labour did not understand.

In those (early) years I don't think there was an understanding in the wider government of the demands of teaching . . . I don't think that, unless you've done it, anybody knows the nature of the pressure in the classroom . . .

And Michael Barber said:

The effect on leaders of the profession and the profession generally was quite negative, and it was much more negative than I might have guessed, you could say naively.

Indeed when it came to the issue of school failure Barber admitted that his own personal experience had an impact on his advice to ministers. He traced the development of the naming and shaming policy not only from the Greenwich Lecture but from his experience of being placed on the first Education Association established by Shephard which took over the running of Hackney Downs School in Hackney.

I'd been through not just the Greenwich Lecture but the Hackney Downs experience . . . and then working with Gillian Shephard and Robin Squire (previous Conservative education ministers) . . . on all the stuff they'd done . . . They put a lot of the framework in place . . . [In] the second half of '95, I went to Hackney Downs . . . that was a very searing experience for me, that I never regretted but it was a very searing experience . . .' (it provided) a sharper edge'

There is a debate about the impact of these early initiatives. As Collins noted, the department itself was amazed at how passively schools accepted the Strategies. This was because, as Chapter 4 of this book shows shows, the introduction of the National Curriculum had not been accompanied by in-depth professional development and, as a consequence many primary school teachers did not feel equipped to teach mathematics. And, in the Literacy Strategy the emphasis on grammar in children's writing filled a knowledge gap for many less confident staff. By and large, whether or not the strategies were embraced by schools was strongly influence by the attitude of headteachers. Those who thought that the strategies contradicted their longstanding practice exerted a strong negative influence on their staff. Staff in schools where heads endorsed the Strategies tended to see the strategies as supportive as well. Yet Michael Fullan, in his evaluation of the strategies (Earl *et al.*, 2003), raised the question of how embedded the improvements brought about by the strategies were.

This begs the question – did the Labour Party have a strategy for the profession prior to 1997 particularly in relation to its capability and morale? Barber admitted that the Labour Party, prior to 1997, did not.

> What is true is that, in pre-1997 thinking, there was no overview of where we were going with the teaching profession.

According to Kevan Collins, part of this lack of a strategy became evident when Labour got into power.

> I don't think morale was ever talked about explicitly or intended to . . . we didn't talk about morale or the quality of the local authority, we just kept our eyes on those numbers.

'Because the department know best', says William Atkinson, head of Phoenix School in Hammersmith, they manage the system through legislation and a range of initiatives supported by money but it means that things move too quickly and they don't get properly evaluated before they're taken system wide or dropped.

Permission for the mandate

There is another dimension to the seismic change which took place in 1997. It concerns the wider trade union movement.

Some will ask what an analysis of education policy making has to do with unions representing employees in the private and wider public sector. There is, however, an organic link between Trades Union Council (TUC) unions which are affiliated to the Labour Party and the permission given to the Blair government to introduce mandated educational reform. Part of that link was and is Gordon Brown's great interest in adult learning and in employers' agreements with unions on apprenticeship and skills training and Brown's lack of knowledge about schools.

Apart from the political need felt by Blair and Barber to convince the Treasury to spend more on schools there were other ramifications arising from Chancellor Brown's enthusiasm for just two of the non-statutory sectors of education; important as they were. The Amalgamated Engineering and Electricians Union (AEEU) had a particularly close relationship with Brown as shadow chancellor as it did with Blair. Achieving adult skills training as part of industrial bargaining was part of that warmth.

John Lloyd as a national secretary for the AEEU maintained close links with the government through Blair's industrial relations advisor Jon Cruddas. He recalled the 'completely criticism free orgy' of the 1997 Trade Union Congress.

> Everybody understood that Blair was going to run it like he wanted it to be run and that we could either take a small part applauding everything he did or do the other thing.

So when asked what the effect would have been had the teacher organisations in the TUC been affiliated to the Labour Party when David Blunkett named and shamed failing schools, Lloyd said that it would have been 'dramatic'. It would however, also have been seen as a 'party management problem'. And he added:

> Of course there was no party management . . . with non-affiliated unions; you could say what you liked to them.

A consequence of this close relationship between the affiliated unions and the first Blair government was that the teacher organisations' early disenchantment with the government over 'naming and shaming' was not greeted warmly by unions affiliated to the Labour Party. As Lloyd says:

> I think that the affiliated unions were very irritable with the non-affiliated unions and that has gone on to this very day.

There is however another reason why the Labour affiliated Unions felt strongly about their new relationship with the government in 1997. As Lloyd put it:

> In some senses, the education unions are in a better position than the affiliated unions when another [Conservative] government comes into power because, even though . . . they don't support the other government, they still get invited to talk, whereas, of course, we get invited nowhere . . . Bang! Down came the thing in 1979 . . .

In short, with the exception of the period when John Patten (secretary of state for education 1992–94) refused to meet most teacher organisations, there has been a history of almost continual contact between teacher organisations and successive governments.

This was not the case for the Labour affiliated unions which had been ostracized by the Thatcher and Major governments because of their relationship with the Labour Party.

Once the Labour Party became the government in its early years at least, key areas of dispute were subject to resolution through party management channels. The Labour Party affiliates were not going to look kindly on non-affiliated teacher organisations who had emerging grievances with the Blair government particularly since when, as Lloyd asked;

> Did you [the non-affiliates] put a ten pound note into the kitty that paid for all this during the dark days and now?

So at precisely the time when mandated reform was at its most intense, and professional anger at 'naming and shaming' was at its most acute, the teacher organisations where bereft of, and isolated from, support from the rest of the Trade Union movement.

In short, the rest of the Trade Union movement did not feel inclined to support the teacher organisations in their concerns about the effects of continual mandated reform.

During the second Labour administration, the TUC sought to remedy this imbalance by seeking agreement with the government to create a replica of the party management model whereby education unions and the government would seek agreement on education policy implementation through a 'Social Partnership'.

Whether a coalition government will bring down the shutters on such a partnership in the same way as a previous Conservative government did in 1979 with unions affiliated to the Labour Party remains, at the time of writing, a moot point.

The uses and abuses of research evidence

Prior to New Labour taking office there had been considerable discussion about the value of using educational research to shape policy and practice (Hammersley, 1997; Hargreaves, 1996; 1997). Hargreaves argued for a research based profession based on a model drawn largely from medicine. Further criticisms of both the quality and relevance of educational research were also voiced by Hillage *et al.* (1998) and by Tooley and Darby (1998) although in the latter case critics claimed the case presented was highly selective.

Kenneth Baker also expressed frustration about the long lead times created by the idea of trialling research informed curricula.

> I inherited certain curriculum groups who'd been studying physics for five years ... it was unbelievable ... nothing had happened ... a trial here and a trial there ... if I'd have to have gone through trials nothing would have happened.

At one point it was rumoured that David Blunkett had designs on that part of the university research budget derived from the 'selectivity exercise' which went to education with the intention of commissioning specific projects which were deemed to have direct relevance to the implementation of key policies in schools. However, the Higher Education Funding Council for England (HEFC) seeking to forestall any such possibility set up its own Teaching and Learning research Programme (TLRP) with a budget of 28 million pounds devoted exclusively to educational research.

The idea of evidence based practice quickly became integrated to the Labour government policy, partly because both David Reynolds and Michael Barber who headed the Numeracy and Literacy Task Forces came from the school improvement stable which aimed to provide a base of 'known to-be valid knowledge as a foundation for teaching' (Reynolds, 1995: 59). Yet according to Judy Sebba, herself an academic before being appointed as an advisor in the Standards and Effectiveness Unit, the translation from this rhetoric to reality proved to be somewhat problematic.

There is plenty of evidence that while government pre-1997 used advisers, some of whom happened to be academics, they did not acknowledge the use of research evidence and their early welcome for collaboration with the academic community began to assume a conditional tenor. As Robin Alexander's tells it:

As soon as Labour got into power in 1997 I wrote to the incoming secretary of state David Blunkett, with whom I had discussions just before the election. It was all very encouraging. I wrote to Blunkett saying how delighted many people were that at last serious educators including academics and researchers who had felt disenfranchised over the previous period because research had been rubbished in a fairly systematic way. . . . at last there was a chance for us to engage constructively with policy. The letter was passed on to Stephen Byers. I wish I had it in front of me to quote but it's said pretty well – Thank you for your letter, we will be interested in having discussion with academics as long as they support our policy.

Judy Sebba offers three main reasons why the link between researchers and policy makers was so fraught with difficulty. The first has to do with the naivety of politicians 'who may intend to use research but find themselves in a very difficult position' when the full consequences of their decisions emerge. Thus the evidence base for effective whole class teaching suggests that it should be carried at pace and include a high level of questions. Out of this came the recommendation for *whole class interactive teaching consisting of questioning* which was to be undertaken at a *lively pace* as the cornerstone of literacy and numeracy lessons. But as Alexander (2004) points out if the purpose of such teaching is to promote what Brophy (2002) terms *thoughtful discourse* then pupils require thinking time so that the exchanges should be dialogic rather than inquisitorial.

Second, researchers themselves are often 'too precious about the way in which they expect their research to be used' and are often too selective in what they present. Sebba describes her own experience on her appointment to a chair of education after her time with the Standards Unit.

When I came [*to the University*] one of my biggest arguments was that people were producing too many papers where their own colleagues were referenced in the first three paragraphs. They didn't show a worldwide view.

In Sebba's opinion this preciousness and insularity among researchers often prevents them from presenting evidence in ways that meet with the politicians' and other influential persons' needs or even prejudices in ways that don't compromise the essential message. In her view researchers need to 'play and understand the game'. As an example she gives an account of writing up the evidence in support of teaching thinking skills.

Cause and effect or a contradiction in terms?

Previous Conservative Party policy as much as early Labour Party policy provided the basis for the new Labour government's educational reforms. However, Labour departed from the previous Conservative government in two crucial aspects. It was prepared to intervene on the nature of pedagogy in the classroom and, irrespective of its lack of statutory abilities, it was prepared to direct reforms in schools from the government's own Education Department. Some feel that educational change has come at the high cost of teachers' professionalism. Others such as Alasdair MacDonald are very clear that there 'has been a transformational change in terms of the quality of what happens in the classroom'.

The euphoria of 1997 was never going to last. No government can ever meet such high expectations. High costs to teacher professionalism and transformational change in children's learning may be cause and effect or a contradiction in terms. The big question for government, as it must be for parents and their children, is whether its relationship to teachers, hinders or fosters their effectiveness. Given the expectations that society has of education, it is a question that governments should ask themselves much more than they do.

3 Can schools do it all?

Talking about resilient children is a cheap solution to society's problems ... But if your handicaps are society-caused the bigger investment is to get rid of the handicaps. So the South Bronx has the highest rate of asthma among any young people in America, perhaps the world. There are 12,000 diesel trucks that run almost all day long at the Hunt Point Market there, which is the big food market in the New York City, and five major freeways criss-cross the South Bronx. The kids who are trapped in there are, some of then can be as resilient as they want but that's, this is not the solution. The solution is that's not an area that's fit to raise children in.

This vivid depiction of life in the Bronx given by David Berliner in interview may seem far removed from the lives of children growing up in the United Kingdom but it is, nonetheless, a stark reminder of the futility of the belief that schools can do it all. It was Basil Bernstein who famously wrote, four decades ago that schools 'cannot compensate for society' (Bernstein, 1977). They cannot repair the ruins of social policy or environments unfit for children and families and however resilient children may be, resilience is, says Berliner, not an inexhaustible commodity.

The Every Child Matters (ECM) agenda, seen by some of its critics as a confused and over-complicated way of addressing the issue, was premised on the belief that redesigning schools means looking outward to the needs of parents and children, forging the missing link between school and community. The Children's Plan which followed from the ECM Green Paper recognised it was a long-term ambition to 'to make England the best place in the world for children and young people to grow up in'.

It places families at the heart of government policy, taking into account the fact that young people spend only one-fifth of their childhood at school. Because young people learn best when their families support and encourage them, and when they are taking part in positive activities outside of the school day, the Children's Plan is based around a series of ambitions which cover all areas of children's lives.

(DSCF, 2008)

Interestingly this was recognised by Michael Gove who, to paraphrase Peter Mortimore, said, that 'schools can make a difference' but that they cannot make all the difference.

Where you have traditional white working-class or, in some cases, welfare depen-dent communities – generations of people who have not been able to rely on steady employment – there can be particular problems which schools cannot tackle alone. This doesn't mean teachers shouldn't try. They should. Schools can provide children who have challenging backgrounds with a degree of structure. Support can be given through breakfast or after-school clubs or by a nutritious school lunch. It can be enhanced by organised games or other physical activities. It can also take the form of literacy catch-up work or a tighter focus on support-ing special needs. These things regularly happen in many schools and can make a significant difference to a pupil's life.

'All aspects of children's lives' implies considerably more than schools are able to 'deliver', in government terminology. In Gove's view the Every Child Matters agenda was not one he would be happy to live-with in the longer term and one of the first acts in the coalition government was to separate 'education' from 'children and fam-ilies', with the departmenting reverting to the less ambitious nomenclature as the Department for Education.

How to respond to, or attempt to manage, the combined impact of social deprivation and the unprecedented expansion of commercialisation on the attitudes of parents and their children? A teacher in a secondary school interviewed during a 2008 study for the NUT, painted a vivid picture of the problems facing some parents.

> Parents do come in upset, angry, expressing a sense of injustice. If you take the time to listen, to be calm and hear them out they eventually confess that they are struggling with discipline. Their children are out of control. Their partners have left. They can't pay the bills. They are fragile, volatile!
>
> (Galton and MacBeath, 2008)

What was once a more secondary-related phenomenon is beginning to have an impact on primary schools. Primary head teachers and staff commented on 'difficulties with a small but significant group of parents . . . [who were] . . . themselves under social pressure and often unable to deal with their own children's behaviour [and who] . . . could be highly confrontational, sometimes resorting to violence in protecting their children's interests.'

Galton and MacBeath noted the prevalence and significance of this phenomenon compared to the comments of staff from the same schools researched five years previ-ously. An interview for this book with a headteacher of a successful and socially mixed primary school in Greenwich added confirmation of this trend. She said that there were now a small but significant number of parents who had no control over their children and described children who would kick and bite school staff as well as their parents.

Five years ago, she said, the number of such children was negligible. Now, she estimated that one in ten of the children in her school had entered without any sense of social boundaries. She believed that these children were now observing worsening social behaviour from their parents and that this was having a profound influence on their behaviour, engagement with the curriculum and achievement.

This head identified long-term, inter-generational unemployment as the trigger to the social disruption of these families. She cited the triangulation of long-term unemployment, the attendant desperation it evoked, and the unprecedented pressures through the media. Commercialisation with its emphasis on sexualisation, she claimed, had impacted so deeply on family life that it was easy for some parents to lose respect for social norms in relation to themselves and their children.

Time Trends in Parenting

The phenomenon of parental control, or lack of it, has been explored recently by the Nuffield Foundation through a research review, *Time Trends in Parenting and Outcomes for Young People* (Hagell, 2009). At first sight the findings of this review would seem to contradict Galton and MacBeath's findings.

The study concluded that deteriorating standards of parenting were not the explanation for the rise in children's behaviour problems in the last quarter of the twentieth century and suggests that trends in problem behaviour would likely have been more marked had there not been the improvement in parenting observed in this study.

Yet Gardner *et al.*'s data analysis also showed that 'there had been a general increase over the past twenty years in self-reported distress among parents, and these increases in distress have affected single parents and parents on low incomes to a greater extent than they have other families'. In fact, the study found that parental distress has increased at a far greater rate for parents in 'very disadvantaged' circumstances (compared with parents in other groups). As the study said, 'this is a crucial finding', adding, 'parent's emotional problems are critical for understanding links between social context, parenting and children's outcomes'.

This is an important finding, highlighting the need for increased support for parents who are desperate and out of control of their own lives. However, as the Greenwich Primary headteacher noted, schools cannot be expected to tackle the root causes of the breakdown of social norms. In short, although they can remedy their effects, schools can't do it all. She did not believe that schools, in themselves, could manufacture social cohesion. Their capacity to foster children's learning and socialisation was bounded by the time that those children spent in school. She was sceptical about a centralised concept of social cohesion which mandated schools to promote social cohesion by requiring them to make connections with local business and community groups. The ECM agenda was one of the top three pressures on her and also on the school and yet it had decreased the effectiveness of her local authority. The job of the teacher might still be doable, she claimed, but only if the school had a culture of focusing on the needs of individual children and on identifying their learning needs.

In another part of London, William Atkinson, head of the Phoenix School, echoed these concerns, inviting Michael Gove, at that time shadow education minister to spend time in a secondary school in 'exceptionally challenging circumstances' so as to gain an insight into the context within which government policies play out. And, Atkinson added, these same issues are likely to play out under a new government legislating for raising standards but with diminishing resources to offer to schools in places such as Hammersmith, Tower Hamlets, South Benwell in Newcastle or Moss Side in Manchester.

Nested lives

There is, suggests David Berliner, an inherent inability for policy to get to grips with the 'nesting' of children's lives in their relentless push to make schools and teachers accountable for social dynamics that lie well beyond the reach of teachers and senior leaders. His comment, made in a US context, nevertheless resonates with the issues at stake in the UK.

> Children and young people live nested lives, so that when classrooms do not function as we want them to, we go to work on improving them. Those class-rooms are in schools, so when we decide that those schools are not perform-ing appropriately, we go to work on improving them, as well. But those young people are also situated in families, in neighbourhoods, in peer groups who shape attitudes and aspirations often more powerfully than their parents or teachers.
>
> (Berliner, 2005)

The concept of nesting is an important one because it places a child's experience at the centre and moves outwards in concentric rings to siblings, peer group, parent, parents or successive partners, the neighbourhood and those who inhabit it. The neighbour-hood effect is one that has received scant attention in research and policy but children and their teachers don't need research to tell them that the culture and norms of the places where children grow up, the other children they meet, play with or fight with are a major determining factor in attitude to and achievement at, school. Peer pres-sures that weigh heavily with children and their exposure to significant adults who model behaviour are, as Kincheloe and Hayes (2006) have shown, typically transcend family effects. Any mitigation of the neighbourhood effect depends on adults who provide resources, opportunities, models of activity and social norms, who provide helpful networks and exert social control over deviant behaviour. The high profile case in January 2010 of two children who tortured two of their peers was, claimed in the press, due to these boys growing up in a 'toxic environment'.

A department for children, schools and families

Successive governments have not been oblivious to the inexorable and mounting evidence of social disintegration and the parental effect. It has been a recurring theme in government reports, in initiatives on Positive Parenting, Parents on Line, Sure Start, parenting orders and parent contracts. Parent Know How, a 2007 £60 million Department for Children, Schools and Families (DCSF) programme, 'seeks to transform the quality, choice, provision and awareness of parental information and support services, where needed, in order to help improve outcomes for children and young people'. The change of name from the Department for Education and Skills to the Department for Children, Schools and Families under Labour was a cornerstone of government policy, which placed 'school' symbolically between 'children' and 'families', apparently a matter of considerable debate within the department at time but signalling what was seen then as the role and purpose of the school.

Irrespective of government and party politics, school does play an intermediary between child and family and so carries with it a burden of accountability.

It means that schools have a legal and moral responsibility to account to children and to their families for the quality of service they provide and for the degree to which they engage families and children in learning as a shared enterprise.

From a government perspective accountability to children and families is policed by an upward reporting through the agencies of the state – the department, National Curriculum testing, performance tables, School Improvement Partners and Ofsted – all subject to continuing changes within and between governments. Yet, as evidence continues to show, disenfranchisement of children and their families is an ongoing concern. The issue is writ large in relation to parents of children with special needs.

The Lamb Inquiry (Lamb, 2009) reported that parents of children with disabilities and special needs 'wanted the system to work for their children as it does for everyone else' (para 28) but that their children's needs were very often misunderstood and, added the report – the quality of communication could generate 'significant levels of hostility'. As the Inquiry noted:

> Good communication was often as much about the capacity of the school or service to listen to them [parents] as to talk to them.
>
> (para 35)

It was in relation to statementing of children with special needs that communication issues rose most saliently to the surface. The process, Lamb found, frequently caused 'high stress and anxiety', often devoid of requisite support and basic information. Statements were, it was claimed, 'cut and paste', written to describe local authority criteria rather than to describe the child. There was confirming evidence from school staff – 'Statements did not appear to be fully conversant either with the child or the special educational need the child had' (para 23–24). Bland and unsupported statements about needs and progress were liable not only to frustrate parents but also to throw into sharp relief the low expectations held of their children.

> There is a tendency for annual reports to say that a child 'is making good progress' without providing any evidence to substantiate the claim or explain what 'progress' means. In a number of cases, parents have reported low expectations over what a child is achieving.
>
> (para 30)

The fact that parental views were often not reflected in the statement served to undermine their confidence in the process and confidence in the system. Nor, the inquiry noted, was the voice of pupils taken into account in the process.

Rather than simply more effective statementing or better communication the Inquiry's conclusion was more fundamental – 'the importance to parents of knowing that those working with their child understood their child's needs and good communication'. This would entail, concluded Lamb, 'a cultural shift in the way the schools and services interact with parents' (para 39).

Can schools do it all? the school effect

Much of the debate nationally and internationally about the place of schools as intermediary between child and family was sparked by the highly influential and provocative 1971 Jencks Report in the United States. The central thesis and conclusion of *Inequality: A Reassessment of the Effect of Family and Schooling in America* was that the 'school effect' was marginal when set against the parents, family, peer and community effect.

The report was to set in train four decades of school effectiveness research in numerous other countries, often reported as contradicting the Jencks' thesis. However, most tend to concur with what was being reported in the US, although with a different spin. The much celebrated finding of the Mortimore *et al.* 1988 study *School Matters* came to a very similar conclusion as the Jencks Report but chose to look at the potential of the 10 per cent full glass than the nine tenth empty glass of the American study. Indeed, hundreds of studies later the school effect remains stubbornly in the 8 to 15 per cent region.

This is a much misinterpreted statistic. It relies on a methodological approach which has evolved in sophistication over the three to four decades since Jencks, and now takes the form of multi-level modelling in which student attainment between given points is used to calculate added value and on that basis to try and attribute changes (effect sizes) to teachers, subject departments, senior managers or the headteacher. These 'black box' studies inevitably focus on the inner mechanisms of the school and on what is most accessible to measurement. The 'effect size', a normative measure between the more and less effective schools, often slides imperceptibly in policy documents, and even among effectiveness researchers, into the language of 'good' schools. It is a distinction that the most scrupulous of researchers have sought to make, given that what may be considered 'good' may not necessarily be effective and vice-versa.

The central question 'what makes a school "good"?' remains a contested issue, dividing those who argue that schools should concentrate on what schools do best and those who see schools as a community hub or as service agencies tailored to what parents want for their children or for themselves. In a world of accelerating social change the view that schools should be outward, rather than inward looking will remain a contested issue. The expectation that schools should provide a 360 degree service to children and parents, and be a key agent in triggering community cohesion, will inevitably remain a recurring theme in local and national policy discourse.

Serving the community

The idea of schools serving the community is not new. The community school movement which emerged in the early 1970s was in some respects a revisiting of Henry Morris' Cambridgeshire Village Colleges created 50 years before. In

Sutton-in-Coalfield the Sutton Centre, opened in 1974 was not to be called a school but a community learning centre incorporating the local library, bowling green, disco and with its completely open plan design putting learning on view to adults and children alike. The Abraham Moss Centre in Manchester also created in the early 1970s described itself as 'a vibrant combination of college and community facilities', home to Crumpsall Library and Leisure Centre with specialist facilities which included hairdressing salons, beauty therapy suites, a fully equipped theatre, IT and multimedia studios, music practice rooms and recording studios.

Much of the enthusiasm for community schools was to dissipate over the 1980s and 1990s with an emerging rhetoric, a standards agenda and an OFTSED regime that wanted schools to be schools and not community playgrounds. This did not prevent schools, particularly those in 'challenging circumstances', from reaching out to their communities but with targets to be achieved and with intensified competition it did constrain a genuine community focus.

A further re-invention of schools began to emerge in the mid years of this decade, expressed in government action to integrate local authority services following Lord Laming's inquiry into the death of Victoria Climbié (House of Commons Health Committee (2003)). The idea of 'extended schools', co-located services, and one-stop shops emerged, drawing on the aptly titled 'new community schools' in Scotland, in turn modelled on the full service school in the United States which promised to parents and community a 'one door' entry to educational and social services.

However, the change in both government expectations and the social environment since the optimism of the early community school movement meant that the second Labour government was never going to backtrack on its target driven standards agenda in order to cope with the lessons of the Victoria Climbié tragedy. Legislation creating local authority Children's Services did not replace school responsibilities but added to them.

Tim Brighouse, up until 2009, leader of the London Challenge and long time advocate of re-invented schooling, envisaged a future for schools in which they would act as a hub or anchor:

> If you were really interested in development of the education of the child then you had to think of schools being a kind of anchor but an anchor orchestrating sets of experiences beyond school.

He went on to describe how in the early 1980s as director of education he had tried to engage debate on the nature of the school day and the curriculum, with a series of 'packed meetings all over Oxfordshire' and extensive press coverage but always running up against the far-reaching implications for social change that would be required. While the school day was to remain sacrosanct these discussions did lead to the founding of Education Extra ('commitment to the needs which all young people have for engaging in enjoyable and supportive learning, above and beyond the curriculum and well beyond the classroom') and to the creation of the Children's University, targeted on children in the most disadvantaged of communities. The Children's University (a rapidly growing organisation today) is a concrete expression of that vision, exploiting sites such as museums, art galleries, docks, airports, farms or factories as validated learning destinations.

Fixing the community, fixing the school

'If you can't fix the community, you'll never fix the school' quoting Bill Bates in *Times Educational Supplement* (Milne, 27 July 2007). He was headteacher of New Manton primary school in Nottinghamshire; a school impoverished by pit closures, a school which had achieved notoriety in the late 1990s because of the behaviour of its pupils. Bates' comment was rooted in the idea that the community has to take responsibility for the attitudes children have to their school and to their learning.

While he could point to considerable success in linking the school to Manton's community, he nonetheless felt constrained to resign his headship because of his local authority's and local MP's criticisms of his National Curriculum test results. His baldly expressed sentiment would have found little sympathy from the architects of the Children's Plan and ECM. While agreeing that schools were a key catalyst in promoting social cohesion in the community, reaching the government's floor targets in literacy and numeracy were also vital.

For teachers, however, the *Every Child Matters* agenda itself was not the issue. Interviews with teachers show that they did not contest the idea of linking children's social care and their education, but the accompanying accountability procedures that came with the ECM were the source of frustration. As one teacher put it:

> [The Every Child Matters agenda] is an improvement because it focuses people on the things that are important for young people and joint working . . . It is a distraction in terms of the paperwork that goes with it and the confusion over who actually fills in that paperwork or who is responsible for each element of (the work).
>
> Accountability procedures are . . . getting in the way of what we have to do with (children) because, if we had too much to do, then little time is really left to spend with them, (to) one . . . build up relationships so that they can impact on others and, two, for them to really achieve at the level we want them to achieve because we won't have enough time to spend with them in the classroom.

The ECM agenda had other unpredicted effects. It was widely suggested that ECM led to a decrease in local authority support for schools, a reflection of a much wider debate about the effectiveness of applying a children's services approach to meeting children's needs. An interview with a classroom teacher at the same Greenwich primary school in south London suggested that ECM's holistic approach to children's well being had raised expectations among some parents about the role of the school. These parents now believed that the school should take over their responsibilities for children's behaviour. Given that schools have extended their remit to cover such issues as healthy eating and action against obesity, why should this not extend to children's well being in general, in and out of school?

How the ECM agenda impacted on parental perceptions of schools in relation to their own parenting is largely unexplored territory. And while ECM may not survive, at least in its current form, the question remains – what is 'doable' by the school in relation to the social stability of families as well as in relation to the wider contribution of schools to community cohesion?

A capital question

Sir Alasdair MacDonald, headteacher of Morpeth School in Tower Hamlets, made an important and similar point to his counterparts in Greenwich and Hammersmith when he referred to the wide differences in educational capital which children enjoy in home and community. 'I think you can raise attainment across the board in classrooms', he said, but 'I don't think you can narrow gaps in the classroom. I think the only way we're going to narrow gaps is by addressing expectations, aspirations and engagement with education.'

How to generate within the school the 'educational capital'– the birthright of the most privileged – is an ambitious commitment.

> The whole thing is about . . . educational capital . . . its incredibly important . . . that's what we need to provide in addition to the classroom, we've got to give young people all the other things that you know our society values and which middle class families provide for their children.

Macdonald's belief that schools themselves cannot eliminate educational disadvantage without addressing parental needs and expectations is confirmed by a body of research covering at least half a century, evidence which has had little positive impact on policy makers who seem unable to address the needs of those, as Johanna Crichton (2005) described them, who are 'disadvantaged, disaffected and disappeared'.

It also coincides with an issue which has only fitfully emerged during the last 20 years of national reform agendas; that of how to tackle educational disadvantage created by social class. As Mongon and Chapman (2008) note, the negative effects of social and economic deprivation on pupil attainment is three times greater than that of gender difference and is further compounded by ethnicity and its counterfoil, racism.

The young people to whom Alasdair Macdonald referred stand in stark contrast to those who benefit from the educational capital of parents, who support their children's engagement with learning, who nurture their children's aspirations, and are able to deal with failure and setbacks. As Peter Mortimore pointed out, two-and-a-half-decades after his seminal study of school effects;

> There are poor pupils whose lives are disorganised but whose parents – or lone parent – are struggling to survive, to find somewhere to live, to feed the family, to get through the next week . . . 'schools can make a difference', but they cannot make *all* the difference.

These are the family legacies which school achievement rides on, but in the absence of such capital schools cannot compensate for the social vacuum into which disruption and disorganisation flow. The issue may be couched as one of parental support but this it to misrepresent the nature of the issue. Goodwill towards the school is not enough. 'The vast majority of our parents will support us', said MacDonald, but what can schools be expected to do?'

> It's the pupils themselves that we really have to work with and know that their parents will support them in that . . . [but] we don't have the resources to change parents . . . you could dissipate so much energy in trying to change the parents in order to get them to support their children . . . I think we have to assume that if we get this a bit right (with). . . . our current pupils, the next generation of parents will actually then be able to provide their children with the kind of educational capital and support that middle class parents can.

Educational and social capital develop over time and are closely inter-related. Social capital relies on networks and connections. It involves norms such as trust and collaboration, and varies in form depending on the frequency and quality of contact and the strength of bonding between people. The fewer the connections parents have to other supportive adults, to sources of information and advice and the less there is trust in those around them and in 'the system', the less the opportunity to negotiate that system on their own and their children's behalf.

The following incident reported in *Schools on the Edge* captures the nature of the vacuum when parents are cut adrift from supportive social networks and lack the resource, self assurance and negotiation skills to play the system.

Anouka's story

> Playing too close and too inquisitively with D-I-Y electrical wiring, Anouka was subject to an intense electric shock and severe burns to her right arm. Her mother, in panic, knocked on a neighbour's door and then on another to see if she could borrow some cream or bandages to put on the child's burn, or perhaps an aspirin to stop the pain. Neither neighbour was willing to open a front door at that time of night. As Mrs Okede's phone had been cut off she was unable to call her estranged husband, now living at the other end of the city. She decided she would take Anouka to the casualty department of the nearest hospital. With Anouka in her arms she walked the quarter mile to the bus stop where she knew there would be late running buses. She was lucky as one came within fifteen minutes and took her quite close to the hospital. The receptionist there was sympathetic to the child's clear distress but advised Mrs Okede that this was the wrong hospital and gave directions to another hospital two miles away. Two bus rides and an hour later mother and child arrived at the casualty department of the second hospital where they waited patiently in an overcrowded room for Anouka to be seen.
>
> (MacBeath *et al.*, 2008: 24)

For many parents it is lack of mobility and navigational know-how, trying to make their way through the thickets of bureaucracies and social institutions with the confidence to deal assertively with authorities in white coats. For parents (often the lone parent) gaining access to social and health services means juggling child minding, employment, and domestic upkeep, including guarding vulnerable property against ever present threats from mounting incidence of street crime and violence yet without adequate financial resources or emotional resilience to escape the oppression of a hostile environment.

The OECD's recent study, *Doing Better for Children* (OECD, 2009), found that in respect of 'protecting children from risky behaviours' the UK is only better than Mexico and Turkey out of the 30 industrial countries surveyed.

For many children and young people success comes with risk and is equally a matter of navigation. For children who bring with them a strong legacy of social capital from family and community, navigation of school rules and conventions is relatively unproblematic. The home culture in many respects coincides with the culture and norms of the school and of their teachers. For others it is a continuing struggle to come to terms with the tacit assumptions of school life, expressions of authority, systems of sanctions and rewards which conflict with the norms and priorities of the peer group and often of parents as well. Success in school is not simply a matter of academic ability but the expertise to understand and 'play the system'. It is reliant on motivation, commitment, perseverance in the face of setback (see for example Dweck, 1986) and a resilience and self determination which is able to defy counter cultural peer group pressure (Harris, 1998).

In Manuel Castells (2000) explorations of the Network Society the lack of social capital leads to what he calls 'perverse integration' – the route back into society through the twilight economy, the 'black' or 'grey' economy. This activity, however much on the social margins is not separable from the wider social and economic context in which these activities find expression.

In short, schools may make a major difference to the overall academic attainment of young people from less culturally rich backgrounds but unless they are equipped with the educational and social capital to use their qualifications the disadvantage gap will remain. Focusing on attainment and results, without fundamental systemic change will simply reproduce disadvantage.

It is becoming increasingly apparent, and indeed urgent, that the role of the school needs to be refocused and that school communities themselves have to be integral to that refocusing. It is those constituencies who need to be engaged in the debate as to what is doable for teachers, for schools and for their communities. It was clear from a range of interviewees that the Children's Services paradigm, with its armoury of top-down accountability procedures would not survive under a new government.

Ours is a vision for children – theirs is a vision for schools

Ministers in the Labour government between 2007 and 2010, defined the Children's Services agenda as creating the political clear blue water between themselves and the Conservative Party. Three major initiatives were imbued with this thinking: The Children Act (DfES 2004), The Children's Plan (DCSF 2007) and the Twenty First

Century Schools White Paper: 'Your Child, Your Schools, Our Future: Building a Twenty First Century Schools System' (DCSF, 2009).

Jim Knight, minister of state for schools (2005–9), described the difference between the Labour government and the Conservative Party on education policy as 'fundamental'.

> If [there is] a fundamental disagreement about a vision for education, then I'd say, at the moment [that] the Tories have got a very much school-based issue for education, rather than school system based. . . . Ours is a vision for children; theirs is a vision for schools.

How far this distinction is invidious and how far it is real merits analysis. Interviewed before the May election, a number of leading Conservatives had strong criticisms of the Children's Services/Every Child Matters Agenda. Baroness Pauline Perry, co-author with Stephen Dorrell, of the Conservative Party's recent review of Public Services (Conservative Party, 2007), described the amalgamation of education and social services into Children's Services as 'a disaster'.

> It's a disaster for both (services) . . . The last thing they needed at this point of time in history was to be re-structured by yet another structural reorganisation . . . when you want better communications between people, you don't necessarily have to merge them into one.

Her view is echoed by Kenneth Baker who argued that he would 'disentangle' social work out of education. 'I think that by combining them', he said, 'you try to make someone who's trained to be a social worker work in schools' and that his number one priority would be to split them. The dangers is a crisis mentality, said Gillian Shephard, arguing that without the split the small group of disadvantaged children will tend to drive the agenda.

> If you don't have, at local level . . . a strong force for what education is trying to do, everybody will be concerned with the smallest group of disadvantaged children, vulnerable children and . . . appallingly treated children at the expense of the rest . . . when there is a crisis in the Social Services bit all the money will go [there] . . . those cases (e.g., the Victoria Climbié case) have brought access to the whole education budget. I am very attached to rigour and intellectual endeavour, aspiration, ambition . . . If you haven't got someone speaking up for education it's not going to get you anywhere.

However, to deconstruct the Children's Services framework, both Shephard and Baker agree would be an enormous task, a political headache.

> I think the Conservative Party's got so much trouble that they can't do it . . . the headache is enormous, the debt is unbelievable.
>
> (Baker)

What I would want to have is for authorities to be able to choose how they ran themselves, so they won't be obliged to have Children's Departments . . . if you said to them that you're now going to reorganise back . . . think of the money and . . . the executive energy that would have to go into all that . . . in fact, I don't know how you would restore at local authority level the zeal for education . . . which has been legislated out of them.

(Shephard)

The disquiet in the Conservative Party about the Children Act and subsequent Every Child Matters policies is longstanding. Behind an apparent unity, some of Labour's key advisers posed similar questions. Michael Barber, as director of the PMDU (Prime Minister's Delivery Unit), said that he had thought the ECM agenda could be both a distraction and a risk. During his time advising Government he had raised the implications of the ECM agenda 'with everybody in the Department at every level'. While not arguing that they shouldn't be doing this, he posed the question – 'If you're doing this, how are you going to ensure this continues to focus on standards?'. He acknowledged also that:

In the current climate with the role of the director of Children's Services, I would not even want to argue that they should prioritise literacy and numeracy above worrying about the very small number of really hard cases . . . their time and attention is bound to be split and distracted from the standards agenda, even though the standards agenda is far from finished.

The Standards agenda has been 'hard won' agrees Estelle Morris. 'I'm very much in favour of a broader Children's Services agenda', but she worried that it could take 'the eye off the ball'. Her concern was whether the director of Children's Services could, in fact, be 'a doable job'.

At the moment, if you're the director of Children's Services, what will you be doing for a lot of your time? . . . You will be checking your child protection procedures. So you should, but while that's happening, you know what happens when you put your best people there because you've been told that's a priority . . . your eye will get taken off the ball . . . What's the alternative . . ? We could have done that (the Children's Services agenda), without re-organising the whole of local government.

Agreeing that the Children's Services agenda was problematic, Conor Ryan, ex advisor to David Blunkett and Tony Blair on education, pointed to the 'two cultures problem'.

It can be difficult at the best of times to put two cultures together but I think what's been lost in all of this is [that] the objective surely ought to be having very simple mechanisms for ensuring that, if there's a problem, it can be dealt with. What head teachers tell me all the time is that there's lots of committees and meetings . . . but, actually, when it comes down to it, [when] the head teacher is worried about a child they want a social worker to phone up.

(Ryan, 2009)

Ryan was also critical of the Labour government for taking a 'more of the same' approach to calling in Lord Laming a second time to review his own report.

The bigger difficulty . . . wasn't so much getting Laming the first time but getting Laming the second time . . . they had an opportunity to second time to get someone to go in and have a fresh look at it.

Laming was going to say you needed more of the same of what he [had] already recommended . . . actually you needed someone to just go in and take a fresh look at it . . . the report might have helped them to pull back some of the bureaucracy and improve . . . contact . . . with social workers.

Kevan Collins, the director of Children's Services for Tower Hamlets, while expressing his commitment to an effective social care system, was deeply concerned about the way in which Children's Services had been conceived and about the Government's leadership in this area. Committed to trying to make Children's Services work, Collins was nonetheless critical of the procedure-based approach to tackling the needs of vulnerable children.

Sometimes we are identifying children who we can support but what it means overwhelmingly is that an agency somewhere is passing their risk or passing responsibility [for] that child to this thing called 'social care' . . . There is a belief that if you just assess, someone gets better but all that happens is that you assess and you determine that the child meets the threshold or not. [You] reduce the profession to believing that what's missing is that there is a key piece of procedure missing.

Collins compared what he believes to be a reductionist approach in creating Children's Services to the government's leadership of the Literacy Strategy.

Whereas the government said . . . we want to do something about literacy in primary schools and we're going to lead this, there has been no leadership, in my view, . . . to create Children's Services. If it goes, and we lose it, . . . I don't think the responsibility lies with local government . . . I think that local government has tried to make this work; central government has not.

Yet what should work is not clear. Collins himself certainly has a vision for the role of the local authority which involves, 'a strong relationship between the schools . . . the settings children spend most of their time in and the community itself' which would also involve 'strong democratic accountability back to the community'. His solution is, 'a broad and clear way of statutory and non-statutory partners . . . required to be gathered together if they are in receipt of state funding to work in a collective interest for children, particularly GPs, schools, police.'

This vision is way out in front of the developing day-to-day experience of schools with their concerns about what is doable. Nevertheless the one thing that is common between the supporters and the sceptics in respect of the Children's Services paradigm is a high degree of dissatisfaction with its demands on schools and local authorities. As Michael Gove put it shortly before the election, anticipating the possibility of inheriting these issues:

> My worry is that the role of local authority director of Children's Services is vast, not just in terms of the proportion of the local authority budget that you're responsible for, but also you are responsible for Children's Services where there is both crisis management and also deep, structural social problems that you have to deal with and there is also the whole school improvement agenda.

Suffused with optimism?

As Michael Gove noted (quoted in Chapter 2), 'Whenever you have a new government, people start off with zeal, enthusiasm and idealism'. There is always a hope for change that will necessarily be for the better. In this chapter we sought to explore the changing expectations of schools over time and the seemingly elusive promise that schools would be on a continuous journey from good to great.

In the mid-1990s the themes which defined the debate about the characteristics of a good school were framed by the school community itself. The relationship to parents focused largely on the effectiveness of home-school links. There was a change in the conceptualisation of the role of the school in 2003, with the government's preparatory work on developing 'extended' or 'full-service' schools. Wilkin *et al.*'s (2003) study, 'Towards the Development of Extended Schools', commissioned jointly by the government and the NUT, is suffused with optimism about the potential for the school to improve the health of the community and vice-versa.

> Interviewees suggested that community cohesion could be increased through the implementation of an extended school approach . . . upskilling the local community, empowering parents and families, contributed to creating more stable and cohesive local populations . . . thus the school was identified as providing a common denominator around which common identities and shared feelings of belonging could evolve.
>
> (Wilkin *et al.*, 2003: 72–73)

For interviewees for this book this optimism seems to have evaporated. There is a clue which points to the reason in Wilkin *et al.*'s study itself. Summarising the 'key messages' that emerged from the study, Wilkin *et al.* concluded that, apart from the need for 'appropriate resourcing and management' and for 'effective discussion and communication with partner agencies, there is a need for: 'a model grounded in the contexts and needs of its local community, not a top-down imposition' (Wilkin *et al.*, 2003: 114).

In fact, the construction of the Children's Services model and its accompanying accountability procedures for children's well being have been nothing if not 'top down'. The procedural approach to meeting the needs of vulnerable children, criticised by Collins, is required of both local authorities and schools. The expectation is that schools should both fix the community and fix standards at the same time. This is an unreasonable expectation as Bill Bates found to his cost and as echoed by MacDonald and Atkinson, although both are tireless in their attempts to bring in and reach out to parents and to foster links with the surrounding community partners. While equally committed to raising standards, 'outcomes' are viewed through a less narrow and constricting lens.

Perhaps the optimism for the community-boosting potential of extended schools and children's services has been lost because, integral to the top-down model of such services is the accountability method of delivery. What is lost in that delivery model is trust. Local authorities themselves are mired in procedural responses to potential child abuse because they are not trusted to establish local approaches which respond to local circumstances. Neither apparently can schools be trusted. If a school does not follow all the new Ofsted requirements for child safeguarding it is not only given a negative judgement in that area but the overall judgement of the school is limited to the level of the safeguarding judgement. As Wilkin *et al.* imply, schools can only utilise the vision for their essential role in the community if they have control of how that vision can be implemented.

It is instructive that successful leaders of schools are in fact leaders who feel competent enough to buck the accountability requirements laid on their shoulders if those requirements do not coincide with their own and their schools' vision of what it means to be successful. Mongon and Chapman's (2008) study for the National College of School Leadership and the NUT on *Successful Leadership for Promoting White Working Class Achievement* highlights the importance of the 'internal locus of control' remaining with leaders and their schools. (Mongon *et al.*, 2009). This conclusion matches precisely Wilkin *et al.*'s resistance to the idea of a top down imposed model of how schools relate to their communities.

An idyll revisited

Once upon a time there was an idyll of the school as the hub of the community, 'a visible demonstration in stone of the continuity and never ceasingness of education'. Henry Morris' 1925 vision of the Cambridgeshire village college, while testament to a different age, remains as a powerful expression of what might, or ought, to be.

> As the community centre of the neighbourhood it would provide for the whole person, and abolish the duality of education and ordinary life. It would not only be the training ground for the art of living, but the place in which life is lived, the environment of a genuine corporate life. The dismal dispute of vocational and non-vocational education would not arise in it. It would be a visible demonstration in stone of the continuity and never ceasingness of education. There would be no 'leaving school'! – the child would enter at three and leave the college

only in extreme old age. It would have the virtue of being local so that it would enhance the quality of actual life as it is lived from day to day – the supreme object of education . . . It would not be divorced from the normal environment of those who would frequent it from day to day, or from that great educational institution, the family . . . The village college could lie athwart the daily lives of the community it served; and in it the conditions would be realised under which education would not be an escape from reality, but an enrichment and transformation of it. For education is committed to the view that the ideal order and the actual order can ultimately be made one.

Islington is far removed from Morris' leafy village but a more holistic view of children's learning is problematic as Richard Marshall, headteacher, suggested:

It will require a complete shift of thinking about what kinds of experiences schools are supposed to be providing for kids and if we started with that question, what is the child to do from the time they get up, they leave the house, they come back at seven o'clock say, what experiences do they have that we'd like them to have and what experiences do we want them to continue having throughout the rest of the evening?

In common with other of our interviewees he argues that it is more about subtraction than addition, about removing what we know to be the blocks and cul-de-sacs rather than yet more innovation.

Target setting, league tables, testing, national strategies, micro-management, the constant stream of publications from the National College, all of that really mitigates against thinking about alternative ways of doing things. The business model we've adopted is a bad model. It's too much like what people imagine running a business should look like and in fact it is no more good for business than it is for education.

The case for something completely different is a compelling one.

4 In the end, teachers are on their own

I came ingrained with the view which I retain, that ministers . . . can say what they like about what teachers should do but in the end teachers are on their own in the classroom and, therefore, they are the most important component in education.

(Gillian Shephard)

You can fiddle around with examinations; you can introduce targets and all the rest of it, but they're not at the real heart of the thing. When a teacher gets into the classroom and shuts the door, that's between you and the kids.

(Pauline Perry)

Self-efficacy or burn out?

These are the words of the Conservative government's last secretary of state before May 1997 and of an ex HMCI, who currently takes the Conservative whip in the Lords and is the co-author of the Conservative Party's review of public services. Kenneth Baker's caricature of a health secretary telling a surgeon how to operate, quoted in Chapter 2, was by way of affirming his view that it ought never to the job of education ministers to tell teachers how to teach.

Give or take an occasional aberration or two, such as Michael Howard's 2005 election campaign commitment to instruct all schools to teach synthetic phonics, these attitudes informed the previous Conservative Party's approach to teachers and have continued to be a matter for discussion within the coalition government.

This is not to say, however, that these three very different politicians shared similar views about the best ways of supporting the professional development of classroom practitioners or the mechanisms for delivering such support. For Kenneth Baker, the addition of five further professional days to the teacher's working year was deemed sufficient. The interview for this book is revealing. He simply assumed that teachers had the knowledge, skills and understanding to teach from day one a brand new National Curriculum. The allocation of the five, what soon became known as 'Baker Days', was therefore judged to be sufficient for teachers to acquire the necessary subject knowledge to teach the National Curriculum. When questioned about this assumption during his interview and asked if anyone thought that teachers might need more extended professional development, Kenneth Baker responded:

> I assumed quite a lot of them had it [the necessary knowledge]. I was asking a lot of them. I understood that. . . . I had lots of training sessions, introduced Baker Days . . . The idea of Baker days was that they'd be bought up-to-date.

Gillian Shephard, however, had a different perspective.

> I thought if the Conservatives had known that they were going to be in for eighteen years . . . the whole of reforms would have been completely different . . . The curriculum in primary and secondary schools would have been the first thing. The second thing would have been to link teacher training in with that.

Indeed her advice to a new secretary of state would have been to 'focus on teacher quality' while Pauline Perry thought that more than anything teachers needed encouragement:

> It needed better in-service training; it needed better initial training; it needed the celebration of things it does brilliantly; it needed celebration of its commitment; and it needed celebration of its professionalism.

These narratives illustrate that previous Conservative governments did not have consistent strategies for teachers' professional development. Yet it was a Conservative government that was responsible for the only full-scale enquiry into the continuing professional development of teachers in the last forty years: the 1971 James Report. Interventions by previous Labour governments had been also been sporadic. In the Callaghan period of office, for example, Pauline Perry persuaded Shirley Williams:

> to adopt a structure for professional development . . . and she persuaded the cabinet to give her £60 million . . . then, of course, it's given to the local authorities . . . to put the thing into practice and what did they do? They scooped it up and spent it on something else . . .

The demise of this decades-old initiative is instructive. Local Education Authorities' (LEAs) squandering of national CPD funding must have contributed to the then Conservative Government's decision to reduce the influence of Local Authorities and to ring fence what became Grants for Education, Support and Training (GEST). The Conservatives' growing distrust of LEAs also led to two of the key James Report's recommendations dying with the Conservative government's introduction of local management of schools; local authority teachers' professional development centres and local authority funded sabbaticals for teachers.

The consequence of the Conservative government's Education Reform Act therefore was that the chance to promote a genuine national professional development programme, defining entitlements and rights of teachers, as advocated in the James'

Report, was lost. In-service grants went to local authorities and schools through GEST but no underpinning entitlement for teachers accompanied them.

New Labour, however, as has been seen in earlier chapters had a somewhat different perspective on teachers. Labour's initial priorities were primarily concerned with literacy and numeracy in primary schools and failing schools in the secondary sector – followed by a dose of the quasi-market in secondary school provision. By their own admission the future of the teaching profession was not given much attention. In Estelle Morris' opinion the government lacked an understanding 'of the demands of teaching' during the first three years in office partly because 'unless you've done it' it is difficult for anybody to know 'the nature of the pressure in the classroom'.

Kevan Collins, who joined the Labour government's Standards and Effectiveness Unit in 1997, couldn't remember a time when the morale of teachers 'was ever talked about explicitly or attended to' because everyone was focussed on the literacy and numeracy targets. On reflection, Michael Barber admitted that:

> What is true is that, in pre-97 thinking, there wasn't an overview of where we were going with the teaching profession.

The Labour government's focus on the strategies was in sharp contrast to the approach adopted by Gillian Shephard during the last two years of the Conservative government. She set up schemes for Reading Recovery and Literacy and Numeracy Projects in 13 authorities but the intentions for the Projects were subtly different from their reincarnation under Labour. In establishing them, Shephard criticised a 'free-for-all attitude' to professional development in the 1960s, which she felt complicated things. Her comment which focuses on supporting teachers is framed by a deep suspicion of state intervention in pedagogy and, by implication, of state intervention into professional development for pedagogy.

> I didn't consider it is a good thing . . . if you shake teachers' self-confidence by saying what you're doing is wrong . . . therefore, (with the projects) I wanted to build on what teachers thought was right.

Labour's narrative, as we have seen, was completely different. In 1997, unlike its predecessors, it had no such ideological suspicion of state intervention in pedagogy. The Literacy and Numeracy Projects were appropriated as a national model and template for securing improvements in primary schools. Despite the protestations of various ministers from both sets of governments in the last 20 years that there was no intention of 'telling teachers *how* to teach' there have been many different approaches to 'telling teachers *what* to teach'; and many of these have certainly sought to engineer from the centre changes in teachers' pedagogy through changes in the curriculum either indirectly or through direct intervention.

It is instructive to list these attempts. In the indirect category under the Conservatives there was The National Curriculum, National Curriculum Assessment, School Performance Tables, the creation of the Teacher Training Agency (TTA) the Schools' Curriculum and Assessment Authority (SCAA) and the introduction of

'Baker Days'. Labour's contribution involved setting National Targets, revamping the TTA in the form of the Teacher Development Agency (TDA) and SCAA as the Qualifications and Curriculum Authority (QCA), creating a National College for School Leadership (NCSL) a General Teaching Council for Education (GTCE) and introducing workforce reform.

Under the Conservatives only three direct interventions were introduced with the objective of changing the way that teachers taught. The first of these was School Inspection, particularly during the reign of Chris Woodhead, the second the pilot Literacy and Numeracy Projects and the third the Grants for Education and Support and Training (GEST) scheme. In contrast Labour has introduced a raft of initiatives. These include the National Literacy and Numeracy Strategies and their re-emergence as the National Strategy with the inclusion of Social and Emotional Aspects of Learning (SEAL) and School Inspection Partners (SIPs). There was, in addition, the 2001–3 National Professional Development Strategy, the setting up of a Standards Fund, the creation of a Masters Degree in Teaching and Learning, Appraisal, Performance Management and an attempt at requiring teachers to regularly take a license to practice, Performance Related Pay and Local Authority Intervention.

Taken together, these represent a battery of government mandated measures. Their impact would seem to be variable and open to debate. Evidence to the Cambridge Review (2009) of Primary Education confirms that many of these initiatives continue to be contested. The list, however, confirms one thing; the Conservatives have been far more interested in indirect measures to improve pedagogy while Labour has been far keener on direct intervention.

With the possible exception of the GTCE, few measures, however, have addressed the question of how teachers can own their learning and how teacher self-efficacy can be enhanced. Why is this important?

OECD's recent Teaching and Learning International Survey (TALIS 2009) reflects on the connections between professional development, self-efficacy and teacher performance. TALIS is the first time OECD has tackled an international study of teacher attitudes to teaching and learning. Ranging through this groundbreaking study are components which collectively could be said to make up the building blocks for any government policy on the future of the teaching profession; building blocks which, at best, still only constitute part of the foundations.

A devastated workforce

The consequences of the Blair government's first education initiatives, particularly the 'naming and shaming' of failing schools did not go unnoticed in political circles. In fact, the government in 1997 did know, in no uncertain terms, about the state of teachers' self-efficacy and morale, as David Puttnam recalled.

> What I was asked to do by David Blunkett was . . . to get out and about in schools and come back to him by December [1997] at the latest . . . I said you probably know this is a devastated workforce. . . . [I] talked about the condition of

staffrooms and that too many people in them were operating sub-optimally a lot of the time, and in ways that the private sector wouldn't tolerate for a second . . .

In the aftermath of his frank assessment, the sound-bite, 'pressure and support', began to be used to characterise the government's relationship to teachers. The 'support' was two-pronged. One prong focused on attempting to raise teachers' self-confidence; the other on the status of teaching. Remarkably one man was at the centre of both strategies, David Puttnam. His analysis of 'a devastated workforce' persuaded the government to back his strategy to raise morale.

Appointed by Blair as a life peer, and seen as someone who was 'media-aware', he was given the job of promoting education to the general public. In making the appointment it is not surprising that the most media-aware of prime ministers should choose an ambassador who himself fundamentally understood the workings of the press and media. Puttnam's initial raid on the shocking state of teachers' staffrooms was only a prelude to his solution to tackling the problems of a devastated workforce, but it was popular.

> David Blunkett agreed to commit to £500 to ring-fencing improvements in every staffroom . . . and to our amazement we discovered that it was changing schools . . . for every £500 you gave them, you got £3,000 worth of value because teachers went and decorated the staffrooms themselves . . .

For Puttnam, a further way a devastated workforce could recover was through a public celebration of teachers' successes in the classroom; a judgement remarkably similar to Pauline Perry's view that, above all, teachers needed a celebration of the things they did brilliantly. Indeed, Puttnam's project was remarkable in another respect; it was consciously cross-party and consensual at a time when the whole thrust of Labour's education 'pressure' policies were highly partisan.

Puttnam's solution, the Teaching Awards, nearly didn't get off the ground.

> My deal with David Blunkett was that we wouldn't go ahead with the Teaching Awards if we couldn't get a sufficient number of nominees. He asked for 1,000 nominees . . . I got him down to 800 and, on the night before we closed, we had 796 . . . so I sat down with Caroline Taylor [the then Awards Chief Executive] and added four . . . well actually we created eight additional nominations . . . I went back to David and said, that was close, 804. He said, that's good enough. You'll be pleased to know that none of our nominations won!

In his interview, Puttnam was very clear about why the media was central to the celebration of the individual. The awards were to imitate the Oscars, indeed:

> Teachers [are] for me more interesting than any group I ever met in Hollywood.

Generous hyperbole as it may have been, there were many teachers who appreciated such a comment. While the attitudes of teachers initially varied from lack of interest to disdain, the agreement by the teacher unions to be Trustees and Puttnam's self-evident appreciation of teachers meant that the Teaching Awards became an annual fixture. For Puttnam, with an eye to media response, there was no point in having any sympathy with the idea of collective awards. The Oscar model was vital if it was to capture the media's attention.

Catching the hospital pass

The other form of 'support' involving Lord Puttnam focused on teacher status. The vehicle for raising status in Labour's policies was the General Teaching Councils in England and Wales.

The campaign to establish the General Teaching Council in England (GTCE) had been longstanding. All the main teacher organisations had policies to establish professional councils; albeit that the detail of those policies were somewhat vague. The core of those policies was, by and large, that the GTCE would stand up for teachers' rights and for teachers' professional development, and would maintain a register for teachers with deregistration for those whose conduct was unbecoming. Key questions were unresolved however. For whom would the GTCE become a voice? Was it representative of teachers? Was it their professional council or was it a council which safeguarded and spoke up, not for teachers' interests, but the wider public's?

Having been established, the GTCE became a classic case for the teacher unions of Oscar Wilde's maxim that you should be careful about what you wish for. For a start, the legislation gave the GTCE a far wider remit than expected. Not only did its remit cover registration, teachers' conduct and professional development, as teachers' organisations had campaigned for, but it included deregistration of teachers on the grounds of competence, and a mandate to have a voice in policy areas as diverse as the National Curriculum, assessment and school inspection. The government also chose to insert a clause which gave the secretary of state a right to add any additional responsibility to the GTCE's remit which the secretary of state so chose.

For teacher organisations, this extended remit rang alarm bells. They had long records of education policy work and were also sensitive to the GTCE being given the power to ban teachers from continuing to teach on the grounds of competence. Teacher organisations' concerns were also triggered by claims, in early GTCE literature, that it 'represented' teachers – leading to legal threats from the NUT to prevent the GTCE being able to describe itself as a representative body. However, the greatest mistake made by the government, teacher organisations and the GTCE alike was the assumption that somehow teachers would welcome not only the establishment of a body which disciplined them, but a body for which they had to pay on pain of deregistration. This led to the NUT threatening to ballot its members on refusal to pay the fee unless teachers' pay was supplemented by the government to cover the cost.

In short, the overwhelming response from teachers to the GTCE was hostility. As an initiative given to teachers with the avowed intention of raising the status of the profession, it backfired spectacularly. However, for the teacher organisations which had to perform rapid U-turns on their enthusiasm for the GTCE's establishment, there was some consolation in the common outcry from teachers, 'Why do we want a GTC when we've already got a union?'

For David Puttnam, being offered the post of first chair of the GTCE was definitely a mixed blessing. He had been provided with 'really good advice' by the long-established Scottish GTC to:

> create a low key organisation . . . that does its job properly . . . that doesn't stray outside its remit and start upsetting people it doesn't need to upset.

Given the controversy surrounding the founding of the GTC, the possibility of it meeting any of those criteria was slim. Indeed, Puttnam believed that the Minister responsible for the GTC's inception, Stephen Byers, by not focusing on legislation had actually undermined it.

> Stephen Byers wasn't all that helpful in piloting through the legislation setting up the GTC and it quickly became a hospital pass[1] because the funding was never properly put in place – it was all a bit of a mess.

Keith Bartley, the current GTCE chief executive, is still dealing with the fall-out of the 'hospital pass'. He was resigned to the hard slog of achieving incremental improvement in support for the GTCE as well as recognition.

> The research that we do tells us that our recognition within the profession is now very high, around 98 per cent . . . and that an increasing minority of teachers, running at . . . over a third, view the existence of a professional regulatory body favourably. . . . Most professional regulatory bodies don't expect to have a very high percentage of favourability rating . . . but they also have to have high recognition and low opposition . . . and our opposition rating is still running at about 27, 28 per cent . . . so that's the bit we have to work at, converting those who feel antipathy towards what they see as an imposition into at least an acceptance of its existence, if not a welcoming.

For such a reform-driven government, the 'support' part of the reform package for teachers was therefore both top down and patchy. It certainly felt tokenistic despite Puttnam's obvious good faith and best intentions. Such 'support' as was available was not only hampered by ministerial neglect but by the policy and promotional agenda of a government which could not be obstructed even by Lord Puttnam.

One example of the primacy of this promotional drive was when Alastair Campbell, Blair's chief press secretary, in an effort to promote specialist schools, told the press that, 'today marks the end of the bog-standard comprehensive'. According to Peter Hyman, who had worked out the phrase with Andrew Adonis:

> Conor Ryan, Blunkett's special adviser, was apoplectic . . . he knew this was too far for Blunkett and would annoy many teachers and unions. In public Blair condemned the phrase as being a bit over the top and would not use it himself.
>
> (Hyman, 2005)

Hyman reported the reaction as 'All hell breaking loose', The reactions prompted Blair to phone Puttnam who in his interview recalled the conversation.

> David, I want to apologise – you must be very upset over Alastair's remarks . . . Yes, I said, . . . upset is right, in one sentence, he just managed to undo six months' work.

Yet despite Blair's avowed unhappiness with a public relations disaster with teachers, the overarching prerogative of Labour's reform agenda meant that Blair privately approved – as Peter Hyman recalls: 'In private, he (Blair) thought it gave us some definition'.

It's more to do with confidence than culture!

On Puttnam's account the lines between 'pressure and support' were, in fact, blurred. The government's Green Paper, *Teachers: Meeting the Challenge* (DfEE, 1999) covered both pressure and support including the Teaching Awards and GTCE. It also made a concerted attack on the collectivist culture of teachers. For the first time a government sought to introduce teachers' individual pay incentives linked to performance management. The government's reasons were explicit.

> Few professions have turned their back on linking pay and performance to the same extent as teaching. The tradition in teaching is to treat all teachers as if their performance was similar even though in every staffroom teachers themselves know this not to be true. . . . The main reasons why the system has rewarded experience and responsibility but not performance is cultural.
>
> .   (DfEE, 1999: 32)

Contained within the 'threshold arrangements', as the performance related pay system came to be called, were both pressure and support; pressure to change a culture through a wholly unproven, individualised, incentive scheme; support, through the addition of hundreds of millions of pounds of additional funding for the threshold.

Introduced after a year–and-a-half of being elected, the Green Paper was Labour's 'Strategy for the Profession', as Barber described it. Alongside the threshold arrangements and performance management, the English and Welsh GTC and Teaching Awards, it contained a raft of other proposals including the National College for School Leadership, a School Performance Award scheme, and a national Fast Track scheme for 'talented trainees and teachers' and national numeracy, literacy and ICT tests for all trainee teachers. Tucked away in the Green Paper was the recognition that:

> a clear and continuing commitment to professional development throughout a career should be at the heart of teachers' professionalism.
>
> (DfEE, 1999)

It outlined a new professional development framework which appeared to have been borrowed from the 1971 James Report's recommendations. The framework consisted of 'three distinct, and equally important, elements':

- the government's training priorities including the literacy and numeracy strategies;
- school priorities; and
- the individual development needs of teachers identified through appraisal.

These various elements of the strategy for the profession have met different fates. Appraisal has evolved into performance management which has now been refined and linked to 'threshold assessment' for teachers' pay. The effect of this complex system of individual pay and performance incentives has yet to have an impact on standards. When asked whether ten years' investment in trying to move to performance related pay had improved teacher quality, the chief executive of the Training and Development Agency, Graham Holley, admitted:

> It's always very difficult to tell and I don't know of any research that proves that . . . it's difficult to prove because there are so many variables . . .

Indeed, Holley recalled the only evidence he had seen on the issue was from another occupational group: the civil service.

> That was a particular group of people, of course, with different motivations and culture but that didn't produce any kind of result which showed that differential pay had an effect on performance.

On performance management Holley was equally downbeat.

> It's more anecdotal than systematic at the moment, but we've got some hard evidence coming through that the introduction of performance management is . . . more to do with compliance than culture.

Holley's comments about the relative ineffectiveness of individual pay and performance incentives for teachers will come as no surprise. Research by Professor Ray Richardson at the LSE in 1998 said that such public service schemes were equally ineffective. He concluded that:

> individual performance related pay in the public sector has been, variously, counterproductive, 'a damp squib', occasionally, 'a very modest success'.
>
> (Richardson, 1998)

Something really worth doing

The fate of the third part of the Green Paper's strategy for improving teacher performance together with professional development, requires more extensive analysis, simply because it appeared to rectify decades of neglect of teacher learning.

Richard Harrison, the DfEE official responsible for implementing the Green Paper proposals on professional development (CPD), reflects that the intention of performance management and the threshold would have been:

something that would force teachers to improve, to up their game . . . and the professional development was a complement to that, but not something that was seen as important.

Harrison, it would appear, was out of step with other DfEE officials. He decided that CPD's lack of importance needed rectifying. He overturned the preliminary work carried out on the Green Paper's proposals and decided to go out to talk to a range of people.

> When I first [began] I had no perception of where teachers were [in their development] because I had not worked in schools at all. I was coming to it completely fresh . . . I tried to use that as a strength . . . I would say, I know nothing about this area, tell me about it . . . tell me what is happening. I was a bit like a sponge in picking up views and I tried to select people to talk to who then told me, would be informative and knowledgeable and balanced themselves . . . so through these conversations, I developed a view which was reflected in the strategy.

This approach could not have been further from Labour's roll-out model for delivering the Primary Literacy and Numeracy Strategies. It was essentially collaborative and, ironically, it reflected the relationship developed with teachers in Gillian Shephard's National Literacy and Numeracy Projects. Another irony was that the freedom Harrison felt he had was created by the low priority given to teachers' professional development outside the drive to implement the Strategies.

> I certainly did have a lot of freedom . . . I think partly because whatever people might have said . . . it's a fairly low status issue . . . it wasn't one [in] which ministers were very involved . . . I was very lucky . . . nobody had definitively staked out the ground . . .

Subsequently, Harrison achieved ministerial backing from Estelle Morris who persuaded Blunkett to support the CPD Strategy. Launched just before the general election in May 2001, it contained a range of innovatory forms of teacher learning that had never been promoted as a government strategy before. It included Best Practice Research Scholarships (BTRS); Early Professional Development for teachers in their second to fourth years of teaching, bursaries, termly sabbaticals for teachers in schools in the most deprived areas and international professional development.

Harrison's 'talking to people' involved drawing on the latest research. A key part of that research were studies which sought the views of teachers on the kinds of professional development that they valued (Cordingley *et al.*, 2003). The research identified the form of professional development which had the greatest potential for raising pupil achievement – collaborative professional development. Described by Harrison as 'a bright spot' against a thin background of research evidence, the EPPI research contributed to a range of innovations in the new strategy.

And it was a new strategy. No government had put together such a holistic programme before. It realised many of the James Report's proposals. And as a strategy, it was successful; or rather it was a successful pilot. While the bursaries had little impact, Early Professional Development was greatly appreciated by teachers who had just left their induction years. The BPRS not only provided a model for the emerging Masters for Teaching and Learning, but the evaluations received from the BPRS programme showed that, for experienced teachers, involvement renewed their commitment to teaching itself.

Tragically, the strategy was short-lived, lasting only two years, despite unprecedented buy-in from representative organisations and teachers themselves. The causes of its demise, in 2003, lay in the very freedom given to Harrison to establish it – the department thought it was relatively unimportant. As Harrison himself said, it was 'part of many other things going on in the department'.

Other structural factors undermined the strategy. The government's new Standards and Effectiveness Unit had its own priorities – the delivery of the Literacy and Numeracy Strategies and tackling failing schools. Indeed, Harrison thought that had he tried to lobby the SEU to raise the profile of the CPD Strategy, it would have damaged its existence. When asked what might have happened, he speculated:

> I think because of the preoccupation of the SEU, you couldn't do anything that was going to get in the way of their work . . . because then they would make sure it would not happen . . .

Philippa Cordingley also highlighted another reason for the strategy's semi-detached relationship to the department:

> The key problem [was] that they assumed leaders would do it. They got completely obsessed with school leadership, and by establishing the college [National College for School Leadership-NCSL] they [thought] they'd sorted the problem . . . we don't have to influence things very far because we just have to influence the leaders . . . they didn't understand they had to take the whole profession with them . . .

The 1998 Green Paper (*Teachers Meeting the Challenge of Change*) gave impetus to the establishment of the NCSL. Influencing leadership through a government agency became a top priority particularly given headteachers' bumpy relationship with the government over the Literacy and Numeracy Strategies. Michael Barber's comment that head teachers didn't 'like the sharpness of results and Ofsted inspections . . . they didn't like being held to account for their performance in literacy and numeracy . . .', provides an explanation for the government's determination to turn them into its levers for improvement.

Making sure head teachers are effective pedagogic leaders is of course a key strategic aim for any government. The OECD's recent study, *Improving School Leadership* (Pont *et al.*, 2008) confirms this as an international aspiration. Effective pedagogic leadership, however, requires governments to be confident in the skills and abilities of its leaders; which was self-evidently not the case as Michael Barber's comments in Chapter 2 of this book attest.

Expecting headteachers to be levers had one purpose and one purpose only; which was to lever in government reforms. As Richard Harrison himself said:

> We did have a professional development agenda but it was around literacy and numeracy . . . this was the sort of training they needed to have and this was the way they were going to teach it . . . that was what priority professional development was.

Harrison was thus in the curious situation of having created a buy-in strategy which had the capacity to bring about fundamental changes in classroom practice. But government itself did not see this innovative approach to professional development as a priority. Its eventual fate, therefore, was all too evident.

Initiatives do disappear

Two events conspired to blow away the government's CPD Strategy in 2003. The first was a minor funding crisis which hit primary schools particularly. Headteachers claimed that they didn't have the money to introduce newly agreed school workforce reforms such as planning and preparation time. Second, under pressure from headteachers, the government decided to remove the ring fence from the vast majority of its grants. This made the National CPD Strategy, which provided specific grants to local authorities and teachers, vulnerable to such pressure.

Judy Sebba, once adviser to secretaries of state, David Blunkett and Estelle Morris, recalls the decision to remove the BPRS scholarships – a key component of the strategy. Her description of the horse trading that went on between the DfES and headteachers' associations goes to the heart of the two questions: how can teachers receive equitable access to professional development and how could a National Strategy popular with teachers be undermined?

> SHA [the Secondary Heads Association] got rid of the BPRS . . . I had this argument with John Dunford . . . he [thought] that headteachers should be responsible for all professional development projects and I [didn't] . . . when the Unions were called to sign the [School Workforce] Agreement, that was the trading point with SHA [now the Association of College and School Leaders] because they said we want headteachers to have control over the money.

This appeared to be a classic example of one section of the teaching profession – a teacher organisation representing school leaders – using its power against another –that of classroom teachers. It would seem that SHA had used its power as a potential signatory of an important government agreement to return to a status quo which, it might be argued, was inimical to classroom teachers' interests. It was also an argument which had a synergy with the DfES's need to create head teachers who would deliver its reforms.

Judy Sebba, who took up an Education Chair at the University of Sussex on leaving the DfES, herself was quite clear about why giving professional development funding to headteachers would damage the interests of individual teachers.

We [Sussex University] had to come up with some means of allocating means to teachers who, for whatever reason, wouldn't be allocated a place [for research-based professional development by their school, or by their local authority] . . . because, otherwise, individual teachers are disenfranchised because they've fallen out with their head.

Judy Sebba's comment about the danger of teacher disenfranchisement highlights the tension in government policy for teachers. This tension remains in, and is exemplified by, the successor to the 2001 CPD Strategy, published by the TDA (2009), entitled *Strategy for the Professional Development of the Children's Workforce in Schools 2009–12*. It showed that the Labour government had come some way to learning the lessons of the previous strategy. It was strong on leadership of CPD in schools. It emphasised its belief in CPD being 'a right and responsibility for all members of the workforce'. It acknowledged the findings of the EPPI research.

International and national research shows that sustained, collaborative CPD which includes a mixture of school based activity, coaching and mentoring and external specialist input has the greatest impact on outcomes for children and young people.

(TDA, 2009)

Yet, nowhere in the document was there any evidence of how an equitable right or entitlement to CPD might be secured. How could the situation where a teacher who has been 'disenfranchised because they've fallen out with the head' become a thing of the past?

The failure to answer this question not only highlights the weakness and inadequacy of government approaches to professional development. It also shows that governments have yet to fully understand that teachers' collective self-efficacy cannot be solely dependent on a leadership structure which completely controls and mediates access to basic professional entitlements. This lack of recognition certainly led to the 2001 strategy being terminated. As Richard Harrison reflected:

The existing funding was chopped . . . we certainly [had] good strong evidence this was worth continuing . . . we lost everything beyond that year.

Despite this evidence, the key players in delivering the then government's initiative had little concern for its demise:

2003 seen from the Delivery Unit . . . was not high on my radar . . .

(Michael Barber)

Yes I think initiatives do disappear and you'll see that happening from one secretary to another.

(Conor Ryan)

Indeed, it might not seem that a long-dead initiative from a previous government is worth much attention. The fact is that to some it was the only initiative which had the potential to solve the problem highlighted by Judy Sebba; that is how to prevent arbitrary disenfranchisement of teachers. Any government with an interest in raising standards has to learn the obvious lessons from the premature ending of something which, as Richard Harrison put it, was really worth doing. First, it has to internalise and prioritise the importance of teacher learning. Then it has to ask itself how can this be done? It has to learn from national and international research on what works and it has to draw on past experiences and histories, both in and outside its own civil service. What must not happen is that such an initiative is prey to internal departmental jockeying or political trade-offs.

'Professionalism and trust'

Reference to political trade-offs highlights the fate of the government's second initiative to do something for teachers, the School Workforce Agreement.

Conceived in November 2001, as *Professionalism and Trust – the Future of Teachers and Teaching*, Estelle Morris described it as:

> the best piece of work I ever did, because it was actually saying that the vision had to be different . . . the booklet was the rationale for fundamentally changing the workforce . . .

The details of the agreement involving a member of education unions and government and its transformation into the Social Partnership is worth a separate study. As John Bangs said in his 2006 article on the Social Partnership:

> There is a developing theory and practice concerning trade unions, employers and Government relationships which has barely been analysed, but which is serious and needs further debate.
>
> (Bangs, 2006: 207)

Based on European concepts of social dialogue, the proposals have sought to deliver 'something for something' by reducing teacher workload in exchange for remodelling the school workforce in order to raise standards. 'Remodelling' has involved the employment of thousands of extra support staff. Their job has been to take on administrative tasks and specified teaching work to cover guaranteed planning and preparation time or absence. It was an agreement which was and is controversial with England's largest teacher organisation, the NUT, refusing to sign because, to use the words of the Plowden Report, there was an 'understandable anxiety about the employment of teaching assistants teaching on an unsupervised basis' (cited in Cambridge Primary Review, 2009 p. xx).

Irrespective of the controversy surrounding it, has the vision worked? Graham Holley's downbeat analysis of it is important since it was his agency's responsibility to service the agreement.

> There is some research evidence, and the . . . evidence is that [teaching assistants'] impact on straightforward educational standards is quite limited. The

evidence suggests . . . that teachers value the presence of other skilled adults in the classroom and that it frees up their time to do things with children more directly . . .

While Graham Holley's analysis is downbeat, the findings of four key studies which analyse aspects of the School Workforce Agreement are downright gloomy. On the impact of school staff on the attainment of pupils with SEN, *The Costs of Inclusion* found that:

> In the absence of relevant training, TAs . . . [develop] a close and caring relation-ship which can easily become one of dependency. Without expert support, they lean more to a nurturing role and find it difficult to extend challenge and risk taking . . . differentiation of the curriculum is typically left to the discretion of TAs. . . . there can also be a tendency for TAs to 'isolate' 'their' child from group or whole-class learning contexts. . . . their care and concern . . . is not matched by the expertise needed to make a classroom lesson relevant or accessible to a child with special needs.
>
> (MacBeath *et al.*, 2006)

These findings are confirmed and expanded to cover the whole pupil population in a DCSF commissioned study, *Deployment and Impact of Support Staff in Schools* (Blatchford *et al.*, 2009).

> We found a negative relationship between the amount of additional support provided by support staff and the academic progress of pupils . . . [in a range of year groups covering one or more key subjects] . . . we can conclude that the negative effect was on progress over the school year as well as end of year attainment.
>
> (Blatchford *et al.*, 2009)

This is a startling finding given the enormous Government investment in school workforce reform. The reasons Blatchford and colleagues give for it are very simi-lar to those in the MacBeath *et al.* (2006) study – lack of training and inappropriate deployment of support staff.

School workforce reform, the findings DCSF and non-DCSF commissioned stud-ies have come to similar conclusions. *Teachers Under Pressure* (2008) found that five years after the School Workforce Agreement was implemented, the average working hours of primary teachers had increased marginally as had the hours of school leaders, whereas the working hours of secondary teachers had decreased marginally (Galton and MacBeath, 2008).

Indeed, in support of this assessment, the DCSF commissioned research from London Metropolitan University, *Aspects of School Workforce Remodelling*, concluded that:

> there has been no overall reduction in teachers' workloads.
>
> (Hutchings *et al.*, 2009)

Both studies concluded that any reductions in workload have been countered by the effects of other initiatives which had added to workload.

From this evidence, it appears that the objectives of school workforce reform have not been met. Teaching assistants are left to support the children with the greatest needs. The vacuum created by reductions in workload has been filled by other initiatives. In short, workforce reform has had little impact on changing teaching methods in ways that raise standards and nor has teachers' workloads being reduced: the two key objectives of remodelling.

The first academic analysis of the School Workforce Agreement, *Industrial Relations in Education* (Carter, Stevenson and Passy, 2010) has come to a wider, and for teachers themselves, a more disturbing conclusion.

> Taken together we argue that these developments represent a continued 'Taylorisation' of teaching in which principles that underpin the division of labour are increasingly applied to the efficient management of the school workforce . . . within this process new hierarchies are created in which a narrow band of managers assume greater control of the labour process of others . . . it is possible to argue that workforce reform represents a further separation of conception from execution in teaching, whereby those with management roles assume increased importance in designing and maintaining teachers' work, whilst the majority of the workforce find their work increasingly codified and policed.
>
> (p. 141)

This conclusion may seem pessimistic but it poses fundamental questions about the role, future responsibilities and professionalism of teachers which have yet to be answered.

'A State Theory of Learning?'

The key government strategy for improving the teaching profession was the Literacy and Numeracy Strategies. Michael Barber's paradigm for improvement of the basics in primary schools has been explored elsewhere in this book. The question here is whether the Literacy and Numeracy Strategies and their successor, the National Primary Strategy, have actually worked; not only as 'the Standards and Effectiveness Unit's professional development agenda' – to quote Richard Harrison, but as a strategy for improving the teaching profession?

Relatively little has been written about the Literacy and Numeracy Strategies. John Stannard and Laura Huxford's book, *The Literacy Game*, is a rare insider history of the Literacy Strategy. It reiterates Barber's reasons for giving this particular initiative priority; 'literacy teaching, along with literacy standards, were on a plateau and neither were good enough'. (Stannard and Huxford, 2007).

Like Barber and Collins, Stannard and Huxford detected little teacher resistance to their introduction. Webb and Vuilliamy's examination of the impact of the National Strategies probably comes closest to identifying why.

They [the strategies] appear to have led many teachers in our sample to a change in their values as to what benefits children's learning. . . . After initially being forced to change their practice, a large majority of our sample of teachers who were trained before 1990 [now argue] for the benefits of a more structured and focused approach to their teaching where lessons are more carefully planned and lesson objectives are shared and reviewed with pupils . . .

(Webb and Vulliamy, 2007)

The impact of the strategies on standards and the quality of teaching and learning is contested. Referring to the findings of the Effective Pre-School and Primary Education Project (Sammons *et al.*, 2009), believes that they have improved teaching quality and pupil achievement.

We found a very interesting, clear and statistically significant pattern of higher observed quality in classes where teachers used a plenary rather than not . . . The observed quality was highest in teachers' classes where a plenary was used in both literacy and numeracy and lowest where it was not used in either lesson . . . this indicates a positive link between greater adherence to the literacy and numeracy structures (as measured by using a plenary) and better quality teaching . . .

She also pointed to 'significantly positive effects of the quality of teaching on pupil progress' and says:

My own view is there's quite a lot of evidence of a positive impact of the strategies on pupil outcomes and teaching quality both from UK research, Ofsted evidence and international comparisons.

This view reflects Stannard and Huxford's analysis of the strategies and also the view of Geoff Whitty, the Director of the University of London's Institute of Education, who said that:

The effect of the mandated change initiated by the strategies had been broadly positive.

(Whitty, 2009)

These optimistic conclusions therefore contrast with the findings of Tymms and Merrell for the Cambridge Primary Review which conclude that reading attainment has changed little since the 1950s (Tymms and Merrell, 2009). Indeed, the Review criticises 'a state theory of learning', and concludes that 'claims that recent improvements in primary education are a direct consequence of the government's standards drive can neither be proved nor rejected'. However, not only do the comments of Sammons, and those of Stannard and Huxley and Whitty place a question mark over these assertions, they also raise an intriguing question; what if 'a state theory of learning' works?

To answer this question, it is worth reflecting on Webb and Vulliamy's analysis of teacher attitudes, which is similar to that of Galton and MacBeath (2002). Despite the strategies being 'viewed very positively' by teachers, they were also 'viewed as an expression of the government's lack of trust in the teaching profession'. The government's decision to mandate change:

> has, undoubtedly, brought about changes in classroom practice which many teachers consider an improvement . . . however, it has done so at great cost to the morale, confidence and creativity of the teaching profession, which is only beginning to show signs of recovery.
>
> (Webb and Vulliamy, 2008: 151)

The Webb and Vulliamy study was a source for Sammons' (2008) conclusion that the National Strategies were viewed positively by teachers because they 'promoted continuity in teaching and learning' and provided 'a structure'. This is then followed by a brief two line paragraph, with no discussion of its implications, stating that, 'nonetheless, the authors note teachers' resentment of perceived government prescription and lack of confidence in teachers' professional skills'.

The arguments that there have been improvements in practise and standards are as strong as the arguments against. However, if the arguments that the strategies have worked are accepted, the question then has to be; will they have a lasting impact?

In fact, in their final evaluation for the Labour government, Earl *et al.* explicitly warned about the dangers of not giving teachers' ownership of the strategies.

> In many cases, the Strategies have not yet produced the needed depth of change in teaching and learning. . . . Such a lag is not surprising given the length of time, but will need continued attention through the provision of sustained professional learning opportunities which should be increasingly embedded in the life and routine of the school . . . LEAs and schools need to have increased scope and responsibility for such professional learning.
>
> (Earl *et al.*, 2003)

To paraphrase Earl *et al.*, self-evidently sustained learning opportunities have not been 'embedded in the life and routines of all schools'. Wider evidence presented in this chapter attests that this shift has not taken place. Indeed, Graham Holley's tacit recognition that there is a very wide variation in school spending on CPD exemplifies this point (Evidence to the House of Commons DCSF Select Committee, 2009). Yet, the withdrawal by the Brown government of the £200 million spent annually on the Strategies from 2011 was met was barely noticed by the media, despite it being a major cut in funding for teacher learning. Some schools are only now asking where their support will come from. In some areas classroom practise may have improved; standards may have risen, but a very big question mark hangs over whether any improvements will last.

And now for something completely different

This analysis suggests that the history of attempts by successive governments to improve teacher learning is patchy, at best, and often misdirected. A key component of Labour's 1997 reform strategy, that of improving standards in the basics in primary schools, may last only a little longer than the life of the National Strategy itself. Hundreds of experienced consultants with a deep knowledge of literacy and numeracy have or will face redundancy or redeployment. The strategies' failure to embed their contribution in the life and work of schools as Earl *et al.* (2003) recommended, will dissipate an invaluable resource.

As Keith Bartley, the then chief executive of the GTCE said:

> The chances of being able to . . . convert some of the money that is being taken out of the National Strategies and ring fence it to enable the effective delivery of a National Professional Development Strategy (are) realistically virtually nil.

A 'culture of compliance', to use Holley's words, dominated the Brown government's final attempt at reviving a national professional development strategy for teachers. Its proposed requirement, that all teachers should comply regularly with a licence to practise, was predicated on the principle that compliance leads to improvement.

The other facets of Labour government reform, which directly focused on teachers changing their practise, appear to have been largely ineffective. Dominated by mandated compliance, the evidence on which they are based was insecure and their implementation has led to unpredicted and often negative consequences.

One thing is clear, however. The history of government support for teachers in the classroom provides ample material for learning lessons for the future. Short-lived as it was, the 2001–3 Professional Development Strategy provides a template for offering entitlements for learning directly to teachers. *Still No Pedagogy?*, Robin Alexander's 2004 pamphlet, remains a very good question to ask. Keith Bartley's comment that, 'It's the place where we (the GTCE) have to stand most strongly and most stridently', indicates wider concern that successive governments have simply ignored the central issue of how to foster teacher learning. The myriad informal developments in pedagogy amongst teachers, in schools, or mediated between local authority advisors and consultants, are atomised or, at best, localised.

Our analysis suggests that there is no central forum for debate on pedagogy, virtual or otherwise, managed and owned by teachers from which teachers can improve their practice. To put it baldly, there is still no pedagogical bank to which teachers can contribute and from which they can draw.

Low motivation, low satisfaction?

Symptomatic of this continuing lack of focus on teachers' professional development needs was England's refusal to take part in the first TALIS study. Michael Davidson, the senior policy analyst at the OECD in charge of the survey, refuses to attribute blame to any non-participants for this decision but his arguments for the participation for countries such as England and the US are telling.

> What we have got is [a] . . . focus on teachers' self-efficacy and . . . [on] . . . how they can and are able to make a difference with the students they teach. . . . Surely, any government would think it is important to know what teachers themselves feel is making them more effective in their work, even if the policy response to that is a bit tempered by the fact that it is self-report from teachers . . .

TALIS' overview of the teaching profession, however, begs a larger question. Why is it that no government has ever had a strategy for the teaching profession which has acknowledged the importance of teachers' self-confidence, self-esteem and self efficacy? Enthusiasm and innovation are reliant on these characteristics. Alasdair MacDonald, a successful headteacher, was under no illusion that understanding these needs is central to his school's effectiveness.

> We valued teachers' professional development . . . we put a priority on that . . . we were generous in the time we allow them for preparation . . . (as a result) teachers felt valued . . . they were allowed to develop their own ideas in an environment which was not overly critical.

TALIS reflects on the connections between professional development, self-efficacy and teacher performance, the first occasion when the OECD has tackled an international study of teacher attitudes to teaching and learning. Ranging through the study are components which collectively could be said to make up the building blocks for any government policy on the future of the teaching profession. The inclusion of self-efficacy is particularly important since teachers' responses to any government initiative are predicated on whether they enhance or undermine perceptions of their own effectiveness.

The TALIS report highlights research which shows that:

> Teachers with high self-efficacy expect to succeed in teaching and to handle students well, and this influences their interpretation of successes and disappointments, the standards they set and their approaches to coping with difficult instructional situations. Strong self-efficacy beliefs can prevent stress and burn-out and teachers' self-efficacy, beliefs and their job satisfaction are linked to instructional practices and student achievement.

The exploration of the factors likely to increase the probability of teachers changing classroom practice in ways that meet government requirements is in its infancy. Nevertheless, Michael Davidson said that some obvious conclusions have already emerged:

TALIS shows that what helps with self-efficacy is feedback, professional development and positive student/teacher relations. If teachers themselves are saying that they are very confident and happy in their work, then that's going to be a really good sign for retaining teachers. . . .

[While] we are a long way from having that kind of data [or any link to self-efficacy and outcomes] . . . perceptions of self-efficacy must be important for retaining teachers in the profession and attracting them as well . . . OK you want to retain and attract the right teachers but that involves another set of policies . . . but you can imagine that you're not going to make much progress if teachers feel that they're just not able to make a difference. Low motivation, low satisfaction.

The debate continues.

5 Inventing and reinventing the curriculum

What the best and wisest parents wants for his own child, that must the community want for all its children. Any other ideal for our schools is narrow and unlovely.

(Dewey, 1916)

So wrote John Dewey in 1916 setting in train a debate on the place and purposes of the curriculum which has been revisited in every generation since. But not always with approbation. In a US compilation of the ten most harmful books of the nineteenth and twentieth century Dewey's *Democracy and Education* is included in the top ten, alongside *The Communist Manifesto* and *Mein Kampf.* During the Thatcher administration Dewey's status as the arch heretic was reified, held responsible for the toxic doctrine of child-centredness. At a Cambridge conference in 2004 Richard Pring recalled being approached in the late 1980s by a furious secretary of state, Kenneth Baker, who accused him, as an ally of John Dewey, of destroying education in English schools.

Under the Thatcher government this charge was applied more comprehensively to encompass headteachers, complicit local authorities, HMI and academics whose embrace of 'progressivism' had left a trail of destruction across the school landscape. The cause célèbre which was to be the final nail in the coffin of 'progressivism', or the caricature which it was to become, was the high profile William Tyndale affair in 1975. Terry Ellis, the headteacher of this Islington primary described himself as a convener rather than a head, as Peter Newsam told Kathryn Riley in her book *Whose School is it Anyway?* (Riley, 1998) – a designation not out of line with many other London primary heads at the time but one deemed by the authors of the Black Papers in particular and the national press to be a sellout of children's futures and headteachers' accountabilities.

The Tyndale curriculum offered children a choice of, among others, English, mathematics, football and tie dying. Featured for over a period of four months in the national media it ignited the debate about 'progressive' versus 'traditional' teaching methods, destined to rumble for more than a decade. Trace evidence of this debate can still be found in current mindset of civil servants, as Mick Waters recalled during his time as director of curriculum at the QCA.

I turned up at a meeting talking about global sustainability, cooking, healthy lifestyles (which would include cooking), civic responsibility and helping youngsters to feel part of their community. We were told at this meeting that these were 'loony left wing, tree hugging pinko, ideas' that weren't sustainable. Financial capability was another. We were told that that was definitely not worth considering.

In Kathryn Riley's interview with Rhodes Boyson, 'pinko ideas' were clearly at issue in the mid-nineties. Eschewing a definition of what progressivism was, Boyson, a former headteacher before he entered parliament and took office as an education minister in the first Thatcher government, chose to define it by its opposite:

> The opposite of progressive education is structured education where the teacher comes into the classroom. The teacher is a teacher and he says 'sit and all sit down' and the pupils all sit down facing the right way, and he says 'we are doing this and we are going to learn something'.
>
> (Riley, 1998: 31)

Real Ale: a primary source

This was conspicuously not the case in primary schools in the 1970s, of which Tyndale was merely the most extreme expression. A visitor to a Berkshire primary school in the mid-seventies recounts a conversation with the headteacher in which the 'curriculum' was hard to perceive or define.

> It was a completely open plan school with children of mixed ages working individually in pairs and in groups, all engaged in their own pursuits, some extending outside through the open doors which led to the gardens and playground. Talking to children about what they were doing I would then ask 'where is your teacher?' Children would then look around, and reply 'I don't know. I haven't seen her for a while'.
>
> In conversation with the head I remarked on the huge variety of activities – reading, pottery, painting, writing, guitar making, stamp collecting – that these children were engaged in and the underlying child-centred philosophy. Her catalogue of different interests being pursued among the children was so extensive and idiosyncratic that I was reminded of a German educator, whose name I had forgotten at the time, in which he extolled children pursuing their own centres of interest as a way into broader issues. He gave as an example beer brewing which could give rise to a host of other sources of learning such as economics, marketing, packaging, art, chemistry and mathematics. 'Funny you should say that', she said, as she led me to cupboard in which a ten-year-old was in the process of creating a new flavour of beer. 'We keep him in the cupboard just in case an inspector drops in'.

The historian, Brian Simon, writing on the evolution of the English primary school notes that it was the abolition of the 11+ examination following the swing to comprehensive education that opened the door to the ideas of 'progressive educators' using the term in its 'broadest and most positive sense' (Galton *et al.*, 1980: 39). According to Simon, the 'nests of the new breakout' were mainly situated in Leicestershire, the West Riding and Oxfordshire and these local authorities attracted a stream of educational tourists from the United States during the early to mid-seventies, prompting the then commissioner of New York, Ewald Nyquist, in 1971 to declare that all schools in the state would become 'British Primary Schools' within the decade. History does not record whether the commissioner had in mind the rather bizarre, and more extreme example of this Berkshire school or the more mainstream versions of 'progressivism' which largely consisted of extending 'infant school practice into the lower junior forms'.

Where politicians dare not tread?

The Tyndale Affair along with the Horizon television programme based on Neville Bennett's book, *Teaching Styles and Pupil Progress* (Bennett, 1975) was a significant benchmark in the curriculum discourse, its ripple effects still extending into a newly elected government. At the time it provided the platform for Labour Prime Minister 'Sunny Jim' Callaghan to launch his 'Great Debate' with a speech on education at Ruskin College in October 1976. He spoke of 'legitimate public concern' over the sense of unease felt by parents and others about the new informal methods of teaching which, he said, 'seem to produce excellent results when they are in well-qualified hands but are much more dubious when they are not'.

Subsequent governments were to be less charitable or discriminating about 'progressive' methods which as numerous commentators have pointed out (Kliebard, 1986; Bennett, 1987; Galton, 1987) is both a vacuous and mischievous notion, bracketing Dewey together such diverse philosophical viewpoints as those of Rousseau, Froebel and Montessori and failing to discriminate when so-called 'informal' and 'formal' methods might be most appropriate. Moreover, research of the period (Galton, Simon and Croll, 1980) demonstrated that although the organisation of classrooms had shifted towards more individualisation (to accommodate the ending of streaming with the demise of the 11+ examination) the nature of the interactions between teachers and pupils remained overwhelmingly didactic. The accusation by one minister at the time that 'children were never told anything but left to find out for themselves' proved to be a gross distortion of life in the primary classrooms of the 1970s.

In a passage which may seem curious and self-evident today, the Plowden Report argued that children need to be capable of being taught as well as learning for themselves (para 496). It was a statement which William Tyndale staff were later to dispute, in their unswerving pursuit of discovery learning, wrote Kathryn Riley, but also it was written to avoid the caricatures of progressivism that were to be the very stuff of media coverage. 'Plowden was far from an anarchist's charter as some of both sides of the dispute at Tyndale later interpreted it' (p.14). And as Neville Bennett concluded:

Nevertheless, it has to be said that the ideological basis of Plowden's theory, aligned as it was to a particular set of political beliefs about the nature of man and society, has meant that the results of studies of teaching styles have tended to generate more political heat than pedagogical light.

(1987: 47)

It was to be another decade before the 1988 Education Reform Act but the seeds that had been sown in Islington were to come to fruition under a Conservative government. The Kenneth Baker tenure of office marks the period when a previous tenant of that office, Sir David Eccles' 'secret garden' of the curriculum was thrown open, never again to be the sanctuary, (as Eccles had claimed in 1960) 'where politicians dare not tread'.

Absurdity and dysfunction

Although ten years on from Tyndale, the national curriculum was built in on a growing disquiet about the absence of consistency in the curriculum across the country and within local authorities and, in too many places, a lack, monitoring and intervention by the local authority.

> I think it was in 1978, going back thirty years, the department did a survey of local authorities; a required survey that asked 'What do you do to monitor the curriculum in your schools?' and the reply was devastating. Over seventy per cent of them said, 'Nothing. We don't do anything, we're not involved in the curriculum in our schools'. Now that to me, I mean that really lit my fire.
>
> (Pauline Perry)

As Pauline Perry described it, much of the impetus for the national curriculum was already being laid under Keith Joseph. She spoke of 'the absurdity and dysfunction' within the newly created comprehensives in which, as a pupil could do 'five subjects – home economics, needlework, basic cookery, fabric design – which were all basically the same subject, while another child 'the high flyers' did maths, physics, chemistry, and advanced maths. Challenging this dysfunction and creating a broad and balanced curriculum was the legacy for Kenneth Baker – a curriculum of entitlements. As Perry claimed under a Conservative administration:

> We'd done all that. We'd done all that thinking and all that work, so that when Ken Baker came, we were able to sort of drop it into his lap as something that needed legislation, needed to be done because it was going to work.

While Kenneth Baker gave credit to Sir Keith Joseph, he disputes the idea that Joseph was genuinely taking forward the implementation of a National Curriculum, more 'wasting time' with vouchers and with endless debates on theory.

> Keith Joseph was much more intellectually distinguished than I was. Much more! Not questioning that at all. But he was not a practical man. I'm a practical man,

and I wanted to do things. And Keith was seduced into discussions by very clever people in the department, wanting to discuss the theories of education. Endlessly. And he was fascinated by it, and it was very interesting, but that is actually for smoke-filled rooms and cold nights where you turn up the gas lamps and discuss it, and toast the muffins.

Baker's impatience with his predecessor lay in Keith Joseph's desire to pilot, 'trying things out', a process which had lasted for three or four years without any tangible results. As Baker admits, unlike Joseph, he could not tolerate the endless consultation that produced little. The professionals, the academics, the teachers and school leaders and the local authorities could no longer be trusted, he believed, to deliver a rigorous learning experience for children.

> I was a great believer in getting things through, because if you allow every possible view to be expressed on an issue, nothing will happen at the end of the day, and so it is true of whatever you change in life, you have to say we'll go through this and this and it may not be the most perfect, but let's get ahead and do it. Because if you don't do it nothing will happen.

A seismic shift

The consultation that did take place under Baker and his successors is described in length and detail in Duncan Graham and David Tytler's book *A Lesson for us all: The Making of the National Curriculum*. 'Consultation' was carried out in a climate of 'unremitting hostility to local authorities' while civil servants were to become the enemy of elected officials and HMI too had to be treated as suspect. 'Headteachers too were ignored if their views were not coincident enough with those of ministers' (1993:10).

Numerous commentators have referred to policy makers' tendencies to look back with nostalgia at their own experience as the benchmark for a good education. As Baker told it, for example:

> I went to a Church of England primary school in Lancashire, right? It was a Victorian building with Victorian teachers, I learnt my tables by heart, my poems by heart, it was a wonderful education; copperplate writing, and we had tests! I got my report. I get marks. And I thought that was very good education.

Inevitably, therefore the notion of what constituted a curriculum was a narrow one. According to Sir Mike Tomlinson, at the time the HMI responsible for secondary schools, Prime Minister Thatcher

> was only interested in three subjects, English, mathematics and science, and in her view those were the three you needed to focus on and the National Curriculum ought to be clear about that. I don't think she minded particularly about frameworks for the rest but she didn't in any way want the vast detail that ultimately appeared.

In their book Graham and Tytler describe the curricular working parties set up under the Baker administration, all working to attainment targets and kept under close and regular scrutiny by three successive ministers – Baker, Macgregor and Clarke – each of them in turn determined to put their own personal stamp on the curriculum. As Baker's own subject was history he construed the 'objective treatment' of history as anti-patriotic. He instructed the chair of the history working group that attainment targets would have to include more facts – more chronology and more British history. When Clarke took over, however, he was to take grave exception to history including present day events as these were not history but 'current events', so leading to protracted debates as to the cut off point for 'history', Clarke's original position being anything up to 1945. He was eventually to compromise to include any event that had taken place up to 20 years ago.

Similar problems were encountered by the geography working group which finally had to compromise with attainment targets that included the naming of all major rivers and mountains in the UK Euro-sceptic Margaret Thatcher made it clear she would be keeping a close eye on the syllabus and its treatment of the European Union and, with regard to history, Thatcher insisted on names, dates and places. In mathematics heated disputes took place over the use calculators, long division ('good for the soul'), and arcane problems such as 'time to fill a bath while the stopper was out'. The first maths curriculum produced by the working group was greeted by Baker as 'an unmitigated disaster' and he sent the working group back to their smoke-filled rooms to think again.

In an interview for this book Baker recalled the battle to get rid of the 'wets':

> I set up two groups. I set up one group on English with the right-wingers; I thought they would come in with rigour with grammar with spelling. Not at all! So I set up another one, and they were a bit wet too! It was very difficult! I thought in maths that this must be an area where there's no passion, not like history or English. Not at all. Armies marched. Those that wanted rote learning tables, those that didn't, those who wanted the children to think like machines, those who didn't, those who wanted trigonometry not taught till after 16. Argh!

The creation of subject groups also meant that each were fighting for timetable space together with internecine warfare as to what context belonged where, with the Science Lobby daring to annexe the geography syllabus. For the first time the professionals were in the position of having to react to pressures from civil servants and ministers and, for the first time a prime minister took a close personal and detailed interest in what children should be taught. The 'Great Debate' that took place at the time was between a prime minster and a secretary for education.

> There was a Great Debate between Margaret and me. Margaret just wanted to do English, maths and science and I said I wanted a rounded education and endlessly long very hardly bitter but bitterly-argued debates. I'm still in favour of a rounded education.

It is a comment which highlights a potential split within the Conservative Party. Baker fought and won his Great Debate with Margaret Thatcher on achieving a rounded curriculum. Before his elevation to secretary of state in the coalition Government Michael Gove argued for, 'an immediate programme to overhaul the National Curriculum in the core subjects of English, maths and science . . . [which will] . . . focus on WHAT [sic' should be taught . . . we will not return to detailed prescriptions of HOW [sic] things are taught.' (Gove, 2010) An accompanying interview in *The Times* quotes Gove as saying that he was an 'unashamed traditionalist when it comes to the curriculum'. His future vision for the curriculum exactly mirrored Margaret Thatcher's which focuses on a core, not a rounded curriculum. Could it be that over 20 years after Baker won his Great Debate with Thatcher, her original conception has come back to bite him and he has lost it after all? Or, now with Gove in the seat of powers in what ways is the curriculum being rethought?

From his own experiences of serving on the various subject committees Mike Tomlinson recalled that:

> Everything was viewed in subject terms and you also put in each of these groups very experienced, very highly regarded subject specialists. And, of course, not surprisingly, by the time it all finished you'd got a curriculum which required 110 per cent of curriculum time and they wanted it specified to the nth detail . . . I remember two things standing out. The only two areas in which there was very, very serious discussion and consideration over some time, first of all when should history end: in terms of what date should it end, should it end before or after the Second World War? And the other was of course, inevitably, was what books within English should they read and how many of those should be Shakespeare?

This was, in Graham and Tyler's words 'The first major education reform in Britain that had not been created by the education professionals. . . . the first evidence of a de facto power shift in the way education was controlled in England and Wales.' (1993: 30). The 1988 Act gave the government 415 new powers over the education system, referred to by critics as the 'Kentucky Fried Curriculum': 'You run the restaurant, we'll set the menu.'

Mary James, director of research at the Faculty of Education in Cambridge, described it as a lost opportunity.

> I thought between the child-centred notions and the knowledge-centred notions and the society-social system-centred notions there was somewhere that we could create a curriculum that was relevant, broad based, deep – have some depth, have relevance and still be somewhat coherent. And I was just very sad; I think it was very sad when the National Curriculum swept away all that debate.

Purpose and political imperatives

Twenty years on from the creation of a national curriculum there would be few indeed who would argue for a return to what preceded it. No incoming government would wish to put back the clock to what is widely accepted by all parties as an age of uneven provision, lack of uniform standards, with content and methodology subject to the idiosyncratic preferences of individual teachers. But as Mick Waters argued:

> I think that the purpose of the curriculum has never properly been considered because, when Baker introduced the National Curriculum it was part of the Education Reform Act which was really an educational retrenchment act. We have got to get a grip of this. We have got to haul it back: the purpose of the curriculum, what's it about, what's it trying to do for the youngsters in the nation for learning?

Now having left the Qualification and Curriculum Authority and able to examine curricula from and interested international perspective he commented:

> In the job I've just left I got the chance to go to ministerial meetings in so many places, from America to Australia, to China to India, to Egypt to Scandinavia, where ministers would unfailingly stand up and talk about how the world is changing, its uncertain technology, global sustainability, rich and poor, economic challenge, movement of people, threats to our civilisation, etc. Then they all say, therefore, what youngsters need to be is adaptable, flexible, ever to cope with change, and words like that. Then, within an hour, all of them are marching to another drum which is about how we hold on to tradition and how we don't let things that we have traditionally tested drift away because they're fearful of their electorate thinking that they've lost what they thought the electorate matters.

The electoral imperative was expressed by Estelle Morris as 'the Shakespeare argument':

> It's the Shakespeare argument. It doesn't matter how good the arguments, no secretary of state is going to allow Shakespeare to be taken off the curriculum and, so they should because that's a reflection of what the public wants.

It is the worry of what might be taken out that drives an essentially backward looking curriculum, argued Mick Waters, so that the starting point for any review is always what we had in 1998, a curricular rationale 'built on the classical tradition, the classical model of public school basis, which is fear all the time'. Indeed Waters agreed that Ministers tend to arrive with few ideas of what a curriculum is for:

> They go with the breeze because there are few overarching curriculum principles.

The fear of losing anything is what produces the overcrowded curriculum, drastically reducing the room for manoeuvre, according to evidence given to the Cambridge Primary Review.

The heavy emphasis on coverage and pace reduces curriculum to content to be checked off, and curtails exploration. It places a premium on the retention and recall of facts, and downgrades [anything] other than superficial understanding. It denies children opportunities to plan for themselves how to approach their learning tasks – a vital ingredient in engagement, cognitive advance and the development of the capacity to learn how to learn. It forces teachers into transmission mode even though they would like, and children need, opportunities for ideas to be properly discussed and explored. It reduces, for both teachers and children, time for reflection and evaluation (2009: 21).

'Thinning down' might be achieved, suggested one submission to the Cambridge Primary Review if it were 'to remove the eccentricities of a long line of secretaries of state and prime ministers'. (2009: 16).

Shakespeare in, dinosaurs out

An interesting footnote to the Shakespeare argument is what might be termed 'the Baker Dinosaur Syndrome.' One of the arguments for a national curriculum as Kenneth Baker told it was to get away from teachers' reliance on the things they liked to teach, prehistoric monsters being a case in point. 'You know, you had the dinosaurs three times because the teacher knew about the dinosaurs', he said in interview. A decade-and-half on, a primary deputy head recounted how she had put a box of dinosaurs in front of a student on placement, suggesting he might bring back the dinosaurs. He regarded it as highly significant that the student didn't have a clue what to do with them having been 'trained to deliver curricular packages designed by someone else' (in Galton and MacBeath, 2002).

What should children learn, when should they learn it? And how can, and should it, be learned? The defining questions of the curriculum prove to be a continuous thread from government to government. 'Who should, in our society, decide what we teach our children? asked Estelle Morris rhetorically, answering her own question with reference to David Blunkett's inclusion of citizenship within the curriculum, and arguing that government has, and should have, a role to say in what we should teach children'. But then the onus on government is to take its obligations in curriculum building seriously and not to be continually introducing changes in response to the media and various pressure groups as in the case that Mick Waters recounted at the start of his period of tenure at the QCA:

I'll tell you where a bit of number ten pressure came from. I remember talking about cooking earlier on and being told, 'No, we don't want to take that on'. Then Jamie Oliver did his thing on 'Turkey Twizzlers' and overnight, it turned into cooking has to be front and centre in the curriculum. I believe youngsters should learn to cook [but] you don't change policy because of Jamie Oliver or TV programmes; you should have coherent, logical views.

Interviewed in late 2009, Jim Knight, then minister in the Labour government referred to Lord Adonis' John Cass lecture, in which Adonis described 'a 20 per cent education system', designed in the post-war period to educate 20 per cent of the population – a school system based around a link to going to university and the majority going to relatively unskilled work. The re-invention for the twenty-first century curriculum would, suggested Knight, work from the following premise:

> The purpose of the curriculum clearly is to prepare children well for the next stage in their learning and the next stage in their development, but also to allow teachers to engage pupils and make them want to come to school and want to learn and develop a habit of learning which, of course, will stay with them. I think this is where the debate has to go. I don't mean it has to go into the curriculum, it has to go into a debate that starts from of a point of saying, 'Ok. What is this world that we are educating children into?'

If there is to be a genuinely Great Debate under the coalition government it could usefully start from such forward-looking premises. It would not only refuse to be bound by pressure groups, by powerful subject lobbies and by fear of *Daily Mail* editorials and *Sun* headlines. It would dare to confront the 'untouchable' subjects up until the age of 16 as Angela Rumbold, minister of state in the mid-1990s asserted. The prospect of Labour government in 1997 heightened the tenor of the political debate on the future of the curriculum. Rumbold, in reply to a Labour politician, is recorded as saying:

> During my twenty years of involvement in education I have rarely listened to three-quarters of an hour of such unmitigated drivel. . . . I hope that my right Hon. and Hon. Friends will take every opportunity to make it plain to young people that the chances that they have under any putative Labour government are nil.
>
> (Hansard, 17 May 1996)

The Labour government, however, was clearly determined from the day of its election to ensure the country, the opposition and the media that the curriculum was in safe hands. Recalling his time with the QCA and dealing with civil servants and policy makers, Mick Waters, said:

> They were all very open to what youngsters need, and considering what to do. But they were endlessly briefed about 'this will be seen as "leftist"', 'this will be seen as lacking in standards', and all the evidence that you place before them counts for relatively little in the face of [these] media briefings.

Touching the untouchables

The reaction to touching the untouchables is exemplified in Bramall and White's series of essays and invited contributions from curricular architects, critics and prophets, each having to make a case for the conclusion of their subject in a compulsory curriculum. 'At point after point', argued John White in his 2005 book *The Curriculum and the Child*, as with mathematics, the standard curriculum has become a totem, a taken-for-granted feature of the educational landscape'. . . . Do we just freewheel lazily across the decades unwilling to consider any alternatives? (2005: 6).

In discussion of mathematics, but also with relevance of the whole of the curriculum, the Cambridge Primary Review concluded:

> Clearly, there is scope for debate here: to date there has been a somewhat deferential silence (2009: 34). In a 'root and branch' review of the curriculum no element or subject should be exempt.

The challenge to what A. N. Whitehead once termed inert 'ideas' is exemplified in Bramall and White's book, *Why Learn Maths?* It was enough to cause a media backlash, prompting Chief Inspector Woodhead to entitle his annual lecture 'Blood on the Tracks' in which the obscurantists, intellectuals and theoreticians were taken to task, naming and shaming Professors Alexander, MacBeath and Wragg as 'at the heart of the darkness in British education'. His literary allusion to both Joseph Conrad and Bob Dylan was combined with what Richard Smith (2000: 134) describes as 'verbal pyrotechnics', 'the manipulation of the audience', and the appeal to common sense as in 'the ascending tricolon (Friends, Romans, countrymen . . .)'.

Geoffrey Howson, Professor Emeritus of Mathematics, in riposte to Bramall and White, writes that 'the present mathematics curriculum cannot be justified solely by the repetition of pious clichés or such foolishness as the National Curriculum's claims of mathematics' promoting 'spiritual development through . . . helping pupils obtain an insight into the infinite,' or 'moral development through . . . helping them learn the value of mathematical truth' (2005: 226). The National Curriculum,' he wrote, 'appeared to be designed not so much to meet the needs of students but rather those of an untried and ambitious assessment scheme.'

Requiring students to simply 'swallow as much of the curriculum as they could before the age of 16', wrote Howson, ignores the 'wise words' of the 1947 Hamilton Fyfe report:

> Whatever be the values of the 'subject' carried to its full term in university study, they cannot be achieved for the child of 16 by simply snipping off a certain length of the 'subject' like a piece of tape. . . . Every course must have its own unity and completeness and a proper realism requires that content and methods alike be so regulated as to reach their objective within the time available.
>
> (Fyfe, 1947)

Howson added, not simply in relation to mathematics but to the purposes of the curriculum:

> The 'piece of tape' mentality still persists and, for example, forces weaker students to learn algebraic techniques that they will never develop into usable knowledge. Of course, such students are no longer being 'denied' the opportunity to learn algebra, but instead are simply forced to learn techniques that might conceivably

[but with a fairly low probability] lead to something more useful and valuable. It is difficult to see exactly what the aims of the present curriculum are.

(2005: 226)

Curriculum: everything children do

Much of the debate around the curriculum refers exclusively to the brief periods of time in which children are contained within classrooms and within subject teaching. It also tends to refer to documents, syllabi, schemes of work, lesson plans and is measured by targets and attainments so that 'curriculumandassessment' become one compound noun.

When the terminology of the formal, informal and hidden curriculum became current in the 1970s, it prompted a discourse around the relative impact of the formal curriculum as against what was learned through voluntary and extra-curricular activities and, most powerfully of all (as it was often argued) through the 'hidden curriculum'. The term, attributed to Philip Jackson's observation of *Life in Classrooms* (1968), referred to those things that children learn simply through the socialisation process of attending school and absorbing the hidden lessons of power, authority, compliance and the dark side of classroom 'underlife'.

It is hard to find amidst three decades of school effectiveness literature a study which deals with 'the curriculum effect'. As the school effect is now widely agreed as falling between 8 and 15 per cent (Rutter et al., 1979; Scheerens and Bosker, 1997; Mortimore, *et al.* 1998), the purposes and impact of the formal curriculum have to be viewed within that context.

> The evidence is that many, many teenagers comply with learning, they don't engage with it. Even the successful youngsters comply and don't engage. They work out the formula, they repeat the formula, they then get more GCSEs, but they aren't fascinated with learning, they aren't there to be influenced by the process.
>
> (Mick Waters)

'Schools spend inordinate amounts of time debating whether 50 minutes is a good length of a lesson or 40 minutes. That's just institutional management, that's not learning, that's not the curriculum' said Mick Waters. The 'curriculum' is, he argued, a wide more encompassing notion which starts not from a syllabus or body of content but from the experience of school in all its social and academic activities.

> If you're the head of a school, the curriculum is everything the children do while they're associated with your school. Everything. That's why you have to question some of the fundamental institutionalized rituals that take place in schools because the events, the routines and what they do after and beyond add up to the curriculum when you put them alongside lessons.

In John White's book on *Rethinking the Curriculum* he referred to the sea change in government thinking between 1988 and 1999, from the 'platitudinous' aims of the former to the more 'determinate' scope of the latter which 'present a picture of the kind of pupil that the school curriculum can ideally help to foster' (2005: 4)

It is instructive to compare Ken Baker's view of the curriculum in 1988 and that of Tim Brighouse who, in 1999, was advising the new Labour government. While Baker argued for an extension of the school day in order to pack in all subjects of his 'broad and balanced curriculum', Tim Brighouse's vision was of a shorter school day, ending at lunch time with the school as an anchor rather than a container.

> My thinking [was] that if you were really interested in development of the education of the child then you had to think of schools being a kind of anchor but an anchor orchestrating sets of experiences beyond school.

While this would have been a bridge too far for any government to cross, the climate of thinking within the QCA has been moving progressively towards a broader vision of the learning in and out of school. Nonetheless, the flexibility, transparency, 'learning lines', and 'open' programmes, with learner choice 'relatively unconstrained', offered by the Tomlinson Review was also to prove a political bridge too far. As Barry Sheerman, a former chair of the Select Committee admitted, this was a missed opportunity. Mike Tomlinson when questioned about this decision explained that it came about as a result of his attempt to build a consensus across all three main political parties on the proposed reforms. He got the agreement of the then secretary of state, Charles Clarke, to send the opposition party leaders an advanced copy of the final report for comment.

> Then Michael Howard made a speech the day before the report was due to be launched. He couldn't say he had seen the report but he interpreted it as a threat to A levels and he made a statement in a public speech that he would defend A levels at all costs; they were not going to go. And remember the timing was that we were coming up to an election. Tony Blair, for whatever reason, couldn't resist that same evening wanting to say something in response to Michael Howard. He needn't have done but he did. And of course we had the wonderful position of a speech given by the prime minister saying, 'I'm not inclined to get rid of A Levels at all' while his secretary of state and his minister, were at another event saying, 'This will get implemented in full'. . . . There followed a lot of annoyance right across the interest groups with that decision.

Driving around the barriers

A conversation with Andreas Schleicher of the OECD in Paris revealled the extent to which the need for a radical review of the curriculum is relevant to any serving or incoming government. He described spending five years in debate with anthropologists, economists, market specialists and educators on what are the 'classes of competences that make people competent'.

> [The challenge] wasn't how do we protect an established body of knowledge, nor how we enable people to acquire knowledge, but how do we enable people

to work with socially heterogeneous groups, how do we enable people to act autonomously?

As someone who has led the OECD's PISA programme over half-a-decade, he defined two major challenges for the future of PISA, with clear implications for where school and curricular priorities should lie in the future.

> The first is to broaden the range of competences that we use as criteria for success and I think having inter-personal competences, whether it's music or the Arts, or social competences, the kind of inter-personal skills in the basket is important. Intra-personal competences, like meta-cognition and motivation and so on. Also, the capacity and motivation to keep learning. That, I think, is one major challenge for PISA.

Analysing the *Drivers and Barriers to Education Success*, in their 2009 longitudinal study, Helen Chowdry and colleagues do not on any one of their 117 pages mention the word 'curriculum' but the growing disaffection of young people which their data reveal has clearly much to do with the curriculum diet as with the context in which it is 'delivered', an apt term for the way in which it is conceived of by policy makers.

As Chowdry *et al.* (2009) reported, children tend to become progressively more negative about their own ability and their future educational aspirations and more prone to engage in risky behaviours. These are predominantly children from the lowest socioeconomic groups, only one in five of the poorest fifth of their research sample attaining five or more GCSEs at grades A* to C including English and maths, compared to almost three quarters of the richest fifth – a gap of over 50 percentage points.

This is a curriculum matter in its largest sense, in the sense of the experience of what education is, through the continued exposure to school and classroom. The disconnect between policy makers and the real world of growing up in Britain was brought out sharply by Mick Waters in a description of a conversation with then minister Alan Johnson:

> I'll never forget Johnson going on about teenagers having to read Austen, Hardy and Elliot as top of the list of what children should do in Key Stage 3: the absolute essentials. This was at a time when the umpteenth youngster was being stabbed in south London.

The teaching profession has not been a passive observer of the curriculum debate. Sir Ron Dearing's (1993) review was a by-product of the then government's response to the boycott by the teaching unions of the excessive workload created by the National Curriculum tests. He sought consensus from the teaching profession on how the demands created by the original National Curriculum could be reduced.

So confident was Dearing that he claimed his reductions would create 'discretionary' time of 20 per cent for schools that was not prescribed from the centre.

This idea that autonomy to develop the curriculum can be returned piece by piece to schools with central prescription reducing to a core has echoed down the years.

Dearing's 20 per cent re-emerges in the Cambridge Primary Review where Robin Alexander calls for a 70/30 divide between a national and local curriculum or a national and community curriculum.

The purpose of Dearing's 'discretionary time' was explored by Maurice Galton in 1997. His research with Ken Fogelman, *The Use of Discretionary Time in Primary School*, found that only 8.3 per cent of headteachers in their sample said that National Curriculum requirements could be met within the 80 per cent of the time available. For most heads it was 'phantom time' really.

Galton's conclusion was that:

> Despite the best intentions of Sir Ron Dearing to reduce the pressures on teachers, this had not. . . . happened, partly because of other initiatives such as the introduction of school performance tables and the pressures arising from Ofsted inspections, exacerbated by the generally negative tone of the chief inspector's comments on primary teaching.

There is a sense of 'plus ça change' in the reasons given. Shaving off chunks from an excessively prescribed and overloaded curriculum is but one solution in a twenty year long debate about the curriculum.

In 1990, Michael Barber, when he was head of education for the NUT, called for a framework curriculum which

> within a decade at most, redefine(d) achievement away from its current narrow academic connotations, which encourages achievement for all and which promotes creativity, collaboration and a sense of adventure.
>
> (A Strategy for the Curriculum, NUT, 1990)

Fourteen years later, the NUT published an Education Statement calling for a curriculum which defined a range of statutory entitlements for young people's learning. Others such as ATL have published similar proposals.

Jim Rose's government-commissioned review of the Primary Curriculum, following as it did the 2004 Secondary Curriculum Review, responded to the government's requirement that prescription and workload had to be reduced by 'reviewing the current programmes of study so that schools have greater flexibility to meet pupils' individual needs and build on their learning'.

The Rose review was, according to Mick Waters, set up in haste because Alexander's on-going efforts were seen by ministers and officials as a potential threat. Sir Jim was chosen because of his consensual approach. As Mick Waters put it:

> Jim's outlook is maximum consensus where he talks about 'line of best fit', which I thought was a good phrase when I first heard it, and then somebody explained to me that it was about finding your way through, get as near as possible to everybody, but not too far from anybody.

Surely a recipe for mediocrity? Rose's view that a National Curriculum which enabled a personalised curriculum to be developed in schools led to proposals that the curriculum should be divided into six 'areas of learning'. This concept is not dissimilar to the Cambridge Primary Review's proposals for a primary curriculum structured around 'aims and domains'. Albeit that the Rose Review was hampered by a set of government requirements, both Rose and Alexander in their own ways argued for greater autonomy for schools.

Yet how schools respond to new curricula freedoms will depend, not necessarily on their ability to use them per se but on the government's school evaluation mechanism, Ofsted.

Ofsted's report, *Twenty Outstanding Primary Schools* (2009) found that:

> Outstanding schools are confident organisations that weigh up curriculum initiatives and local and national programmes before deciding whether they are right for the school, not being afraid to dispense with them if they are not . . . (they) have the confidence and imagination to take the statutory curriculum and make it their own.

Few schools have the confidence for curriculum innovation if they are deemed to be 'inadequate' or 'satisfactory' by Ofsted. Subjected to intense scrutiny through local authorities' new powers to intervene and to no-notice inspections every three years, schools in these categories are hardly in charge of their curriculum destiny. They epitomise Barber's argument that their improvement has to be driven from Whitehall.

The current accountability model has led to a two-tier division of schools. The first tier deemed 'good' or 'outstanding' weigh up curriculum initiatives and decide whether or not to use them; the second tier have their futures determined for them by School Improvement Partners, local authorities and Ofsted.

Goodbye Taiwan, Itella Finland

The Rose Review sought to compare different National Curricula. The comparisons contain interesting information but they fail to identify the essential differences between Government mandated and bottom-up curriculum development.

Of the European countries' National Curricula, the Finnish Curriculum is one of the closest in content to the English National Curriculum. It is the curriculum of a country which, according to the OECD, is at the top of the league table for student achievement in the literacies. Finland's curriculum is similar in size and content with separate curricula for primary and secondary schools. It has an overarching set of aims and values for the curriculum followed by subject orders which describe what should be taught, and it contains a set of stages for assessment.

Yet the Finnish and English National Curricula are radically different. The differences arise, not from content or pedagogy, or whether they are assessment defined curricula, or indeed whether they focus on values. The difference is whether the government trusts school communities to develop the curriculum. Indeed it is explicit in the Finnish Curriculum that schools are expected to develop the curriculum so that it is tailored to meet children's needs. In England, the curriculum is used more to define and raise standards. Trusting school communities to develop the curriculum is only implicit at best.

In one sense, the public story of the National Curriculum is different from the idea that it is evolving steadily towards ever-greater curricula freedom for schools. As Waters' comments show, the curriculum is a canvas on which political parties paint their aspirations for society. The use of the statutory curriculum by schools is heavily influenced by Ofsted ratings and the embrace of the Taiwan model. The National Curriculum is an occasional vehicle for public debate about values and a benchmark for schools if external evaluations deem it necessary.

This uneven and inequitable approach to the curriculum surely has to change. The ability of schools to improve is fostered, not inhibited, by the confidence to innovate. The National Curriculum needs to be restructured as a framework curriculum which defines children's curriculum entitlements. The expectation of all schools, not just some, should be that they are responsible for curriculum innovation and development. In *The Coalition: Our Programme for Government* (2010), the document setting out the agreements reached during the Conservative and Liberal Democrat coalition negotiations, both parties accept that all schools should have greater freedom over the curriculum thus appearing to reject their predecessor's centralised, 'top-down' approaches to reform. At the recent general election the Liberal Democrats wished to replace the rigid National Curriculum by a slimmed-down version with a minimum entitlement for all pupils. The Conservatives also wanted a simplified curriculum, accompanied by strong pressure for all primary schools to teach synthetic phonics. In contrast, the coalition have opened up the possibility of 'greater freedom over the curriculum', a direction in which according to the Cambridge Primary Review some headteachers have already embarked in response to Robin Alexander's reminder that schools should not assume that 'reform is the task of government alone.'

And still no pedagogy

Michael Gove in his first message on his appointment as secretary for education told staff that he 'wished to refocus' the newly formed Department for Education 'on its core purpose of supporting teaching and learning'. In bemoaning the lack of any serious discussion during the tenure of the previous governments of the relationship between teaching and learning and of the moral considerations and values guiding decisions of the 'what' and the 'how' of teaching, Robin Alexander (2004) echoed the concerns of Simon (1981) some two decades earlier. Simon suggested this lack of interest arises because of two main influences. The first, a historical factor, concerns the role of the Public schools, and to a lesser extent, the grammar schools, in the late nineteenth and early twentieth century. Their prime purpose was to educate successive generations to serve in the far corners of the Empire where fraternizing with the local population, particularly the female members, could undermine the moral superiority of those in positions of authority. Consequently, a liberal education, was an essential requirement in preparing future generations to rule an Empire, since reading a good book or listening to music could help while away the hours during the lonely evenings and strengthen the moral fibres.

Second, and more important was the introduction of selection in the development of mass education. During the period when most children's' experience of schooling ended at the elementary stage the onus was on the analysis of what did or did not work well in the classroom; in short, on pedagogy. But with the advent of selection, particularly the introduction of intelligence testing as a means of weeding out those unsuited for an academic education, the onus shifted to the pupil's weaknesses as a prime cause of children's failure to learn. Even after the abandonment of the 11+ in the 1970s the notion of 'readiness' in Piagetian theory and more recently the promotion of 'disadvantaged groups' due to race, gender or impoverished home environment, still promotes the idea that reason for school failure lies with the child's limitations rather than with the pedagogy. Hence the raft of schemes such as Every Child Matters which were designed to compensate for these disadvantages.

Alexander (2004) put forward a further reason why interest in exploring aspects of teaching is limited. He also blamed the advent of the 'standards agenda' which largely determined whether teaching was good or bad in terms of the scores achieved on the Statutory Tests and the pressures created by Ofsted in enforcing this regime. Teachers faced with these pressures teach to the test mainly using well-tried coaching techniques as evidenced in their accounts of their practice (in Galton and MacBeath, 2008). Furthermore, as discussed earlier in the chapter, politicians largely conceive of the curriculum in terms of delivering subject knowledge and the kinds of classroom organisation best suited to meeting this requirement. Thus the emphasis tends to be on whole class teaching rather than on other arrangements.

Getting your rainbow right

In the advice to teachers on how to solve the problems of an overcrowded curriculum in the document, *The Curriculum in Successful Primary Schools* (Ofsted, 2002), teachers were advised to adopt the three-part lesson for all subjects. In art, for example, the teacher was to tell the class:

> Today I want you to paint a picture of a rainbow. Here is a chart showing the colours, a piece of white paper, a brush and some watercolours. Paint your rainbow as beautifully as you can. You are painting the rainbow to practise using your brush to blend colours. This is an important skill in art. Write this learning objective next to your title.

Included with this recommendation are helpful notes for the teacher who is advised to:

> Display the learning objective
> > Get children to repeat it
> > Ask 'So what am I looking for?' 'Why are we doing this?'
> > Assess at the end of the lesson, how well pupils have met the learning objective.

> (Ofsted, 2002)

Three years later with *Excellence and Enjoyment* the message had changed. Creative lessons were now about teaching children to think differently. Pupils were expected to 'think or behave imaginatively through purposeful activity to generate an original outcome which must have value' (QCA, 2005).[1] Now Ofsted (2006) was no longer recommending that pupils should produce identical rainbows but in their evaluation of the government's Creative Partnership initiative were praising instances where children were encouraged to develop their own ideas and to produce a range of different products using a variety of media.

In his interview Sir Mike Tomlinson concured that Conservative ministers of state, apart from Gillian Shephard showed little interest in pedagogy. He credited Chris Woodhead during his period as HMCI with bringing the issue to the fore, so that 'he alone made the discussion of teaching a legitimate discussion', albeit in ways that many commentators would argue eventually constrained the debate. According to Tomlinson:

> It [teaching] had been a hidden agenda and he brought it to the forefront and said it's important and we ought to be talking about it. Now the talk got to, well I think teaching should be of this sort but that I can forgive. But the fact was that for the first time the profession was talking about teaching which was at the heart of what it was doing.

According to Lord Puttnam, who was given the task of boosting teacher morale in the wake of the 'naming and shaming' episode as chair of the newly formed General Teaching Council, Michael Barber regarded Woodhead as an asset in helping to drive the strategies forward and believed that his leaving was one of the reasons why the results plateaued. Puttnam, however, in the light of his own experience, strongly disagrees with this verdict.

> He [Michael] was wrong on this. I was on the sharp end visiting school after school-the difference within months of Woodhead's departure was palpable. The flaw in Michael's argument was that the regime was essentially 'fear based'. In the end that can never work. It felt to me as though the early progress had ground to a halt – mired in rigidity and statis. We'd reached a point where nothing was moving.

Bridging the gap between research and practice

> If they had listened more openly to the academic research community back in 1997, they might not have spent eight years pursuing policies with such perverse consequences for a supposedly progressive political party.
>
> (Whitty, 2006: 168)

In Chapter 2, we discussed some of the reasons why research has been largely ignored, or used highly selectively by successive governments. There may also be another more fundamental reason why policies designed to result in evidenced based practice can never be realised to any great extent. McIntyre (2005), for example, argues that:

The gap between research and practice is wide, not primarily because educational researchers are self-indulgent or irresponsible in the kinds of research that they do or in the ways they report it, nor because teachers are unprofessional or anti-intellectual in their approach to practice, nor even because of inappropriate organizational arrangements, but primarily because the kind of knowledge research can offer is of a very different kind from the knowledge that classroom teachers need to use.

(McIntyre, 2005: 359)

There are three reasons given for this claim. First, the kind of pedagogical knowledge teachers need is knowledge *how* whereas researchers tend to generate propositional knowledge or knowledge *that*. While the latter can contribute to practice it can never simply translated into pedagogical knowledge. So rather than research based practice we can have research informed practice.

Second, knowledge of how things get done is essentially pragmatic. Teachers therefore evaluate ideas on their practicality. Researchers, on the other hand, prioritise in terms of 'the clarity and coherence of the arguments and the truth of their conclusions'. Finally, McIntyre asserts that research based propositions 'to have potential value must be abstract and theoretical or in some other way generalised'. In contrast, pedagogical knowledge is highly contextualised so that what works for one teacher with one class may not work with another.

McIntyre offers a number of ideas for bridging this gap between the work of researchers and teachers but, on his own admission, the one with the greatest potential is that put forward by David Hargreaves (1999) based on Gibbons *et al.*'s (1994) model of knowledge production. They call this Mode 2 research in contrast to the more traditional type which they term Mode 1. Mode 2 knowledge is produced 'in the context in which it is to be applied, not in the laboratory, is transdisciplinary and production is heterogeneous in terms of the different skills, knowledge and experience participants bring to it' (McIntyre, 2005: 375). Based of these ideas Hargreaves suggested networks of schools: a knowledge-creating school system having the characteristics of a spider's web in which

Each node is a problem solving team possessing a unique combination of skills. It is linked to other bodies by a potentially large number of lines of communication. To survive each must be permeable to new types of knowledge and the sector as a whole becomes increasingly interconnected.

(Hargreaves, 1999: 122)

During his interview for this book David Hargreaves gave an example of this kind of approach.

We started the nine gateways for personalising learning that came from grass roots . . . that meeting with heads around the country put it together and then we converted them to what we call four Deeps. But what we hadn't realised is we didn't know what the interactions would be when we started and they proved to be quite interesting. . . . We said openly we invented the four Deeps in the bar the night before a presentation and tried it out and the Deeps were an attempt to give them some coherence . . . I went to a conference and some guy came up to me and said 'I just thought you'd like to know, the head's re-organised the school because of a lecture he went to when you talked about the Deeps'. He said 'yeah, we've abolished all the deputy titles, we've now got a deputy Deep Learning and a Deputy Deep Support and Deputy Deep Experience'

A week later I heard of another school, again by an indirect route . . . and then we discovered people were doing it and we never advocated it and we brought them together and asked them why there were doing it, why they were using it as an organisational device or a planning device . . . There were people writing their development plans around the Deeps. . . . We got the people doing this to speak at the SSMT [Secondary School Masters and Teachers] national conference last November and the sessions were completely sold out and I tell the story because we thought we were doing something as a conceptual simplification, the kind of things I would do as an academic, making it slightly catchy but what people were doing were saying, these were not stupid people, they were saying it made a kind of sense if you look at the list of why they did it, at the top of the list is because it reminded us of our moral purpose.

It is interesting to remind ourselves that the essentials of the Literacy Strategy (both the framework and the subject didactics) were put in place by John Stannard during a pilot with a similar approach involving cooperation and sharing among schools in several local authorities. Had it continued there might have been every chance that a suitable pedagogy appropriate to the new curriculum and recognised as such would have been embedded. But once the Literacy and Numeracy Strategies had been 'rolled out' the dye was cast. The adoption of a top down dissemination strategy secured the prize of the 'low hanging fruits' and can claim to have increased teachers' subject knowledge and their confidence in handling literary concepts, but it has failed to develop an embedded pedagogic rationale to go with this new found awareness. Contary to David Puttnam's claim that it has resulted in 'statis', recent studies of classrooms (Alexander, 2004; Galton, 2006; Hargreaves *et al.*, 2003) actually suggest that a significant number of teachers may have retrenched to a more direct didactic style. The verdict on Labour's early pedagogic reforms may well be, too many political initiatives; too little knowledge of teachers and teaching. It remains to be seen whether Michael Gove's declared intention of refocusing the Department for Education's efforts on support for teaching and learning will yield different outcomes.

6   Assessment

Get me out of here

I went back to a seminal assessment paper written in 1992 by Wynne Harlen, Desmond Nuttal, Patricia Broadfoot and Caroline Gipps and I thought has anything changed as a consequence? We've been saying the same thing over two decades but we can't seem to convince anyone that the negative consequences of high stakes testing are so powerful they risk undermining the very thing you're trying to do, which is school improvement.

(Mary James)

In the previous chapter we argued that of all the issues which have added to the pressures on teachers, that of the high stakes testing regime has been one of the major impediments to teachers' attempts to improve the quality of their teaching. Instituted originally under the Thatcher government, but ratcheted up by New Labour, there has been a running battle with the teacher unions and with academics whose expertise in assessment has been consistently ignored. The contribution that these tests make to a valid and viable school accountability system has been undermined from the start of New Labour's time in office by naming and shaming poor performing schools.

In *Teachers Under Pressure* (Galton and MacBeath, 2008) nearly all practitioners interviewed (whether teaching at Key Stage 2 or 3) complained of a loss of confidence, a loss of creativity and spontaneity, an increase in stress and feelings of losing control. As Mark, a primary teacher who eventually left the profession, explained:

I think if you're not careful everything is geared to one week in May and I question the value of it. Is that what education is about? I don't think it is. I think you don't end up delivering a broad and balanced curriculum because I think your whole focus is on science, maths and English because that's what you're being tested on and we put a lot of pressure on children and on ourselves.

In the last few years, within the various bodies responsible for education policy in the United Kingdom, there has been a greater degree of flexibility in the approach taken to assessment policy. In 2005, teachers in England were given more responsibility for pupil assessment of 7-year-olds. In Wales, testing of 7-year-olds ceased in 2002 and in the summer of 2004 it was announced in the Welsh Assembly that national tests would be abolished for 11 and 14-year-olds. In Scotland teachers have never been subjected to a similar testing regime. Instead national assessment tasks are drawn from a large bank of items and the test scores are no longer collected by the Scottish government.

When the changes to the mode of assessment of 7-year-olds were announced in 2005 the then Schools Minister Stephen Twigg, claimed that the government were 'putting all our faith in teachers'. Prior to the 2010 general election, Secretary of State Ed Balls announced the ending of testing at Key Stage 3 and his then shadow, Michael Gove floated a proposal to abandon testing at the end of primary school and transfer it to the start of the secondary school immediately after transfer. The Report of the Expert Group on Assessment, a body commissioned in October 2008 following the announcement that the KS3 tests were to be discontinued, came down on the side of retaining the KS2 tests in English and mathematics. It recommended that testing should take place towards the middle of June rather than the middle of May as was the case prior to 2010. Asserting, without offering any supportive evidence, that 'the English and mathematics tests at the end of Key Stage 2 are a good test of the key skills which pupils need in order to access the secondary curriculum' (para 2.14) the Expert Group concluded that:

> Simply removing the externally marked Key Stage 2 tests now and replacing them with teacher assessment only, would represent a step backwards for pupils' learning and school accountability. The accuracy and consistency of teacher assessment is improving. However, it is not yet sufficiently robust and consistent to be used in place of externally validated assessments at the end of a seven-year phase of education.
>
> (DCSF, 2009: para 2.8)

The coalition government appeared at first sight to be odds on these matters. The Conservatives wished to retain Key Stage 2 testing and League Tables but will reform the latter 'so that they are more rigorous'. The Liberal Democrats were pledged to 'scale back' Key Stage 2 tests and to use teacher assessment with external checking. League tables would, however, remain but would provide 'more meaningful information which truly reflects the performance of a school. It would seem that while the Conservatives, as in the past, want to continue to judge schools largely in terms of the pupils' performance in the core subjects their partners in the coalition seek a more rounded approach in defining success. The coalition agreement committed the government to reforming league tables in order to show 'progress of children of all abilities' and, perhaps in the context of the 2010 union-led boycott of the Key Stage 2 tests, to reviewing 'how Key Stage 2 tests operate in future'.

A bit of assessment history

Leaving aside the question of how far summative assessments, such as those undertaken in the National Key Stage Testing Programme, represent a valid measure of a pupil's performance, there have been noticeable problems associated with the delivery of these test scores. Secondary schools continually complain that they come too late for use in assigning Year 7 pupils after transfer. In 1994 and then in 2002, teacher unions succeeded in ensuring that the testing process was supervised, administered and marked externally. More recently, with the granting of this contract to the American Educational Testing Services (ETS) Consortium there were considerable problems in producing consistent results on time and many commentators felt this was one of the unstated reasons for abandoning testing at Key Stage 3.

It should not, however, be thought that the desire to measure a standard was a preoccupation of the last two decades. As early as the late 1970s the Assessment and Performance Unit (APU) was set up with the intention of discovering whether standards were falling or rising. At the time, two possible methods of determining these standards were being developed. The first, using a procedure known as Rasch analysis (1966) attempted to deal with the problem that in a typical standardised test candidates could get the same mark by answering a different set of individual items which might be assessing different aspects of whatever the test was designed to measure. The Rasch methodology attempted to solve this problem of 'non-equivalence of candidates' test scores' by placing each item on a unitary scale such that a correct response to any question depended only on the candidate's ability and the difficulty of the question. This allowed any question to be represented in terms of an absolute ability score. Thus a teacher could select items from a large bank to cover the range of content being taught in his or her classroom. Provided these items had face validity, namely a group of experts had agreed that the items, although measuring different content areas tested the same ability or skill, correct answers could be given a score on this absolute ability scale and therefore scores between pupils or between schools could be compared irrespective of the content tested by individual items.

The second method looked at by the APU was developed by the National Assessment of Educational Progress (NAEP) which was the body responsible for co-ordinating new test procedures in the United States. NAEP thought to develop what was termed 'generalisability theory'. Again the idea was to develop a bank of items such that any sample could be related to the population scores of all the items. The idea here was that again, providing the test items had face validity, then the score of an individual or of a class could be likened to a sample mean which would in some way be related to a series of population parameters (Johnson and Bell, 1985). Providing that there were enough items it was therefore possible to use these sample scores to estimate a true population score for the individual or for the class of pupils.

Outflanking Mrs T

When Paul Black and his colleagues were given the task of providing a means of testing standards in the new National Curriculum various issues connected with both the Rasch and the NAEP approach were still to be resolved. Those advocating an approach based on generalisability theory found that in order to create population parameters a very large bank of items was required. In Science, particularly, many of the items were found to be heavily content dependent (Linn *et al.*, 1991) which meant that they infringed the RASCH principle that only difficulty and ability level mattered. Nevertheless, when Professor Black's Task Group on Assessment and Testing (TGAT) commenced its work it sought to develop its thinking on the same principles elaborated by the APU. This rested on the belief that the tests could both be diagnostic (they could provide teachers with a formative assessment of the stage that the pupil had reached) and also they could be normative (they could provide the government with an indication of how well a particular school was doing in relation to national norms).

Only Harvey Goldstein (1993) appeared publicly to contest this argument, partly because many of those in the assessment business were concerned that if Professor Black and his committee were not successful in persuading government to adopt the APU approach, ministers might be minded to return to a simple 11+ pencil and papers tests, particularly because it was thought that Prime Minister Thatcher was inclined to this latter course of action. Certainly this was confirmed by Kenneth Baker who, when the interviewer asked if he had 'bounced Margaret Thatcher into the TGAT Report', laughed and replied:

> I think that probably was the case because I think Margaret just thought of pencil and paper tests. I had to educate myself into all the different theories of testing and that was quite an exercise. Teaching her something, I had to learn myself because there are great theories of testing, sorts of testing, the way it's done, I had to grapple with that. I felt that what I was being given was essentially correct so I had to get it through.

However, Baker's attempts to master the background to the current assessment debate did not appear to be totally successful. Commenting on their early meetings to discuss the direction that TGAT might take, the chairman, Paul Black, recalls:

> It was quite difficult to find out what he wanted. We met on two or three occasions during that early period and I thought either I'm not communicating or listening or you are being deliberately vague. Or perhaps you are vague. In hindsight I think he was perhaps trying to leave it open to me because I knew he had an agenda which was different from his boss's.

The timetable for the study was incredibly short. TGAT first met in September and the report was handed in on Christmas Eve 1986. Paul Black remembers walking out of Elizabeth House (then the headquarters of the Education Department) with the job finished and wondering, 'what am I going to do about Christmas shopping, and how do I buy my wife a Christmas present at three o'clock on Christmas Eve?' The committee met with Kenneth Baker and his officials in the first week of January and after a period of not very intensive questioning it was decided that the report would be published in the following week, the purpose being to outflank critics including Mrs Thatcher. The report was then passed to the Working Parties on science, English and mathematics. Apart from one or two meetings with these committees work on the assessment system then ceased.

Where it all started going wrong

According to Wiliam (2001) problems began at this stage when the subject panels began to determine the kinds of assessments needed to ensure that there was content validity with the intended curriculum. TGAT proposed that at 7, 11 and 14 much of the assessment would be carried out by teachers as an integral part of normal classroom work together with nationally prescribed tests for all pupils to supplement the individual teachers' assessments. Teachers were required to mark both the written and the classroom assessments but these would be externally moderated (TGAT, 1987: 11). TGAT tended to emphasise the formative and diagnostic aspects of assessment which enabled teachers to plan the next stages of work and to remedy any weaknesses. It was argued that these could be combined into a summative record which would represent the overall achievements of pupils in a systematic way. Each subject would be reported in terms of 'profile components' such that the number was preferably no more than four and never more than six (TGAT, 1987: 35). Profile components were to be thought of in terms of skills, knowledge, understanding and exploration in science or writing, oracy, reading, comprehension and listening in English.

The difficulty for those constructing the profile components was that they needed to be such that they catered for the full range of ability but had to be sufficiently challenging so that, while not de-motivating low attainers, they would provide sufficient stimulation for the most able. Two solutions then presented themselves. One was to have a reporting structure such that the benchmarks at each of the four age groups were specific to those age groups. The alternative was to have a set of common benchmarks that could apply across all ages and achievement ranges such that the profile scores at any one key stage were directly related to those at other key stages. Solutions to such problems were complex and beyond possibility in the time given to the TGAT Committee for its deliberations. Consequently much of this work had to be left to the subject committees. According to Paul Black, 'It should have been a year's debate, not three months'.

In the event, many of the profile components suggested by TGAT, for example, the component which grouped together a number of attainment targets concerned with the practical application of mathematics, were rejected by ministers on the grounds that they were difficult to test. More fundamentally, however it was because they did not concentrate on the knowledge of mathematical skills, so wrote Duncan Graham, the first chief executive of the National Curriculum Council, in his 1993 book *A Lesson for Us All* (p. 36). In it he describes how this resulted in the attainment targets being made very specific because any suggestion of a profile which would assess understanding was considered to be 'too woolly'. This was a position, according to Graham, that reached its full expression under Kenneth Clarke. This also had a further consequence. According to Wiliam (2001) the increased emphasis given to specific knowledge components contributed to tests being increasingly based on the content of the programmes of study rather than on the attainment targets as was originally intended by TGAT. Wiliam concluded that:

The fact that these programmes of study are different at different levels means that comparing results at Key Stage 3 with those at Key Stage 2 makes no more sense than knowing that someone must have got worse because they got a C at GCSE and an E at A Level.

(p. 10)

As a result, argued Wiliam, TGAT proposals were never fully implemented. By the time that New Labour came to power, running through the adopted attainment system was a catalogue of errors. He concluded:

> The first error was not to understand the key idea contained in the TGAT Report which is that a student's entitlement should depend on their achievement rather than their age. The second was to compound this by the decision to base the tests not on attainment targets but on programmes of study. The third error was to misunderstand the nature of standards and particularly that they are fundamentally arbitrary both between subjects and within subjects, which led government to drive policy in directions that are simply not supported by evidence.

In Wiliam's view successive governments have created a situation in which policy is currently based on assumptions that are not merely unsupported by evidence but just plain wrong. Rising test scores demonstrate little more than teachers' increasing abilities to teach the test, and to the power of high stakes testing to distort the curriculum.

The new labour approach

When Labour came to power, therefore, it might have been thought that the mess that had become assessment policy would have been subject to review and that one of the people to have been consulted might have been the original designer of the system, i.e. Professor Black. In particular there was a need to sort out the question of attainment targets. Because the targets were eventually defined largely in terms of content the working groups came up originally with some 17 attainment targets for science and some 20 for mathematics. TGAT never intended that all the targets should be reported separately but that they should be combined into profile components. However, according to Black at interview:

> Nobody noticed until late, that is until the groups had done their work and published, that the legislation was so drawn up that you had, like GSE lower down, to report the result on every single target and not on the profiles. The guys drafting the Bill had missed it.

The natural consequence was that the politicians said there were too many targets and that these would need to be reduced to three or four at each level. This meant that the targets were amalgamations, so losing their detail and becoming generally too broad for teachers to assess reliably. Under New Labour, the formative and diagnostic parts of the original TGAT proposals, now developed into Assessment for Learning (AfL) were strongly embraced, but were seen as separate from the setting of attainment targets. The consequence was that the original idea of combining teachers' assessments and written tests was not reconsidered. Even in this area Professor Black was not consulted. As he recalled:

> We were not involved except marginally. We approached guys from this private agency, the government farmed out the writing of the stuff for schools. These two guys asked us if they could talk to us about the stuff and sent us some drafts and we mustn't copy it to anyone and we mustn't show it to anyone, it's handed back to them when we've talked to them and we mustn't tell anyone we'd seen it. This was Kafka as far as I was concerned. I mean we had a talk. They were perfectly good. They understood it, they were keen, they wanted to get it right. There were things in it we didn't like and we said so, things we thought they'd got wrong and then what they used eventually was better, but it didn't do what we would have wanted. But the weird thing is they couldn't own up to having talked to us at all. I don't know if they were told not to but they certainly were not told to do so we were pushed out.

Black contrasted this treatment by DES officials with their Scottish colleagues.

> We got a similar invitation from Scotland to talk about assessment. It was Dylan [*Wiliam*] who went to talk to some people in the Scottish office. He was met off the plane and taken to see the minister. He was gobsmacked, we'd been nowhere near a minister here. They then set up one clutch of several different development projects because they were newly independent and the education minister was trying to do the job. What they did was to get a group of schools, one from each authority, each region, nine schools, and we went up there and planned and conducted a training programme for them. They then brought in a group from the Institute to give an independent evaluation of the project and what came out as the most popular among teachers was the formative assessment. So they then rolled it out in Scotland. Ever since there's been a far more intelligent approach. That's the way it should have been done. Here [*in England*] the thing was captured to tie in with the frequent testing agenda, or that's how it seemed.

Black's own theory of why his work on assessment was ignored had little to do with the fact that he had worked for the Conservative government. Rather it concerned the issue of Tony Blair sending his children out of the catchment area to a well-known Catholic school. Black saw fit to criticise this in the Catholic press and he felt that this, more than anything else, had led to his being ignored. However, Black's theory may be wide of the mark. The lack of any interest in consultation about the usefulness of using the existing statutory tests for accountability purposes, even extended to the body responsible to the government for matters to do with assessment, the QCA. When asked about the extent of consultation on such matters between QCA and the Standards Unit, Mick Waters response was:

Virtually nil. There are perfunctory meetings.

Judy Sebba, who, before she joined the Standards Unit as an adviser, worked in the Department of Education at Cambridge University, disputes Paul Black's interpretation of events. During her time in Cambridge she was familiar with the work being undertaken on assessment for learning through her colleague, Mary James, who along with Black and Wiliam was a founder member of the Assessment Reform Group. She claimed that Paul Black was consulted but the apparent differences in their interpretation can be put down to the form and nature of consultation which took place.

Black's interests and research were about finding ways in which the formative assessments, at the core of AfL, could be combined into a series of profiles so as to provide a summative score which could be used to assess standards. There was never any consultation on this issue, because the tasks of monitoring standards and of enhancing pupils learning through the use of regular classroom assessments were seen by New Labour as two completely separate matters; the former was not even considered as problematic whereas the latter was negotiable. As Sebba, herself, admitted:

> The strategies' adoption of Assessment for Learning was not true to the research. Well, you know, I think it's as true as policies ever get to research.

Thus, while Black was consulted on matters to do with AfL he was never asked to discuss the fundamental problems associated with the statutory tests, even though there was an awareness, at least among advisers in the then DfES and elsewhere, that problems existed. As Judy Sebba confirmed:

> And this is where the NFER[National Foundation for Educational Research] comes into play. If you talk to any of those people . . . anybody, they'll tell you the government's treatment of scales showed a total misunderstanding of how these assessments were constructed.

Sebba's account of being told to write a paper showing that initiatives such as thinking skills and AfL resulted in improved scores on the statutory tests was required as a prerequisite for departmental support. This is confirmed by Paul Black and is a clear indicator of the mindset prevalent within the government.

She [*Sebba*] said, 'I can't sell this to my guys in the department. . . . until you've got evidence that it improves the scores'.

> And we worked with schools, it was a two year project, and they had to choose a target class and we collected data on the intake and the score every year . . . So we ended up with 19 different classes from several different schools with different teachers showing significant learning gains. And Judy said, 'Right! Now I can sell it' and she did sell it and they picked it up but they didn't come back to us.

Keeping the rats at bay

The government's decision to seek advice on assessment from an Expert Group followed the fiasco of Key Stage 3 test results failing to be delivered on time in

2008. In 2006 it had been decided to award the contract to an American consortium, Educational Testing Services (ETS), which is responsible for carrying out much of the testing in United States schools. According to the then chief executive of the Qualifications and Curriculum Authority (QCA), Ken Boston, who resigned on the issue, the subsequent investigation of this failure by Lord Sutherland (2008) was flawed from the start. This was partly because the DCSF, in determining the terms of reference for the Sutherland Report, restricted the inquiry to the behaviour of the QCA and the ETS alone and it did not include that of the government. Boston argued not only some of the evidence given by ministers was inaccurate as to dates of meetings, but that the extent of the participation of government observers, who had knowledge of the problem but whose conduct on returning to the ministry was outside Sutherland's terms of reference, needed to be the subject of further investigation. According to Ken Boston while it was right that bodies such as the QCA were accountable for their decisions, he believed that it was important that observers should be also there to represent ministries and departments and that there should be a genuine exchange of views.

> Problems arise, however, when they are conveying ministerial impressions and where we are actually negotiating the QCA's advice with them rather than listening to what they have to say, challenging it and pushing it hard, since the tendency is not to write the advice so that ministers know what these bodies think and need to hear, but rather simply what they think they might want to know.

Paul Black confirmed that this kind of behaviour existed even before New Labour came to power. During his time in charge of the TGAT committee he was consistently warned by officials of the need to accommodate 'forces out there' and that 'the rats might get at it, although I never quite found out who the rats were'. Boston concluded in his evidence to the House of Commons Select Committee:

> I am quite uncertain what the observers do when they go back to departments. Do they sit down and brief ministers and write notes for them or do they brief other sections of the department which might probably be very helpful. In short there needs to be clarifications of their roles. We do not want organisations that are distant and apart but a good exchange of information between them. We do not want to be too cosy if finally bodies such as Ofqual has to assert true public independence and accountability to parliament.

This tendency by advisers and civil servants to protect their political masters from unpleasant truths is another reason why the weaknesses inherent in the construction and application of the statutory assessments were not explored in any great detail – neither when New Labour came to office or subsequently when critics provided further evidence that the system was not working. It is worth noting that in two lengthy interviews with Michael Barber he expressed little interest in the debate on the validity of National Curriculum assessment, only in attacks on the reliability of the tests – attacks which he took personally.

It's a myth that people like [*names the two critics*] propagate endlessly . . . That we the government [*sought to influenced the QCA*] It would have been completely impossible and wrong, morally wrong. We wouldn't have done it because there wasn't anything problematic. What really shocked me in the reaction was that basically quite a lot of people were willing to deny the improvement of results, including primary teachers, on whose efforts the improvement of results depended. You'd think they would celebrate their success in improving the performance, and you'd think that's what leaders of the profession would do, but in order to slug it out with government they'd rather undermine their own membership, undermine their own profession.

On first joining the QCA, Mick Waters also reflected on his early impressions of the defensive behaviour of officials at meetings with the 'social partnership':

They said, will you come to this and I said fine . . . I went over beforehand and there were several items on the agenda and the officials coming to the meeting with me were quite quirky. . . . Their aim was to survive for the next hour, not to have a debate, not to have a discourse, not to have a genuine engagement, but to just survive the next hour. One thing on the agenda was the diploma and it was face and repaper and force it on, leave little time for questions. . . . I think that's where the department has got into this 'how can we survive the next hour, the next 10 minutes?' It's self-defeating in the end.

A different kind of model

The success of the assessment for learning approach and its incorporation into the strategies, once ministers and others were convinced it didn't get in the way of raising the national test scores, has interesting parallels. There are parallels with the initial development of the Literacy Strategy at the pilot stage and of the development of 'deeps' as recounted by David Hargreaves at the end of the curriculum chapter. Following the debate about the validity and utility of the TGAT approach, Paul Black and Dylan Wiliam produced a pamphlet seeking to clarify some of the unresolved issues. Titled *Inside the Black Box*, it sold well over expectations and on the back of this interest they were able to secure funding to put some of the ideas to the test. Paul Black in interview for this book recalled that the approach adopted was to establish networks of schools where the stance taken from the start was to tell teachers:

We've got all these ideas from the start but we don't know what to do. You guys can tangle with it, try it out . . . it will provoke, suggest to you things that may be worth doing but when you do you will create new learning and we will learn from you in learning together.

Initially, according to one local adviser, involved with the project, teachers didn't believe this message but thought that Black and Wiliam already 'knew the answers and were trying to see if they [*the teachers*] can work it out'. However, according to Paul Black:

They got over that eventually and near the end as the project progressed they took over the agenda and everything and we were just gathering goodies out of which we wrote the book.

Subsequent projects, conducted in a similar vein, have focused on the dialogue involved in carrying out these assessments, such as steering discussion; 'when to close down, when to let it flow?' and on the creation of suitable tasks for carrying out summative assessment using profiles. Combining formative and summative judgements in normal classroom settings results in what Black terms 'dynamic assessments' in which 'you pick out the child's "best shot" and that goes into the portfolio'. According to Black, one of the things that emerged from this work was that:

> The National Curriculum levels are useless. They were too vague. When we tried to bring them down to specific activities. . . . they're full of inconsistencies.

He thus saw the development of this type of assessment framework as problematic as long as governments continue to look for the easy fruits on the lower branches. Indeed, he argued that already the adoption of AfL officially has led to a notion of formative assessment as something 'essentially static' so that a campaign for more dynamic summative assessment is 'I feel in the next millennium'.

Wherefore now the future of assessment?

At the beginning of the chapter mention was made of the Report of the Expert Group on Assessment. Sir Jim Rose appointed as chair of the group, came with the reputation, according to Mick Waters (quoted in the previous chapter) of someone who gets as near as possible to everybody, but not too far from anybody. It was not surprising, therefore, that in its main recommendations on Key Stage 2 there was encouragement for those wishing to move towards teacher assessments but reassurance for those favouring conventional pencil and paper tests.

Rose's report specifically endorsed the work of Black and Wiliam on formative assessment (para 1.6–1.16) but had nothing to say about their more recent attempts to link formative and summative assessments; thus endorsing Paul Black's pessimism as to the viability of such an arranged marriage.

That the conclusion of the expert group appeared to be largely a reflection of Jim Rose's own position was borne out by Mary James who worried at the lack of any assessment experts on the group, the rushed nature of the consultation and lack of opportunity for alternative views to be heard.

> Jim Rose was really orchestrating it. The expert group had very little time to do it, I know Tim Brighouse was rushing around, trying to consult as much as he could because he thought the chances of headteachers in schools being able to get out and talk was very minimal so he did a lot of that. But apparently when it was written it was mostly written by the secretariat. I believe that the people on the expert group were given 24 hours notice of when it was going to be launched. It was Jim who presented it, basically just re-iterating what is current government policy.

She added a further note of scepticism.

> Although the Select Committee was doing this extensive and detailed review on the assessment and testing, at the same time the Department for Children Schools and Families decided to appoint its own expert committee to review this. Just at that very same time, virtually to undermine it I think.

For some members of the assessment group the attempt to link summative and formative assessment was always going to be a strained relationship; some argued that summative assessment involves more than solely aggregating a series of formative ones into a profile. It required teachers 'not just to sum up a series of judgements or completed assessments but [*also*] to sum up the evidence' (Harlen and James, 1997: 375). What, is broadly agreed, however, was 'that there is common evidence which can be used for the different forms of assessment' (Stobart, 2001).

> Ken Boston was asked how many purposes of assessment were there and he said 22! Because that's what Paul [Newton] had actually identified, but it was more than that. If you just took one of Paul's 22, for example, institutional monitoring, it's used for at least another 12 purposes, including seeing whether providers of services to schools have actually met their target. So the idea is if you have an assessment which is really about assessing where individual students are, in terms of their learning and acknowledging their improvement or whatever it is, then that's aggregated and used for all these other purposes to monitor teachers, headteachers, schools, support services, local authorities, the government itself. It then completely distorts the original purpose.
>
> (Mary James)

The Expert Group ultimately rejected such critique arguing, as we have seen earlier in this chapter, for a continuation of the Key Stage 2 National Tests, justified on the grounds that Year 6 marks the end of a phase and needs such a measure (para 2.3). The tests themselves (in English and mathematics but not science) are it contends, 'a good test of the key skills which pupils need to access the secondary curriculum' (para 2.14), adding that teachers are not yet sufficiently skilled in the use of assessment techniques to warrant replacing the written tests (para 2.8).

Despite this latter reservation the Expert Group were happy to recommend that testing in science be carried out by 'high quality, supported teacher assessment' (para 2.17). Nowhere was there given an explanation of why teachers were likely to be better at assessing science skills rather than those of English or mathematics. The unstated rationale appeared to be that while there was 'weak trust but demands for high accountability' in respect of testing (para 2.8) public concern is with the 3Rs. Thus there is less public pressure to retain conventional measures in the case of science.

The Expert Group also made the radical suggestion that the timing of Key Stage Tests should be put back to mid-June on the grounds that the gap between mid-May and the move to secondary school meant that 'pupils start their secondary education unprepared and out of practice' (para 10). The assumption here seemed to be that primary schools collude in not teaching mathematics or English once the tests finish in May because of the narrow focus of the tests, rather than the possibility that the levels at Key Stages 2 and 3 are not compatible, so causing apparent drops in attainment. This would explain why secondary teachers cannot equate the Key Stage 2 test scores with the initial performance of pupils on entering Year 7. In doing so the Expert Group recognised the present backwash effects that arise because of teachers teaching to the test in a high stakes situation. Nevertheless, the group expressed the hope that:

> Schools ensure that any preparation or the tests is proportionate and appropriate and that any broader activities which might typically take place after the tests are sensibly spread over the year.
>
> (para 2.10)

In order to reinforce this view it proposed that a School Report Card should be developed 'which would recognise the broader range of outcomes to which schools contribute as well as giving credit to those schools which focus on the progression of all their children rather than focussing on borderline pupils' (para 2.5). In addition the report recommended that an extended 'bridging study' be started in Year 6 and carried over into Year 7 (para 1.30) so that the second half of the summer term is not devoted solely to revision for the tests.

The report contained a number of interesting and radical ideas, particularly in the suggestion that at Key Stage 3 the tests used for determining standards should not be linked to school accountability (para 4.4) and should be independent of government or its quangos. It argued also that the tests should be based on the same sampling frame as that used in the international comparative studies such as TIMMS and PISA. (para 4.6). However, in the matter of testing at Key Stage 2 it is difficult to reconcile the recommendations with either the research evidence or the comments of Tim Brighouse who was also a member of the Expert Group. Describing his time as chief education officer for Oxfordshire he said in interview:

> I was convinced that examinations only tested a small part of what kids could do and it was in the early 1980s that I began to speculate with colleagues in Oxfordshire, particularly Harry Judge, who was more a kind of critic and facilitator than necessarily a convert to the particular point of view I was putting forward . . . I was arguing for an abolition of exams at 16, and said, and thought, that being in Oxfordshire, if I could get the university to produce a certificate of education with the crest of the university on it, validated by the university, it should be possible to produce some sort of different configuration of what you said about a kid when they left school.

Out of these deliberations arose:

> [a] thing called the Oxford Certificate of Educational Achievement – OCEA – and it had three parts, it had a personal part about recording things kids did, trying

to get a whole person, trying I suppose to get at things that would mirror or cast a picture on what they were like as human beings. There was a graded assessment part and because I couldn't get rid of it there was an external examination a bit like balanced score cards are appearing for school.

These ideas are very much the forerunner of the now defunct report card since it is clear when talking about the certificate during his interview that Brighouse's views about assessment have not changed to any great degree since his Oxfordshire days. Yet it would appear that to sustain these ideas, a price needed to be paid, the price being the retention of Key Stage 2 tests.

What I've tried to use this latest Expert Group to do is for people to realise that assessment is crucial and that the prime and most important bit of assessment is that between the teacher and the youngster . . . to mark and promote the next stage of their learning and development . . . you know formative assessment and that all the other kind of needs of assessment, summative, that's kind of summative in there but the kind of accountability thing are kind of secondary to that. Now I know that they're not at the moment. What I've tried to do is to shift the thinking, that is to say, we keep talking about transformation and we have got transformative schools building, we've got transformative curriculum, or we're trying to get it, the assessment is not in anyway transformative. It's routed in 100 years ago in its methodology and therefore surely there are things that can't be assessed by a pencil and paper test and therefore we ought to move towards validating teacher assessment and using teacher assessment as the main means of assessing kids' achievements. Now I think that the report . . . it moves in that direction but it doesn't get there.

Mary James' earlier speculation, that the Expert Group came into being largely to 'undermine' the anticipated recommendations of the House of Commons Children, Schools and Families Committee's review of the education system, starting with Kenneth Baker's stewardship and ending with that of Ed Balls, would appear to have some substance, given that a similar tactic was used in response to the Cambridge Primary Review directed by Professor Robin Alexander. A further coincidence was that the man with the reputation for 'a safe pair of hands' was chosen to lead both enquiries. In the event the House of Commons Committee (HCC, 2010) takes a very different line from the official position, in most cases siding with the government's critics. Thus while endorsing the principle of national testing the committee report was strongly critical of the present tests which it argued 'address only a limited part of the National Curriculum and a limited range of children's skills and knowledge' (appendix 1 para 3). They are also strongly critical of the government's assumption that 'one set of tests can serve 'a range of purposes at national, local, institutional and individual levels' (para 4). As a consequence, the committee believed that the system is 'now out of balance' because target setting 'has become a goal rather than a means to an end' (para 7). In the committee's opinion, this had resulted in teaching to the test, a narrowing of the curriculum and too great a focus of resources on borderline pupils.

There were other criticisms regarding the use of 'contextualised value added scores (paras 8, 9 and 10) and the manner in which Ofsted has applied the data from performance tables in its judgements of school effectiveness (para 11).

The previous Labour government's proposals for 'single level test' also came in for a great deal of criticism mainly on the previously stated objection that one test cannot perform both a summative purpose and be also an integral part of personalised learning, assessment for learning and a measure of institutional accountability. The committee also sided with those who argued that any national monitoring system should be carried out by 'a body at arms length from government' and that this exercise 'is a task for the new regulator or a body answerable to it' (para 23). All in all, therefore, the committee was highly critical of existing policy.

However, in the hiatus before the general election many of these initiatives, including the introduction of school report cards, were dropped from the Children Schools and Family Bill and on the first day in office the newly formed coalition government posted a health warning on the Department for Education's website to the effect that the current content may no longer reflect current government policy. It remains to be seen whether the views of the Liberal Democrats, who are in favour of a broader definition of a successful school; views which would appear sympathetic to many of the recommendations of the former select committee, will eventually see the light of day in the face of the more traditional Conservative approach to accountability and testing.

A corrupted system?

The chapter has concentrated on the issues surrounding statutory testing at Key Stage 2 but there are also issues related to the assessment of students at the top end of the secondary schools. In illustrating the way in which carefully prepared proposals can be scuppered in the cause of political expediency, Sir Mike Tomlinson's account of the demise of his proposed secondary diploma was discussed in a previous chapter. It is interesting to note in passing that Hong Kong which does extremely well under the present system of A levels has gone further with its reforms and chosen to close down this avenue of entrance to the university sector. The A levels have been replaced by a diploma which requires students to display a broad range of subject knowledge in the arts, science and humanities. It is known locally as the '334' scheme, because pupils will now spend three years in the lower secondary and three years in the upper secondary school before entering a four year university course. Various pathways are available for those who leave schools early to re-enter the system at a later date. Even though Hong Kong's situation was not as dire as that in the UK, Mike Tomlinson's rationale has an echo. In the UK, the biggest fall out (is) at 17, a long tale of underachievement so that at the end of Year 9 into Year 10 some 10,000 kids disappear off the school role. Thus the impetus which has caused Hong Kong to effect these changes is exactly the same as that which drove Tomlinson's thinking; namely low staying on rates from post 16, and considerable demotivation among those who continue.

Sir Mike Tomlinson's proposals, however, were not as radical as those of Hong Kong. A better comparison is with the Baccalaureate in which every part is graded but not separately qualified. They were not, as Michael Howard argued in the speech referred to earlier, designed to water down traditional A levels by seeking to establish equivalence with newer vocational courses. Tomlinson's stance, reiterated during his interview, was unequivocal on this point.

> We have an obsession with wanting to make everything look alike, with this nonsense term, 'parity of esteem'. You can mouth that all the time you like but you don't get it and you don't want it I don't believe. What we should have is vocational education for someone who's interested, which is credible in its own right and an academic line which is also credible in its own right. We should not try to say that three A levels in physics, chemistry and biology are equivalent of two other [*qualifications*] or vice versa. Nonsense: what we should have is distinct. Equally I don't want lines which don't allow students to transfer across and take some credit with them so you need a credit framework.

Whether we will see these ideas resurrected at some later date must be a matter of conjecture. The House of Commons Committee in its 2010 report also urges the government to make clear its intentions with respect to Diplomas and other 14–19 qualifications, and in particular whether there is eventually to be one overarching qualifications framework as suggested by the Tomlinson Working Group on 14–19 reform. Some, however, like Mick Waters, drawing on his experience at the QCA, think there are too many vested interests involved to allow changes of this magnitude to proceed. His comments from inside the key government advisory body on examinations highlighted the examination boards' disturbing response to a high stakes system.

> Before I went for this job, I used to think that all this criticism of exams that they were being dumbed-down was unfair. You know, the old argument, more people passed than ever before. Since I've been there, I think the system is diseased, almost corrupt. I don't mean QCA or Ofqual or anybody. We've got a set of Awarding Bodies who are in a market place. In previous jobs, I had seen people from Awarding Bodies talk to headteachers implying that their examinations are easier. Not only that, we provide the textbook to help you through it.

The current stated intentions of the new secretary of state for education, Michael Gove, do not appear to assuage all of either Mike Tomlinson or Mick Water's concerns. The Conservative general election manifesto promised to develop 'proper vocational and technical education' and to establish showcase 'Technical Academies' in at least 12 cities to lead the way- an aim highlighted by the coalition.. All schools will be able to offer a wider range of qualifications and the Liberal Democrats would go further in combining these into a General Diploma as a leaving certificate. The distinction that Tomlinson made about equivalence and parity of esteem is not addressed by either of the coalition partners. While Michael Gove said he intended to give universities and academics more say over the form and content of secondary examinations, in an effort to restore rigour, there is as yet no mention of tackling what

Mick Waters saw as a corrupt system as the different examination boards compete for custom. The Liberal Democrat manifesto proposed the setting up of a truly independent Educational Standards Authority to supervise such matters but the coalition government's agreement focussed on simplifying 'the regulation of standards'.

Even if such a Standards Authority did eventually emerge, following a decision to split the Office of the Qualifications and Exam Regulator (Ofqual) from the QCA in line with the recommendations of the Sutherland (2008) enquiry, Mick Water's final comment on the possibility of better regulation was equally pessimistic:

> I think the Ofqual split is a good move; to take regulation away from the development agenda. I fully support having a regulator who can ask awkward questions. So, what I'd now want to see is a regulator asking the questions. I'm not sure that's going to happen.

However, Waters did not believe Ofqual would have the capacity or the nerve to tackle those vested interests.

> I don't think they've got the nerve and that's where it's so similar to the economic problems where the regulator did nothing new because the big names went to the government and moaned. They should immediately look up whether the chief examiner should be allowed to write the text with regards to pupils' questions. That's insider dealing. You shouldn't be allowed to do that.

It was this disquiet, both publically and from inside the previous government's own organisations, that triggered the following response at interview from the then Liberal Democrat education spokesperson, briefly chief secretary to the Treasury, David Laws. In proposing an Education Standards Authority Laws' argued

> I think we should be getting at these things [*standards*] and I shouldn't need to guess. We should have a completely independent body . . . an Education Standards Authority that answers these type of questions but that is not tied up as Ofqual is and is not as distrusted by many people as Ofqual is in terms of doing the job. It should be really trying to tell us what has happened to standards and also be capable of marrying existing domestic statistics and international statistics . . . We need some system for judging educational standards which is not as distorted by the targeting of educational results in the way that it has been over the last 30 years.

If the Liberal Democrats were eventually able to persuade Michael Gove of the wisdom of this viewpoint then the demise of the testing system in its present form could be a catalyst for much needed changes. Mike Tomlinson at secondary level and the Assessment Reform Group at the primary stage have repeatedly urged such changes on successive governments. Perhaps Paul Black's conclusion that reforms of this magnitude will not take place within the present century might turn out to be too pessimistic an assessment.

7 Promoting and delivering value for money?

> How can you reassure those who elect people such as us that if we got rid of Ofsted tomorrow, there would be a real worry about the quality of a child's life? Looking across the history of Ofsted, where it came from and why it was introduced, are you sure that it represents value for money? Is it doing anything to make the lives of children in our country better?

This question, put to Christine Gilbert HMCI by Barry Sheerman, chair of the House of Commons Select Committee in 2008, lies at the heart of the debate over inspection, its purposes, its effect and its future under a new government.

Inspection of schools has survived for over a century and passes seamlessly from one government to the next and no prime minster or politician could relinquish a commitment to externally driven quality assurance, audit, review, or inspection by any other name. The question remains. 'What would you lose by not having Ofsted? asks Tim Brighouse. What convincing rationale is there for a 'service' that will cost the tax payer two hundred million in 2010?

Ofsted have their own answer. 'Promoting and delivering value for money' means a return on investment in the following respects:

> Ofsted makes sure that its inspection and regulatory work helps to make a difference for children and young people – securing their educational, economic and social well being and contributing to our success as a country.
>
> (Ofsted, 2007: 42)

This is a bold claim and one that has to be tested both in retrospect and prospect.

Inspectors: ornaments of the profession

The history of inspection is one of constant re-invention, a continuing search for the right formula, yet never quite able to satisfy all of the people all of the time. About one hundred and twenty years ago an article in the teachers' newspaper, *The Schoolmaster* carried this report of testimony given to the Cross Commission in 1888:

The inspectors of schools were the subject of many hard sayings, and the men, who under a system founded on common sense, who would be deemed ornaments of the professions, are derided for their unfitness and irregularity.

(Ascham, 1888)

'Unfitness and irregularity' remain a charge laid by some against Ofsted's contracting out of inspection, producing uneven standards across the country and something of a lottery as to the quality of the team who will visit your school. In the words of one Islington headteacher:

I think the main criticism of Ofsted is that they're not reliable, it's all dependent on who you get. They must be the only organisation in the whole wide world that is absolutely accurate in what they do. They have never ever made a mistake. Solid every time. This cannot be. Who are these people?

This view is endorsed by evidence from the Cambridge Primary Review:

As with any large organisation the expertise of inspection teams ranges from outstanding to inadequate, notwithstanding the training which is supposed to even out such differences. In the review community soundings, several groups raised doubts about the competence of inspection teams – a view echoed in those submissions which questioned the ability of some inspectors to make valid assessments of the quality of teaching and learning.

(2009: 337)

Primus inter pares?

Hostility to the inspection regime in the nineteenth century had much to do with the inequality of the relationship between inspectors and schools together with system of payment by results, eventually abandoned to give way to a more collegial approach. By the end of the nineteenth century HMI opened negotiations with the National Union of Teachers in an attempt to re-establish trust and to pave the way for a more collegial approach. A 1922 report by the Board of Education offers a telling statement which may be set against what was to come under Ofsted 170 years later, and what is now being seen by some as the desirable shape of the future.

The inspectors do not make any claim to be abler or better teachers or schoolmasters than many whom they meet in the course of their work, nor have any such claims been preferred on their behalf. So far as that aspect of things is concerned, they are no more than equals among equals.

(Boothroyd, 1923)

If 'primus inter pares' may be the shape of the future it will have to redress the inequitable relationship between the profession and the inspectorate. Fast forward to 2002:

Ofsted was created to challenge the producer interest, and that, for better or worse, is what under my leadership it did (Woodhead, 2002).

Challenging 'the producer interest', that is teachers, heads and the educational establishment, was an explicit purpose underpinning the creation of Ofsted in 1992. As he saw it, Chris Woodhead was tasked with 'a responsibility to expose failure' and he was, ten years on, unapologetic as to the 'the trauma of failure', arguing that shock, and shaking up were the catalyst needed to tackle the deep seated problems of failing schools and failing teachers. He added:

Prickly, confrontational, arrogant, incapable of working with anyone'. Yes, that is me. But it is what the chief inspector has to be if Ofsted is to maintain any semblance of independence.

(2002: 108)

'Miraculously', said Barry Sheerman, the government kept him on in 1997, a 'ruggedly independent pain in the arse'.

Remember he said he was only responsible to the Queen because he was Her Majesty's Inspector. And some people laughed and said, no, he means to God. Of course what we said [as the Select Committee], was a modified position because the Privy Council told him he couldn't keep saying that. He was actually accountable to parliament through our committee.

Ofsted and its chief inspector were, in Conor Ryan's words, 'a fairly persuasive mechanism'.

We wanted to make moves quickly on it, it was important for us to get things moving, we were going to do it through exhortation and actually we have got, in Ofsted, a fairly persuasive mechanism.

As Estelle Morris describes it, the incoming Labour government had to shift the perception from party of the producer to the party of the consumer – as 'citizen focused'. So the retention of the Tories' favourite chief inspector and the continuation of the 'naming and shaming' policy was intended to give two clear messages to two different constituencies – to the public that it was on the side of the user of the services and not the producer of the services; and to the teaching profession that, 'if they hadn't realised it, they would realise it now. That we weren't the same Labour as last time we came into power, where we would just be in favour of what they did'.

That they weren't the same Labour party of old was to become abundantly clear as, in Mary Bousted's words, the 'delight' and anticipation had begin to turn sour.

Within six months, Blunkett, even within six weeks, had just destroyed that through naming and shaming and also that phrase which I'll never forget, 'Kids in Inner City Schools fail because the teachers have no expectations'. I thought that was a shameful thing for Labour minister to say.

The language of failing schools and underachievement, a legacy of the Conservatives, became embedded in government speech and in Ofsted rhetoric. As Pauline Perry ex-HMI said, it is a language which carried tough messages but was counterproductive in respect of school improvement.

> I hate that kind of language about under-achieving, failing schools. I've never visited a school which I would describe in that way. I have visited parts of a school which were patently under-achieving. I've visited individual classrooms where the teacher was clearly struggling and wasn't keeping discipline. . . . Yes, of course, there were bad examples but they were the exception.

The last hurrah or dog's dinner?

The act creating Ofsted was almost the last act of the first John Major government. Originally, the intention had been to give schools money to pay for their own inspections but this was rejected by the House of Lords who felt it would lead to schools taking the 'soft option' and appointing teams of known sympathisers. At the behest of the bishops the lords also added the requirement that the social, moral, spiritual and cultural ethos of the school should also form part of the inspection. Thinking they would be out of office shortly, the government was forced to accept these changes to the bill in order to secure the royal assent before parliament was dissolved. The result according to Mike Tomlinson, then senior inspector for secondary schools was 'a bit of a dog's dinner'. When John Major was surprisingly returned for a second term of office it was left to Her Majesty's Inspectorate to 'try to make it into some sense' and then for the newly formed Ofsted to make this flawed scheme operational.

According to Tomlinson, right to the point when the policy decision to create Ofsted was taken, HMI under the then chief inspector, Eric Bolton, had been working on an alternative model; one where:

> HMI worked with local authority inspectors and doing joint inspections in an effort at some point of accrediting what the authority did. . . . We worked with five authorities and that was beginning to show some real signs of success. That was the model put forward but what you have to understand was at this point in time HMI were seen as part of the problem, not part of the solution . . . and therefore there had to be something radically different.

The decision to restrict HMI to the inspection of teacher and adult education left the newly formed Ofsted with a logistics problem. Their solution was to invite a whole host of external bodies to form inspection teams. These consisted in some cases of local authority inspectors, who were able to report on schools in other LEAs, members of Higher Education Institutions, private companies and hastily formed consortiums consisting of a mix of retired HMIs, local inspectors and teachers. Training was minimal so that, unsurprisingly, the experience of individual schools at the hands of these Ofsted teams varied enormously. As neighbouring schools swopped inspection stories, considerable resentment was generated on account of this inconsistent treatment. Mike Tomlinson confirmed that 'one of the biggest concerns we had within Ofsted in the early days was consistency'.

The Ofsted regime inherited from the Tories, in fact survived virtually untouched from one political administration to the next. During the next decade under Labour the nature and purposes of inspection were, however, to undergo a series of changes, in part driven by financial necessity, in part due to much needed rethinking of efficiency and effectiveness, in part due to a series of government reviews of the work of Ofsted and the impact on their thinking by high profile coverage in the media.

In 2000, the Government Select Committee's Fourth Report called for a 'more mature' debate, citing the level of rhetoric conducted through the media and including in its report an assemblage of lurid headlines.

- **Traumatised teachers hit back** *The Observer,* 23 April 2000.
- **The day of reckoning:** nothing strikes fear into a teachers' heart like the news that the inspectors are coming. *The Guardian,* 3 July 2000.
- **Fear forcing teachers to quit** *The Guardian,* 2 August 2000.
- **Fresh start after fear** . . . Teachers, like most people, need to be led, not driven. But Woodhead, by his own admission, chose fear as the chief means of raising teachers' expectations. *The Times Educational Supplement,* editorial, 10 November 2000.
- **Hope for a new humane reign** *The Times Educational Supplement,* 10 November 2000.

Endorsing inspection as 'a vital part of the education system' the Select Committee added the caveat:

> But it is time to end the sterile controversies which surround Ofsted's work. We now need less heat and more light. A mature debate on the strengths and weaknesses of the inspection system is essential.

The conclusions of the committee echo the sentiments of the 1922 Board of Education, calling for 'the development of a professional dialogue between inspectors and teachers'. It suggested an increase in the numbers of serving teachers who train as Ofsted inspectors, complemented by lay inspectors who could bring another perspective to the inspection process by asking 'Is this a school which I would wish to send my child to?'. The committee made a number of recommendations:

- A clearer focus on quality in the contracting system for school inspections.
- The period of notice for inspection to be reduced to the shortest period which is practical.

- Consideration to be given to unannounced visits to schools–'snap inspections'– by external agencies such as HMI or LEAs.
- School governing bodies to be allowed to nominate an observer to the inspection team.
- The Inspection Framework to be amended to take account of the quality of the self-evaluation procedures used by schools.
- The Inspection Framework to better take account of major factors which affect school performance, for example, high pupil mobility.
- 'Light-touch' inspections for high quality initial teacher training providers.
- Parliament to play a more active role in scrutinising Ofsted's work, including an advisory role in the (re-)appointment of HM Chief Inspector.
- Strong consideration to be given to the establishment of a Board of Commissioners for Ofsted.
- HM Chief Inspector's advice to ministers, and his or her public statements, to be clearly backed up by inspection evidence gathered by Ofsted.

In conclusion, the co-chairman of the Select Committee, at that time, Malcolm Wicks MP, said:

> The chief inspector should be concerned to improve morale and promote confidence in the teaching profession. The Select Committee feel strongly that low morale among teachers inhibits the drive to raise standards. The chief inspector can best contribute to educational standards by ensuring inspection of schools is positive and purposeful.

The chief HMI did not serve much longer, having both outstayed his welcome and as having done the job he was brought in to do. David (Lord) Putnam described the end of an era.

> Gordon Brown's wedding and the celebration afterwards – I was just leaving, and a somewhat pissed John Humphries comes up to me . . . very amiable. I've always got on very well with John, and he said 'Great news about Chris isn't it!'. Somehow or other he'd got it into his head that Chris and I were friends. I simply said 'Yes, isn't it good John'. He went on, 'Yes, this deal he's got with the Telegraph sounds fantastic'. 'Yes it sounds great'. I said, 'When do you reckon it's going to start?' 'February', he replied. A week later and I'm at No. 10 for some entirely different reason and I mentioned it to the PM that Chris Woodhead's been saying he's going to work at the Telegraph. (Blair said) 'What are you talking about?' 'I picked it up last week . . . he'll be leaving in February.' (He said) 'I can't believe it. I've always gone out of my way to protect him.' He went ballistic! 'How can I be sure it's true?' I said, 'you know what I'd do? You should ask Andrew (Adonis) to take him to dinner . . . Chris is an honest man. Get Andrew to ask him . . .' At the end of the dinner, Andrew asks the question and Chris says 'Who the hell told you? It's none of your business' and really takes off on poor old Andrew. From that point on, things moved very quickly. Blunkett had had it with him by then. He was gone within days.

In a telling postscript Michael Barber says:

> You can read the Blunkett Diaries. He doesn't say a lot about Chris, but there's one line that says, 'Chris Woodhead had many qualities which he sought to hide, but among them were not collegiality or generosity', which is one of the finest back-handed compliments I've ever read!

Restoring the professional dialogue

Restoring the professional dialogue was a key concern of Woodhead's successor David Bell. In an interview with him in 2006 he conceded, 'I have always been cautious in saying inspection causes improvement because frankly we do not', but then added this caveat as to the importance of the collegial conversation.

> To say inspection causes improvement is fundamentally unprovable. I think there are examples of where you have greater evidence of improvement being brought about by inspection, but again it's still not quite the same as saying it causes it. For example, our monitoring of schools with special measures is not causing improvement but most headteachers say to us that the process of professional debate and discussion with HMI brings some real bite to the improvement process. I think it's a bit too simplistic to say that either Ofsted does cause improvement or Ofsted doesn't cause improvement.
>
> (MacBeath, 2006: 30)

By this argument it is in the dialogue (dia-logos 'meaning flowing through it') that the improvement process is engaged. It is what the Dutch academic Leeuw terms a 'me-too-you-too' reciprocal interchange, or what the 1922 Board referred to as 'equal among equals'. It describes what some inspection systems such as Hong Kong's process of external review, for example, strives to achieve.

For Michael Gove, its fundamental purpose ought indeed to be improvement but with sensitivity to the social context of the school and the exigencies of staffing.

> The whole point is that Ofsted should be there not to say right, you are satisfactory and goodbye, but in the report, as well as accentuating the positive, it should say, for example, the quality of teaching and learning in the maths department is good, it's only satisfactory here and we appreciate that's because of the high turnover of the staff and would recommend that x and y are done and we would support the head master's goal.

Are two Ofsteds better than one?

It is hugely difficult to engage the debate as to the contribution of Ofsted whether to school improvement or to the professional dialogue, so contested and emotionally loaded is the notion of 'inspection' and so contentious is its reincarnation as Ofsted in particular. Commenting on the Janus face of Ofsted during the Fourth Select Committee hearing, a member of the panel said:

> I am very much struck when I go round schools that there are two Ofsteds really. In the schools normally, with some exceptions, there is an extremely professional, relatively calm process going on with more feedback than I would have expected. Yes, there is quite a lot of stress but there is an acceptance of the need for the international evaluation. There is that Ofsted, which is rather calm and professional and, maybe to journalists, rather boring. Then there is another Ofsted which is somewhere higher up, which is all blood, thunder, guts, tears and big giants stalking the land, firing at one another. That last bit would be fun if it was not for the fact that it may be associated with what I perceive to be a major problem, namely pretty poor morale among teachers.

How Ofsted is perceived has rested to a significant degree on its history and surrounding rhetoric and by a concerted policy during the Woodhead regime to maintain a high profile, with radio, television and newspaper, always welcoming of controversy and sound bite but ever on the ready to bite back.

> The media has teeth but can only snarl. The committee tried to snarl, but was too comic to intimidate (Woodhead, 2002: 108).

This public theatre did, however, serve to undermine the often effective low profile dialogue with schools and classrooms which continued below the radar, as data show and many witness attest to, inspection could be a welcome and positive experience. The problem, as Sir Alasdair MacDonald (Head of Morpeth School in Tower Hamlets) described it, was the systemic approach which, while rightfully addressing underachievement, created resentment among schools that were doing well by the children in their charge.

> If you're the secretary of state for education and there's children who are achieving abysmally, I think you have an obligation to those pupils in those schools to try to give them the entitlement that is theirs. I think the problem is the only tool you've got, as a government, is to make something statutory. If you make something statutory then for the twenty per cent of schools that are not doing a very good job you have to do that to try to help the children in those schools. The eighty per cent of schools that are really doing quite well, you alienate them because they resent it.

Achieving success 'below the radar' is, for David Hargreaves, a mark of self confident schools. They are not intimidated and oppressed by Ofsted nor by 'the centre' because with imaginative leaders and committed creative teachers they follow their best professional instincts. There is, he claimed,

> [A]n extra-ordinary generation of some school leaders who have bucked the trend and have not taken the line of feeling oppressed by the centre and who don't say

I'd love to do innovation but I can't afford to because of Ofsted or the league tables or whatever and they've just got on innovating and doing exciting things and running very good schools and also schools that tend to do very well by conventional criteria because they're exciting places for teachers and kids to be in.

No more sprucing up

Few may remember the name Maurice Smith HMCI. His was a short interim tenure but with a social work rather than school background he brought a different perspective to the role, marked by a willingness to work positively with teacher unions, for example. In 2006 he reasserted the place and value of dialogue.

> The great majority of headteachers felt that the dialogue between the inspection team and senior staff was helpful. It is perhaps ironic that, although few teachers would claim to enjoy inspections, many now feel short-changed if their own teaching is not observed.
>
> (Ofsted: The First Term of the New Arrangements, January 25, 2006)

Indeed, as headteachers told us, there were teachers who felt shortchanged by not being observed but it was ultimately a tradeoff between weeks of preparation and anticipation and the short notice short inspection which freed them up to deploy energies into more productive channels.

> Weeks of anxious pre-inspection preparation and sprucing up are a thing of the past. We want teachers and pupils to concentrate on teaching and learning, not on preparing for inspections, and we want to see the school in its normal state, as it is from week to week through the year, not as it wants to be seen. . . . These are short, sharp inspections, by small teams. The days when a dozen inspectors would camp in a school for a week are past.
>
> (Smith, 2006)

While short notice creates a number of problems, says William Atkinson (Head of Phoenix School in Hammersmith and Fulham), the benefits for him outweigh the disadvantages. The downsides are the difficulties in getting governors at short notice, bringing parents in, avoiding an Ofsted visit when there were school trips, visits out of school, sports days, the loss of Year 11 in the summer term and the serendipity of who's there and who's not on any particular day. On balance, however, the absence of stress and frenetic preparation more than compensate, he claims:

> With all those downsides short notice takes a lot of stress out of it. You've no longer masses of paper to get together. People haven't had time to be psyched out, feeling miserable week after week, their weekend's been ruined, the temperature just rising and rising.

Speaking at a conference in Nottingham in 2006 Maurice Smith HMCI went a step further:

I especially like the story of one headteacher who, on hearing on Friday that his school was to be visited the following week, decided not to tell his staff until Monday morning: he was confident in their abilities and didn't want to ruin their weekend. It is a refreshing approach, which others might do well to copy.

A 2007 report by the National Foundation for Educational Research (NFER) found that three quarters of the schools surveyed said that the new form of inspection had already contributed to improvement and 85 per cent of schools agreed that the new inspection system was likely to contribute to school improvement in the future. 66 per cent completely agreed with Ofsted's recommendations for improvement and 92 per cent of respondents thought the recommendations were helpful.

Shorter inspections are only a part of the solution. For some the positive endorsement is due to a less confrontative Ofsted regime that has helped to restore teachers' confidence, said Mick Waters – 'I think overall some of the morale in the people in the profession is better than it was a few years ago. I think it has been rekindled. I think there is a lot of enthusiasm in schools'. It is, he suggested, reflected in a more open attitude among HMIs with whom he worked closely while at the QCA.

> We've got on well with Ofsted at QCA. They've been very, very willing to think about what learning is about because the HMI in Ofsted typically are people who are really committed educationalists and want to make a difference in all sorts of ways.

HMI today are a different 'animal', from those who 'came in for a cup of tea and biscuit and a quick trot around the school', says William Atkinson, recalling a regime which roused the ire of the Thatcher government and initiated an era of 'big cats prowling the educational landscape' (Learmonth, 2000: 15).

And then there was the revised framework

If, as some argued, that by 2009 the shape of Ofsted inspections was about as good as it was ever going to get, the Revised Framework appears to have undone such optimism. There seemed much to applaud in the June 2009 announcement of a revised framework focused more on teaching and learning, on dialogue with teachers, and on improvement and capacity building. It promised that:

> 'Inspectors will spend more time in classrooms observing teaching and learning and the progress made by different groups of pupils'
> 'We will double the amount of time we spend in classrooms observing teaching'
> 'We will engage staff in discussion about ways to improve'
> 'They [the inspection team] would also look very closely at whether the school has the capacity to improve'.
>
> (Ofsted, 2009)

This, it was said, would be realised through a ten point plan which would be characterised by – proportionality; promoting improvement; wider focus on well being; learning and teaching; equality of opportunity; safeguarding; engagement of headteachers and staff in the process; taking account of views of pupils, parents and teachers; partnership with other providers.

These measures would also be accompanied by a raising of the bar – higher expectations and greater rigour with inspectors given greater latitude to interpret the new guidelines and demonstrate that they could get tough on standards.

A few months into the new framework and two months prior to a general election the embedding of the Revised Framework in practice was proving to have less than happy consequences. A data gathering exercise by the NUT on the impact of the framework on schools that had been inspected offered some damning evidence.

While there were a few positive comments, reflecting the serendipitous nature of the lead inspector's qualities and sensitivities, the consistency among teachers and headteachers' accounts tell a powerful story. The same words reoccur with painful regularity – belittled, stressed, exhausted, vulnerable, disappointed, frustrated, devastated, demoralised, bruising, distressing, 'a crushing experience'.

These strongly expressed feelings provide an interesting counterpoint to the ten key aspects of the Revised Framework.

1. Snippets of lessons. Very rarely was an inspector present for a whole lesson, typically reported as between 15 and 20 minutes. Judgments, it was said, were made without knowledge of what had gone before or what was still to come. 'I didn't recognise the description of the lesson'.

2. Progress. The possibility of measuring progress was frequently questioned: How could an inspector make a judgement about pupil progress in the space of ten to twenty minutes in a class, without evidence of prior achievement or previous lessons? Without looking at pupils' work? These were common comments.

3. Negativity. Looking for fault rather than for the positives was often couched in strong language – 'a tirade of negativity about my lesson', 'Questions seemed all calculated deliberately to catch me out', 'Looking for reasons to fail'. 'Am I really such a crap teacher?' one member of staff asked the deputy head following a demoralising classroom observation.

4. Intimidation. The aggressive nature of the 'interrogation', as it was described, often, it was said, left teachers disorientated and undermined, in some cases 'leaving staff in tears'. It was undertaken, as it was claimed, in 'a culture of fear' and 'blame'. 'Bullying' was a common charge.

5. Feedback. Feedback was very widely seen as unsatisfactory cursory, rushed or offhand. One teacher described an inspector 'giving me feedback while we were walking down the hall.

6. Omniscience. 'Who made Ofsted infallible?' wrote one teacher, commenting on the definitive nature of the inspector's judgment. It was clear from numerous accounts that inspection teams did not expect to be challenged – 'The inspector did look surprised when I questioned her judgment'. As another teacher wrote: 'They appear to be accountable to no one'.

7. Triviality. One of the most disturbing aspects of 'raising the bar' was schools being downgraded or failed for a variety of reasons, described as 'trivial'–entries on an incorrect speadsheet, failing to cover everything on the lesson plan, the plenary running two minutes too long, the height of the school perimeter fence, the classroom door being left open.
8. Pre-judgment. Evidence, it was said, was adduced to support prior judgments, made before the school visit, with, it was claimed, 'looking specifically for evidence to fail the school'.
9. Inconsistency. Teachers made comparison between what the local authority or the School Improvement Partner had reported, querying the widely differing judgments made. There were also complaints about reports given at the time of the visits and those that had been revised and presented a few weeks later.
10. Generalisation. While a visiting team might visit three out of eight teachers in a department, there was discontent over 'sweeping judgments' that included all staff.

As one deputy head wrote, in summary of his two page submission:

> I spent yesterday evening going through the Ofsted Code of Conduct from their site and it was clear that they had broken just about every single one of their regulations.

It would be easy to dismiss these stories as minority reports from disgruntled NUT members. There is, however, such consistency, such depth of feeling and from such a broad range of respondents (not all NUT members) that these stories cannot simply be dismissed. They point to some inherent problems in trying to simultaneously 'raise the bar', allowing what this means to be interpreted by individual inspectors, while also promising to promote improvement through dialogue and formative feedback with teachers. Add to this mix the high priority given to safeguarding and it is not surprising that there is confusion and conflict. In interview David Laws, then front bench spokesman for the Liberal Democrats made this comment:

> It worries me actually that Ofsted are spending so much of their time thinking about the safeguarding. . . . When I saw the chief inspector the other day, I didn't see her because I wanted to talk about the safeguarding but what she was talking to me about was the safeguarding part of their agenda and because it's been so politically high profile, and because one mistake could cost people right up to the top of the organisation their jobs, it must be taking the eye rather off school improvements and its difficult enough to improve the education of young people let alone sort out everything else.

Mary James, confirming the twenty minute norm, also provided support for teachers' accounts and, in particular, concerns as to the visibility of 'progress' in pupils' learning.

In schools I've been in this term and last term teachers were really anxious about the new inspection framework, particularly the focus on observing in classrooms and expecting to see movement in children's learning. Well, this is fine, but defined as movement on levels? I would expect to see evidence of learning in a classroom but I would expect it in more narrative terms, such as is there evidence that children have grasped a particular idea or don't seem to understand something. The problem is there is evidence of some inspectors coming into classrooms and expecting the teacher to tell them where children are on these APP criteria and expecting to see movement in those achievements in the course of the lesson. Now that's really interesting, because if you've got eight levels according to the National Curriculum plus exceptional performance, that's nine levels, and if you've got three sub levels, that's 27 levels.

A question of purpose

The purpose, or purposes, of inspection will continue to be a matter of debate. Is it about improvement or accountability? Can it serve both masters? Can it do so while continuing to expand its remit? Renamed in early 2010, The Office for Standards in Education, Children's Services and Skills regulates and inspects registered childcare and children's social care, including adoption and fostering agencies, residential schools, family centres and homes for children, all state maintained schools, non-association independent schools, pupil referral units, further education, initial teacher education, and publicly funded adult skills and employment-based training, the Children and Family Courts Advisory Service (Cafcass), and the overall level of services for children in local authority areas. A remit too far, said ex-HMI Pauline Perry.

> I respected Ofsted and indeed have gone on respecting Ofsted. It's only a matter of enormous regret to me that they have been loaded up with all kinds of responsibilities for which it will take them a long term to fix themselves, if ever they can, and I believe that to load them with all this extra kind of social services stuff detracts from their role – their role to enforce or encourage rigour.

It is a remit unlikely to last under a new government determined to recast both inspection and children' services. Interviewed before his appointment as secretary of state for education, to the Cabinet Office Michael Gove agreed with Pauline Perry's caveats, adding his endorsement to the need for a more tighter more focused review of school practice.

> My view is that Ofsted could have an explicitly tighter focus on teaching and learning and so on and that some of the other things for which it inspects at the moment are superfluous. It's not because I believe that it doesn't matter what children eat, but my view is that if you ask a school to be judged on eighteen different criteria, that robs the people leading that school and people within that school of the ability themselves to set the regime.

However, there is a paradox which confronts inspection. With a broadening social agenda and the progressive demise of other agencies of socialisation such as churches, youth clubs, youth organisations and traditional family/extended family influence, a narrowing school attainment agenda may be a regressive step. In the new slimmed down Ofsted the key discriminator which separates full and cursory inspection is measured by pupil 'outcomes', yet, as we have learned from half–a–century of research, it is the social and economic context of the school that is the primary determinant of what pupils achieve in school. Contextual value added measures and PANDAs (Performance and Assessment Reports) act as a proxy for neighbourhood, family and 'community' but are thin gruel compared with the rich mix that comes from a deep first hand insight into the life of inner city or rural communities. Giving evidence to the Parliamentary Sixth Select Committee in 2007, the NUT reminded the committee that criteria used to evaluate effectiveness and achievement were 'predicated on schools' ability to address wider, societal issues such as the prevailing culture of the neighbourhood and the socio-economic profile of the community from which the school intake is drawn' (House of Commons. Education and Skills Committee. 2007).

Once upon a time in Alberta, Canada, the inspection team were required to spend a day at least in the local neighbourhood before entering the school. Mick Waters offered a compelling contrast to such an immersion model.

> When an inspection team goes to do a report, it writes a report and then the Lead Inspector sends it to the reader and the reader sits miles away, never having been near the school, and says, 'If you say this, you can't say that'. They determine the report, every report.

At the other end of equation an Ofsted team will come armed with a portfolio of statistics which, as Mick Waters argued, prejudge the issues and enable inspectors to view the school through the narrowest of lenses.

> It is the consequences of the assessment regime because Ofsted judgements are made based on results. I think it's a shame that they have access to all the scores before they go in. They should say whether it's a good school and then be told the school is not. Not the other way round.

While Gove' argument that a plethora of indicators is overburdening and potentially deskilling, and that schools and inspection systems should therefore focus exclusively on attainment misses the point, said Mick Waters.

> If we believe that health, civic participation, respect, capacity for further learning, being responsible are all what we want, we should measure schools on that, not be measuring schools on a very, very narrow range.

The NUT made the point to the Select Committee that while *Every Child Matters* outcomes are intended to broaden the angle of view, there was an essential contradiction in attempting to marry the inspection schedule with the ECM indicators, 'as the two have very different starting points, over-arching philosophies and purposes. The much broader and less easily measurable concerns of the former cannot be adequately captured by the "snapshot" approach of the latter' (para 16).

Education by numbers

In his book *Education by Numbers*, Warwick Mansell demonstrated the extent to which 'hyper accountability' has been dominated by an obsession with numbers; from pupil testing to Ofsted gradings, 'a brutally efficient system'. Looking back on origins of this addiction to simplicity, Pauline Perry laid the blame for 'numbers game' on Ofsted's predecessors.

> I think this is the key mistake that was made. It was made by the Inspectorate before it became Ofsted but Ofsted inherited it lock, stock and barrel. This was the argument of assigning numeric ratings to individual schools and colleges, and that was totally wrong. In the heyday of HMI, we did not do that. We gave a descriptive account of a school because, again, you cannot reduce the whole of the school [to a number]. You might be talking about eighty teachers and one thousand three hundred kids. How can you say there are a three or they are a two or they are a nine or whatever number it is . . . when it moved to Ofsted, Ofsted thought 'what a good idea', or ministers told Ofsted it was good idea, and so they were off and away.

The response to the limitations of single numbers was seen as a balanced 'scorecard'. As a metaphor it suggests greater coverage than a single 'snapshot' yet carrying within it unfortunate numerical connotations. Since the initial publications in a business context in the early 1990s, the notion of the 'balanced scorecard' has been widely adopted in commercial companies, governments and non-profit organisations. Its purpose is to provide a profile rather than a single number, a range of indicators or 'core yardsticks' that attempt to gauge the quality and effectiveness of the organisation – business, college or school.

Marking your card

Protracted discussion within government and in consultation with the profession came from a recognition that the complexity and richness of school life could not be captured by a single statistic, letter grade or catch-all descriptors such as 'satisfactory' (a term of ultimate ambiguity). So, enter the concept of a balanced score card, once more an idea borrowed from the corporate world. The score card (despite its unfortunate name) offers a step forward by offering a profile of relative strengths and weaknesses, 'balanced' because it gives weight and credence to much more than headline attainment measures.

Originated by Kaplan and Norton of the Harvard Business School, it was seen as a framework that added strategic indicators to the narrower singular financial data so as to give managers a more 'balanced' view of overall organisational performance. The framework was designed not only to provide performance data but to help managers to identify what should be paid attention to, what should be measured, and what should be done to take account of these data in forward planning, referred to at times as a 'strategy map'. There is, however, little, if any, empirical evidence to show that over the ten or so years of its use it has led to improved corporate outcomes although succeeding generations of BSC have progressively tried to make it a more sensitive instrument.

For Estelle Morris it offered a way of demonstrating the breadth of a school's purpose and achievement. A scorecard could, she claimed, convey a set of values that the Labour Party had always espoused but was unable to convince its critics.

> What I think the report card does. What it might do is what we didn't. We couldn't find a mechanism to show we valued the things we didn't test. That was the problem. We always valued the other things. We always valued moving children up from an E to a D. We always valued those things but we couldn't find a way of showing it, that's the problem. Now, the hope for the report card lies in whether or not it's the way of showing we value these things and if we can get to a situation where there's a way of showing how much we value dancing, music, sport and PE; how much we value how much improvement children make and that really gets into the public consciousness.

Michael Gove, however, remained unpersuaded.

> I worry that the report card mixes up hard and soft data. It's not clear who is going to be responsible for the ultimate mark, it's not clear how that's made up. A proportion of it is more attainment, what proportion of it is CVA, what proportion of it is the quality of relationships with other institutions and so on? So, at the moment I'm totally unpersuaded by the case for it because I don't necessarily believe that there is a sufficient relevant agreement that the application of marks will be fair.

The Children's Society's Good Childhood Inquiry, conducted early in 2009, was also less enthused.

> The new 'report card' system being proposed by the government, which would rank schools according to a wider range of measures than exam results, does offer some concession to the point that there is more to school life than simple exam results statistics. In that sense, it might be more 'balanced' than the current rankings. But it really is just another form of league table, which does nothing to address some of the underlying and fundamental problems with this approach. It seems to me to be just another expression of the belief by the politicians, and their advisers that the way to improve something is to publish a new set of indicators and then cajole the profession with a mixture of carrot and large stick into trying to improve on these measures. There are deep problems with this approach.

The Third Commons Select Committee after it heard extensive evidence from both advocates and critics, cautiously welcomed the move away from simplistic attainment measures to a balanced school 'report card' with this caveat.

> A school report card is not, and in our view never can be, a full account of a school's performance, yet the inclusion of an overall score suggests that it is.

A 2005 doctoral dissertation – The Balanced Scorecard: a critique (Hoerle, 2005) referred to 'the desperate search for the right strategic measurement tool', one which proves elusive because of 'measuring the right things right', a perennial issue within a business context but even more acutely dissatisfying when applied within an educational setting. Alasdair Macdonald foresaw a danger in replacing one 'game' with another, given a long tradition of schools' ability to play the system.

> But if it just becomes a game, and it will become a game, some schools will work out that there's a magic formula by which you can get a very high score here and to what end? I think it's a really good example of a policy which is pretty superfluous.

Invisible children

Superfluous? Confused between its improvement and accountability purposes? Or simply inadequate to capture the richness of children's school experience? For parents of children with special needs the problem is that 'the game' appears to be played with loaded dice. As they reported to the Lamb Inquiry in 2009, the notion of accountability by 'the system' (and by Ofsted in particular) to their children was conspicuously absent. Evidence to the inquiry found that Ofsted inspections typically bypassed their children, producing bland and, often misleading reports. According to the inquiry, in a random sample of 35 inspection reports, only one made reference to outcomes for pupils with SEN (Special Education Needs) or disability while 29 made no references to SEN or disability at all.

> Many disabled children and children with SEN are not visible in the key stage threshhold measures because they are working below these levels (Inspection, Accountability and School Improvement, para 9)

What the inquiry described as Ofsted's 'thin evidence base' had a number of consequences. Positive judgments in the inspection report on the school proved damaging to parental confidence when they found that their concerns about the provisions at their child's schools were overlooked, or dismissed. The inquiry cited one inspection report whose evidence about SEN provision relied on the quote from one parent. Nor, in many instances, were SENCOs asked to provide information for the inspection team, quoting a SENCO – 'I felt SEN was not even given a cursory glance'. It conveyed a clear message to parents about the nature of accountability to them and to their children.

Less rigorous standards of accountability for this group of children convey a message to parents, schools, local authorities and others that outcomes for this group of children have a lower priority than for other children.

(Lamb Inquiry, 2007: para 24)

By virtue of Ofsted failure to monitor provision on their behalf, parents told the Inquiry that it fell to them to 'police the system'.

It was also said that a good or outstanding Ofsted report could also run at cross purposes to the work of the local authority advisers whose attempts to identify, advise and resource special needs provision could be undermined by the public availability and perceived 'authority' of an Ofsted report. The Lamb Report also highlighted conflicting evidence from Ofsted and other more informed sources.

Among their recommendations was that all inspectors receive training in SEN and disability and that all SIPS (School Improvement Partners) working in mainstream schools also should receive similar training.

'Not all schools monitor the progress and attainment of pupils with SEN', concluded the inquiry (para 36), an issue that may or may not be addressed by the introduction of a balanced scorecard, but it does point unambiguously to a failure in the school's own approach to self evaluation.

You still have to have one

All schools at the time of writing have School Improvement Partners, or as they are commonly known, SIPS. These local authority appointees, described as 'critical friends', visit a school three times a year for one-to-one conversations with the head. They come with a pre-determined agenda, focusing on performance data, looking for anomalies, underperforming subjects against national norms, breakdown by groups of pupils, gender and ethnic differences. Critical friends? A misnomer, writes Sue Swaffield (2009) on the basis her research.

You get one whether you like it or not, said William Atkinson, insisting that this is no reflection on the personal and professional qualities of his own SIP, rather a matter of principle.

> They [DCSF] still have this notion of one size fits all and one of the things I've spoken to them about is SIPS. What they do with these people is they throw them at everybody on the system, whether or not there's a need for this 'additional capacity'. Where schools have been judged to be outstanding and management capacity is outstanding, capacity for development is outstanding and value for money is outstanding, they are nevertheless subjected to the same degree of intervention by the SIPS as a school that is in special measures or deemed to be satisfactory. You have no choice in the matter. You still have to have one. Why don't we just think about where that resource would be best spent?
>
> Even though the indicators all point in the right direction, and it's stuff that in a good or outstanding school you are doing all the time they still have to go through the process and write a report and respond to the LA and the LA in turn

have to account to central government so you've got this massive amount of activity which is not value for money and is deflecting people's time and energy from raising standards.

The fall and rise of self evaluation

Is the scorecard a form of school self evaluation, an accountability mechanism or an attempt to ride both horses? Scepticism as to the purpose and place of the scorecard is in part a reaction against a further, and 'superfluous', addition to a self evaluation and inspection system still in the process of bedding down. While now widely used in many countries of the world, and has continued for more than a decade to be at the heart of SICI policy (The Standing International Conferences of Inspectorates) in Europe, its beginnings in England were inauspicious.

In the mid-1990s the notion that schools could evaluate themselves was roundly derided in successive talks, conferences and conversations, not only by then HMCI Woodhead but also by Conservative ministers. Memorably at a Conservative Party Fringe meeting in 1996, Eric Forth Junior Minister apologised to his audience for not giving his prepared speech and launched a fierce polemic against self-evaluation, arguing that 'rotten schools and rotten teachers' need the tough hand of an inspectorate to sort them out. Only weeks before, at the Labour Party Conference, Estelle Morris had promised that self evaluation would be at the heart of Labour educational policy, and a year into a Labour government. In 1998, Chief HM Woodhead was obliged to preface the publication of *School Evaluation Matters* with a commitment to self evaluation. The *Handbook for Inspecting* in the following year contained the words 'Ofsted is committed to promoting self-evaluation as a key aspect of the work of schools' and suggested:

> It is advantageous to base school self-evaluation on the same criteria as those used in all schools by inspectors. A common language has developed about the work of schools, expressed through the criteria. Teachers and governors know that the criteria reflect things that matter.
>
> (Ofsted, 1999: 138)

Whether the criteria used by Ofsted reflect 'things that matter' to teachers, pupils and parents is more open to debate. The NUT approach, published in 1995 as *Schools Speak for Themselves*, began with the voices of those key stakeholders and built its criteria from the bottom up, defining core themes valued by all parties. Schools could then measure themselves by what they valued, a challenging remit to go beyond the easily measurable and to keep in touch with what became known as the 'acoustic' of the school. Constantly alive to its values and the quality of school classroom life, self evaluation strived to find the bandwidth through which differing voices carry, the secret harmonies as well as discordant notes.

'I do think in any ideal world all schools would be self-reflecting, would be good at reflection, would be continuing improving', said Alasdair Macdonald, reminding us that self evaluation and improvement are integrally related, not an event, not simply a prelude to an inspection visit, but a way of seeing, a way of thinking and a way of being.

Now virtually used in every school, the SEF (The School Self Evaluation Form) is illustrative of the way governments capture a good idea and reduce it to a simple formula. During his tenure of office HMCI David Bell tried to remind heads that the SEF was not of itself self evaluation and neither was it mandatory. Having been the first director of education to embrace *Schools Speak for Themselves* in his own authority, Newcastle, he stressed that he would welcome approaches to self evaluation created and owned by schools themselves, rather than simply slavishly following a template.

This was a recurring theme in evidence to the Cambridge Primary Review.

> The review's national soundings of practitioners revealed support for more emphasis on self evaluation as part of the inspection process – provided this met the school's own needs for evaluation to inform its improvement agenda and not simply Ofsted's requirement. The present system of self evaluation prior to inspection was seen as an imposition, limiting evaluation to those aspects deemed important to Ofsted, but not necessarily to the school.
>
> (2009: 338)

There are some clear guidelines from the latest of Government Select Committee Reports. The most recent, in January 2010, contained some uncompromising health warnings and some good advice:

> We are persuaded that self-evaluation—as an iterative, reflexive and continuous process, embedded in the culture of a school—is a highly effective means for a school to consolidate success and secure improvement across the full range of its activities. It is applicable, not just to its academic performance, but across the full range of a school's influence over the well being of the children who learn there and the community outside.
>
> (para 53)

This advice was followed by the recommendation that:

> Ofsted should do more to encourage schools to be creative and produce evidence of the self-evaluation process which works for them and speaks to the true culture and ethos of their own school. Ofsted should ensure that its own inspection processes are flexible enough to accommodate and give appropriate weight to alternative forms of evidence of self-evaluation.
>
> (para 59)

Endorsing the tenor of the *21st Century Schools* White Paper, the Committee agreed that schools should be empowered to take charge of their own improvement processes but that this would inevitably require releasing schools from the pressures of inspection, targets and a range of improvement programmes which stifle, rather than support, autonomy and creativity. 'We have consistently noted the adverse effects that targets have had on the education of children and young people', it concluded, but argued that this is unlikely to happen if teachers themselves are not accorded the professional respect they deserve.

> The government should place more faith in the professionalism of teachers and should support them with a simplified accountability and improvement system which challenges and encourages good practice rather than stigmatising and undermining those who are struggling

(para 266)

Quo Vadis

The Ofsted strapline 'Improvement through inspection' is one that has been treated with some caution by researchers, teachers and by HMCI themselves. No incoming government will abandon inspection but it could rethink its costs (human and financial) and benefits (human and financial). William Atkinson offered a scenario which would both build professional capacity while at the same time assuring quality and vouchsafing improvement.

> Inspection is very different from school improvement and I believe what we need to have in schools are teachers trained to do their own internal auditing or evaluation and I also think that those people should also have that remit in neighbouring schools so that they will also look at the processes and practices and evaluate the effectiveness of practice. And it should be that in each local authority there are people trained up to do that. So it would be people who are in the business, currently who are doing it internally and externally. That would have tremendous staff development opportunities and would add significantly to the credibility of the process.

This would give a new role to a slimmed down professional HMI, 'very smart people' in their new would, as William Atkinson described them, able to oversee the process with that most desirable of rhetorical epithets – 'rigour'.

There are interesting precedents elsewhere in the world[1] which provide a compelling case for a very different form of inspection and self evaluation. It remains to be seen whether a new government will have the vision and take the risk to give back ownership of quality assurance to the profession and to a new generation of HMI.

8   Going global

I think, now, it's not fashionable for ministers to say that things are good because it sounds complacent, but I think we are in good shape. When I look at some of the international comparisons and when I talk to ministers from other countries about how they're doing and about how we're doing and when I look at Ofsted's rating of the profession, I think we are in good shape, but we could do better and always do better and we're not yet great.

(Jim Knight, Education Minister of State for Schools 2006–9)

As a country, and in comparison with other nations, we are, on this evidence, 'in good shape'.

A restrospective review of achievements under the Labour government left succeeding governments with much to build on, according to Knight.

What we can be really, really proud of is if we take how a disadvantaged kid is doing. We can be really proud of the fact that, if you look at areas of disadvantage, council-by-council, we have narrowed the gap hugely between the richest and the poorest. If you do the same by school, we've made a huge step forward and we've done that whilst significantly improving standards overall. To pull that trick off is something we'll never get any credit for, but is a fantastic achievement.

Improved standards? A narrowing gap? A 'fantastic achievement'? What evidence may be adduced from the testimony of our witnesses in Britain and in other countries to support these claims? How, on somewhat firmer sources of evidence, does the UK compare internationally?

All political parties draw on international comparisons to affirm or to challenge our right, as a nation, to celebrate. As Michael Gove said, prior to the 2010 general election:

I think the most important frame of reference is an international comparison . . . The critical question for me is, are we giving our young people the same degree of opportunity (as those in) other countries?

> Of all the things that I think have happened in the course of the last five or ten years is that we've developed a better understanding of what works in other countries and, therefore, there is an increased appetite for trying out some of the lessons from other countries.

The aforementioned quotes from Labour in office and Conservatives in opposition draw heavily on international examples but come to diametrically opposite conclusions. Both, however illustrate that, as OECD's Andreas Schleicher says, whereas 'ten years ago, we lived in a very different world in which education systems tended to be inward looking, where schools and education systems typically considered themselves to be unique . . . [now there is] . . . the willingness of governments to engage in international debate'.

In short, the debate about standards has gone global, with both government and opposition parties seeking to strengthen their arguments with international examples.

This chapter explores the implications of this heightened international awareness and considers its impact for children, teachers and the policy-making process itself. The bias towards comparisons with OECD countries reflects the nature of the benchmarks used by government to assess itself. It is also evident in the sources we have drawn on in this book. Their identification of the issues which impact on opportunities and constraints in reinventing schools will inevitably be open to alternative explanations.

Up until recently the Westminster government has ignored the potential for learning from education systems outside the industrialised countries. So have the opposition parties. The relationship with less industrialised countries and with Commonwealth countries in particular is of a different order. The work of such organisations as the British Council, Voluntary Service Overseas and the QCDA have done much to encourage the exchange of ideas, curriculum practice and teacher placement. But it has been largely left to the world teachers' organisation, Education International, through its Commonwealth Teachers Group, the Commonwealth Institute and its joint work with HEIs such as Cambridge University and the Commonwealth Secretariat to try and draw the Westminster government's attention to existing educational developments in countries outside the OECD loop. This divide between OECD and non-OECD is nowhere more obvious than in the almost total lack of joint working between the Department for International Development and the Education Department.

Even more extraordinary is the fact that the Westminster government has steadfastly chosen to ignore most educational developments in the educational jurisdictions of the UK. No formal body exists on a UK basis to share lessons and national debate on UK-wide educational developments.

Improved standards?

The primary reference source on standards internationally are successive PISA (Programme for International Student Assessment) reports from the OECD which compare the UK with other OECD countries. As Jim Knight said, Britain performs above average on key performance measures such as literacy, mathematics and science. Indeed in the 2006 PISA Report the UK was eighth out of 31 nations on the science scale, thirteenth on reading, and eighteenth on mathematics, although on a variance measure (that is, degree of variance within schools) and on the relationship between socio-economic status and school attainment the data are less positive. On most indices the UK is outperformed by Finland, Australia, Canada, New Zealand, Hong Kong, South Korea, Ireland, Poland, Lichtenstein and Sweden. There are many different ways of reading the data and many people have expressed considerable caution about making over-ambitious claims for the apparent success of one system against the relative failure of another. The Finnish PISA Report itself[1] is cautious in attribution of success. Barry Sheerman (Chair of the Commons Children, Schools and Families Select Committee until 2010) added his own health warning:

> All the time we look to international comparisons, but I always make the point that I'm always more impressed by countries more like us – big, urban, high migrant levels – none of which Finland is. All the Nordics are slightly strange because they're small countries, they have a very different tradition. They are people who will pay 50 per cent income tax and 25 per cent VAT – it's not true in France, Italy, Spain, the US, Germany. Now I sometimes just want to compare ourselves to places and countries like us. I'm very happy to learn the lessons, it's all over, the stuff we're doing on children, if you look at the Danish system for children there's so much to learn from, so I pick it up. But you've always got to realise it is a different culture that you're translating it into.

Andreas Schleicher made precisely this point.

> The biggest concern I have often is where people just say, well, PISA's scores are low so the quality of the education system is low. . . . You take the most extreme case of the Russian Federation on TIMMS (The International Mathematics and Science Study) for example. . . . They do really well. In PISA they perform below-average, because students have difficulties with extrapolating from what they have learned and apply it in a novel context which is what PISA is about. So the results tell you something about the criterion that an evaluation system can apply.

It's culture, stupid

Is it the structures of system or is it a set of deeply embedded beliefs and cultural values that account for the relative positioning of countries in the OECD tables? There is substantial agreement that cultural factors explain much of the difference in attitudes to children, to their achievement and to the essential purposes of education. For example, Nordic countries believe that exerting pressure on children at too early an age is likely to be dysfunctional, while in Britain the impatience to compete and deliver results has a long, and sometimes dishonourable, history.

> Our impatient government wants to start early and then confront children with early failure, from which it's very hard to go back.

Peter Mortimore made this comment in light of a lifetime's work in English schools and, in recent years, his research in Nordic countries. In those countries, he claims, children are less subject to impatient governments who want demonstrable results within their short tenure of office. School retention and lifelong learning in Denmark is, he suggests, related to children's self belief, either nurtured or destroyed from an early age.

> Danish schools – through avoiding widespread pupil failure – capture the interest of children and keep them in the education system. Schools send a high proportion of their students to university and the country ends up with a highly educated working population. If you look at the international adult literacy scores, Denmark performs very well.

In the UK politicians apparently believe that the earlier the pressure on children to perform, the greater the likelihood of immediate returns, he argues. However, international evidence supports the Rousseau paradox– 'lose time to save it'. Countries in which children start school later tend to do better on a number of indictors. In Finland, for example, the nine year comprehensive school takes children from seven to sixteen with a more informal pre-primary stage for children aged 6–7. Similarly in Sweden children start formal school on their seventh birthday. Much depends on what a country, or its political leaders, regard as pre-eminent in the lives of its citizens and its next generation, and a cultural legacy on which those judgments rest.

The hunt for the unicorn

Since the 1996 Panorama programme in which David Reynolds sat at the back of a Taiwanese classroom and attributed the success of that country's education system to its embrace of interactive whole class teaching, policy cherry picking has been relentless. Indeed both Labour and the Conservatives have been drawn to citing and replicating Sweden's independent or 'free', schools to support their policies for choice and diversity in school provision.

In their book *The Seven Cultures of Capitalism* Hampden-Turner and Trompenaars discuss 'the hunt for the unicorn', an elusive quest for a solution that is always, it seems, just beyond our grasp. 'The magic bullet', 'the boutique solution', said William Atkinson, are a ready made recipe for failure.

> Because they're after the magic bullet you can always find something in the States or elsewhere, that is working and so let's bring it across. But they don't look at the context, they don't look at the time scale and many of those initiatives have not been properly evaluated or many of these initiatives will work well as a boutique solution but when you then scale them up then there are problems. They just haven't worked out the necessary scaffolding or what it needs to make it work.

He cited the enthusiasm for the balanced scorecard as a case in point, an import from the United States but without the accompanying information to help schools and parents make a reasoned judgement as to its scope and fairness.

> They import this but never telling us about the unintended consequences. They only report on the good things. Where hasn't it worked? What is the collateral damage as part of this process? At the end of the day, as with any medicine, you have to weigh up whether the adverse side effects outweigh the treatment. What else are they not telling us?

What they are often not telling us is the cultural and historical context of 'good practice'. A TES leading article discussing Reynolds' findings from a study of class-rooms in Taiwan (7th June, 1996) highlighted this point. 'Children have a longer school day, more homework, many also attend crammers. There is more parental pressure to achieve. The society as a whole is more obedient and conformist'. Similar caveats have been made in respect of Finland, a much more socially homogenous country than the UK or many of the other countries with which it is compared.

There is a seductive temptation to reference other countries' education systems as models for England, so falling into the trap of seeing simple solutions to complex problems. It is easy to be misled by what we see and don't see and to be blind-sided by the policy rhetoric. While coherence between rhetoric and school practice seems often conspicuously absent in the UK we are by no means alone. The discrepancy between espoused values and policy implementation is exemplified in the quote from Mick Waters in chapter 5 in which he described attending ministerial meetings in places, from America to Australia, to China to India, to Egypt to Scandinavia, in which ministerial rhetoric on the changing world, new technologies, global sustain-ability, divides between rich and poor, economic challenges, movement of people, and the need for young people to be adaptable, flexible, ready to cope with change, would give way to a contrary discourse:

> Then, within an hour, all of them are marching to another drum which is about how we hold on to tradition and how we don't let things that we have tradi-tionally tested drift away because they're fearful of their electorate thinking that they've lost what they thought the electorate matters.

Such ambivalence is unlikely to be found in Finland where the major political parties take a consensual approach to the values which, it is agreed, should inform Finland's education system. Irmeli Halinen, the head of Finland's Pre-school and Basic Education Department in 2008, described these values as 'cornerstones'. They focus on comprehensive education, 'no streaming, no dead-ends'; Autonomy, 'empower-ment of municipalities and schools' and 'a spirit of trust and support'; Flexibility, 'local solutions and common basis, flexible and supportive curriculum; Support, 'minimis-ing low attainment and helping every one succeed'; and Teachers, 'high status and quality of teachers'.

According to Andreas Schleicher, Finland is not alone in having a strong values-based educational system which all major parties share.

> The Nordic countries in Europe . . . have very strong systems . . . they have clearly defined values . . . they have coherence in what they do and what they say and they have this link between their intentions and what is done and what is achieved.

What they don't have, he says, are 'layers and layers of unfinished and incoherent reforms all on top of each other'.

One of the indicators used by The World Values Survey is social trust – measured by questions such 'Do you think most people can be trusted?' From the 1950s to the 1990s this showed a decreasing percentage of people across all countries agreeing to that proposition, from 60 per cent in 1950 to 29 per cent in 1990. In Finland the percentage was 59, in Sweden 68 and in Norway 74 (the UK did not take part in the survey).

Social trust is a vital part of any country's education system as it is for its society as a whole. It is also worth asking whether social trust is hermetic or inclusive. Barry Sheerman's caustic comment about his visit to a Finnish prison stands as corrective to the temptation to see any society as a holy grail.

> I was in Finland looking at prison education and skills and the lovely governor, female governor, walking through the main prison and I said 'no brown or black faces here, do you not have any?' and she said 'oh no, we're a very xenophobic country, they would be torn to pieces, we have to have a special one for them'.

Measures of a nation's worth

Debates about values and education are meaningless unless they inform the work of education systems in changing children's lives for the better. The preface to the 2007 OECD Report on *Child Well Being in Rich Countries* opened its findings with this statement:

> The true measure of a nation's standing is how well it attends to its children – their health and safety, their material security, their education and socialisation, and their sense of being loved, valued, and included in the families and societies into which are born.
>
> (An Overview of *Child Well Being in Rich Countries*, 2007: p. 3)

It is in this respect that many of the Nordic countries appear to most closely meet the criteria. While none of the other Nordic countries perform as well as the much celebrated Finns on OECD comparative student attainment tables cited above,[2] they do rank very highly on measures of child well being. For example, on *material well being* (a measure of relative income poverty, children in households where parents have jobs and with educational resources) the four Nordic Countries top the table, with the UK eighteenth out of 21 countries.

Relative child poverty (children in households where family income is less than 50 per cent of the national median) is regarded as key indicator by OECD and the European Union's Social Inclusion Programme, a measure on which the UK falls to second last ahead only of the US. On health and safety (infant mortality, death from accidents and injury) Nordic countries also perform well while the UK is in fifteenth place.

On the *educational well being* indicator the UK is in seventeenth place. This is a composite indicator which includes attainment in literacy (in reading, in mathematics and in science) but also includes remaining in school beyond 15, the percentage not in employment, education or training, and 15-year-olds expecting to find low-skilled jobs. This is a close ally to the composite indicator – young people's peer and family relationships, a measure on which the UK occupies bottom place. This index is based on parents spending time talking to the child, having a main meal with parents more than once a week, and the percentage of children in lone parent or step families, together with children who find their peers 'kind and helpful'.

The UK also occupies bottom place on the fifth and sixth indicators – *behaviour and risks* (health, diet, obesity, smoking, drunkenness, drug taking, under age sex, use of condoms, fighting and bullying) and *subjective well being* (liking school a lot, self rating on a life satisfaction scale, on health and on personal well being).

These data come from UNICEF's *Report Card 7* which provides a comprehensive assessment of the lives and well being of children and young people in 21 nations of the industrialised world. Its purpose is to stimulate discussion and development of policies to improve children's lives, informed by the United Nations *Convention on the Rights of the Child*. Described as 'the handrail of policy' the report argues that comparisons demonstrate that given levels of child well being are not inevitable but policy-susceptible.

Overall on the six indicators of child well being the UK is placed twentieth out of 21 rich nations ahead only of the US. Taken together these point to a quality of life which is explained by the complex relationship of children' lives in and out of school. While, as famously claimed by Basil Bernstein, 'schools cannot compensate for society', there is little, if any, dissent from a belief that schools should be able to enhance children's sense of self efficacy.

One example of the power of schools to enhance children's self-efficacy is in the area of anxiety about the environment. PISA 2006 found that:

> Students' optimism regarding environmental issues is negatively related to the environmental science performance index ... the lower students perform in environmental science, the more optimistic they are that the situation will improve over the next two decades ...
>
> (Green at Fifteen? How fifteen year olds perform in environmental and geoscience in PISA 2006) (OECD 2008)

In other words, the more children are aware of the environmental crisis, the more pessimistic they become. The solution is the optimistic school, as the Cambridge Primary Review makes clear. Drawing on its research 'Community Soundings' (Cambridge Primary Review, 2007) the review found that young children 'displayed some of their parents' pessimism concerning the future, expressing worries about global issues, including climate change, pollution, world poverty and terrorism'. However, some schools in the research had 'involved children in environmental action and energy-saving projects that had given them a strong sense that they can do something about it' (p. 56).

It is schools, in seeking to, 'unfailingly . . . celebrate the positive' (Alexander, 2010), which are key to equipping young people with the optimism to tackle the global problems humanity faces.

A narrowing gap?

Yet the gap between richest and poorest, most and least privileged, highest and lowest achievers, remains as stubbornly wide as ever in many countries including Britain.

'You've had a Labour government since 1997 and despite the enormous ambitious initiatives there is more socio-economic segregation now than when Tony Blair took office', commented Karen Seashore, (Rodney Wallace, professor at the University of Minnesota), comparing Britain and the United States.

> Elite ownership in positions of privilege are more deeply embedded in England than in the US but in both countries, when you look at results and disaggregate them by race and class and look at them over time, both countries are struggling with insufficient commitment to eradicating social and economic discrimination. And we do so under a rhetoric of providing equal opportunities, a rhetoric of meritocratic language used to cover over very deep problems in an unequal society.

Yet, she argued, there are some relatively inexpensive solutions which are too threatening to the status quo, vested interests and the timidity of politicians. One is the school year and the other is school starting time. Spreading school attendance more equitably across the year would, she claims, close the achievement gap by up to 10 per cent, due to the now well established summer loss which hits disadvantaged children hardest. Starting school at 10 o'clock would also benefit many children whose brains are still dormant first thing in the morning.

The 'steepening incline of disadvantage' described by PISA is susceptible to policy intervention, said Karen Seashore, not by what is added but by the obstacles that are removed. The 'steepening incline' is created and sustained, suggest a number of our witnesses, by the inexorable pressure of targets, league tables and comparative attainment data. In England, said Peter Mortimore, children are subject to as many as a hundred formal tests or examinations in their school career, not all of them high stakes as far as the school is concerned but from the child's perspective any one, or an accumulation of all, may send powerful messages about identity and self worth.

> High-stakes testing is inevitably focused on failure. Our system used to be dominated by selection (and in some parts of the country still is). The eleven plus was

about the system managing failure - as most people failed. Many who did subsequently dropped out of education. Not all; some who failed went on to succeed. They did well and are to be commended but, it must be realised, they are the exceptions. Most young people who fail at school accept the verdict that they are no good at learning. This enforced failure is strong in the English system. In the Nordic countries there is a much more democratic view of education which tries to minimalise failure. There, the education systems encourage the maximum number of students to continue into further and higher education. These countries end up with literate populations and 'can-do' societies.

As classic studies (for example, Marsden and Jackson, 1962; Hargreaves, 1967; Willis; 1977), carried out in the 1960s to the 1980s, showed, perceptions of social class and ability were so intertwined that to negotiate the system required an extra layer of skills, self confidence and advocacy. Mary James' description of her interview for grammar school is testimony to just how deeply rooted the class system was in its effects on education.

> There were these men in these black gowns who interviewed me and I do remember them saying 'I don't think you will find it very comfortable here'. I knew then, at the age of 11, that this was a social judgment. I did have a sort of country accent and they knew my background I guess.

The continuation of grammar schools into the second decade of the second millennium is owed to its rigorous defence by politicians and by the reticence of a Labour government which would not risk alienating its middle class electorate. The hurried removal of David Willetts, shadow secretary for state for education and skills, following his declaration that the Conservative Party would not be introducing more grammar schools, was confirmation of Conor Ryan's view that no government could afford to distance themselves too far from the assumptions of middle-class grammar school educated parents. While David Cameron backed Willetts' speech and accused his critics of 'splashing around in the shallow end of the educational debate' and of 'clinging on to outdated mantras that bear no relation to the reality of life', the *Daily Mail* and the *Daily Telegraph* spoke more compellingly to the prejudices of the middle class heartland and Willetts had to be quietly, and quickly, shuffled aside.

The nostalgic attachment in England to the grammar school explains the negative connotations of the 'comprehensive' school. Peter Mortimore blamed politicians and the media which they thrive on for allowing the myth to be propagated.

> They allowed the myth to be propagated that comprehensives have failed. 'Comprehensive' has become a dirty word, whereas anyone who examines the figures, notes the raised aspirations, or observes the culture of schools, will see that the transition to a largely comprehensive system has been a great success. Much of the blame for the denigration lies with London journalists who, having personally opted out of the state system and invested a lot of money in private education for their children, perhaps do not wish to acknowledge the success of the local comprehensive school. It is very sad.

As Peter Mortimore described it, the 'pecking order' of schools allows a form of 'intelligent choice' by parents and by doing so maintains and locks in the gap between the highest and lowest achievers.

> I think that over the last twenty or thirty years in most local areas parents have recognised the pecking order of schools and, very intelligently, have chosen accordingly, playing with the counters: religious or non-religious; selective or non-selective; specialist or generalist schools; city technology colleges with new buildings or 'bog standard' comprehensive. Naturally, they hedge their bets in order to obtain the best they can. I don't blame them. Given the system, that's what they are forced to do. But it makes for a ramshackle system.

In this respect there are close parallels with the US with parental choice and their very own confusing 'pecking order' of schools. 'We say we have a comprehensive system in the United States but we don't and you don't have one in England', said Karen Seashore, pointing to the proliferation of specialist schools in her country.

> In the last fifteen to twenty years a proliferation of different types of schools serving special populations have emerged in the States. Based on my experience parents become quite confused and in their confusion their choice between schools, as in England, has reinforced socio-economic segregation. This then actually diminishes opportunities for lower class students and reifies the belief that some schools are good schools and some schools are bad schools – even when they're not.

It was widely agreed that the voucher system, promoted in the US as the solution to the 'pecking order' of schools, although floated at one point in the early years of the Blair's government's task force on standards, would prove to be a disaster in the UK. It would, argue heads such as William Atkinson, head of Phoenix School in Hammersmith and Fulham, simply reinforce and extend the invidious workings of the market.

While Phoenix school rose from the ashes of the chaotic Hammersmith School, it was soon apparent that not only does a stigma live on for a generations but that the mantra of 'turning a school around' requires a decade of sustained work, a sustained campaign of parental and community education and a sea change in policy mindset. Pointing to the dangers of going down the market economy route, parental choice and voucher systems, Atkinson compares his school to its near neighbour – the Oratory School where Tony Blair sent his son Euan.

> I've got a voucher that says £5,000, I'm going to go to London Oratory to spend it. Now I come from a really good background, I've not got special education needs, London Oratory might take my voucher but there are a thousand kids with their voucher who want to spend it at London Oratory this year. Are schools suddenly overnight going to grow that capacity to accommodate those children? That's not going to happen, so that is a blatant lie, a misrepresentation. And if I turn up to London Oratory with my voucher, I'm a pain in the neck, very low

prior attainment, my parents are indifferent towards education; the likelihood of actually getting me to come to school is going to be very challenging, so why does London Oratory want to take me to add to their problems?

In Nordic countries, in Japan, Hong Kong and Canada, there is no such terminology because schools – 'Folk' schools and high schools – are for everyone. Nor is the 'comprehensive school' a term used in Scotland where, since 1970, 97 per cent of all children attend a 'high school' or 'secondary school'. The explanation for their success appears to be, said Andreas Schleicher, a combination of a lack of stratification, support for children and the quality of a profession which they are able to attract.

> Whether you look at Japan, Canada, Finland, they all have ways to recruit teachers from the top end of the grade distribution. They develop very strong child support systems; they are very strong systems of lateral support. They tend to be systems that are not highly stratified.

It is 'the bog standard' school which, after all, appears to be the recipe for success.

The problem with teachers

The problem with teachers is that they won't do what they're told. That at least is a policy maker's view. It was not, however, Philippa Cordingley's view nor that of many academics. From their standpoint the problem is that teachers *do* do what they're told and therein lies the problem. Peter Mortimore, speaking in an English context, finds a loss of self confidence within the profession and a fear of risk taking.

> I don't meet so many teachers in the UK these days but I fear that some of them really don't trust their own judgments. It has to be validated by Ofsted for them to really believe and that I think is desperately worrying. And the contrast with the Finns is absolutely huge, where the Finns rely on their own judgment and have the confidence to act on it. Again it induces compliance. Heads I've spoken to over the years have said I'd love to do so and so but it's too risky. Ofsted are coming in and it's just too risky, so they play safe.

The parallel with the US is striking. As David Berliner, Regents' Professor at Arizona State University, described it:

> They [teachers] think those accountability systems and those government mandates are what teaching, as a profession, is like. And they're being socialised to a profession I don't like. And they scare me more than anything else because I think we're going to get a group of teachers that are more scripted, more passive, seeing themselves more like factory workers than as professionals.

In contrast to Berliner's gloomy analysis, OECD's TALIS study (in which the US did not take part) showed that teachers in Norway, Iceland, Italy, Bulgaria and Australia were most likely to take risks and had the highest levels of self-efficacy, while among the lowest on these measures are Korea and Estonia. Unfortunately for statisticians and policy makers the correlations with pupil performance are, in Michael Davidson's words, 'all over the place'. Italy is a low performing country on PISA pupil attainment while Korea and Estonia perform well.

Whether this is a measure of complacency is an open question but a follow-up TALIS question is revealing. In response to the question 'In this school, the sustained poor performance of a teacher would be tolerated by the rest of the staff' in Ireland and Norway the figure was 60 per cent and in Malaysia 53 per cent. 'Not a very happy finding', said Michael Davidson.

It is difficult to know what to make of such data or where they lead and to what extent they are embedded in widely differing historical and cultural contexts. These data rely on teacher self reports, not only problematic within a national context but the reliability of such data in a comparative context is compounded with each new country which is added to the mix. What does appear to hold up well across all countries is fairly consistent evidence that espoused beliefs (or at least reported espoused beliefs) and actual practice do not match. As Michael Davidson said:

> It's fascinating in TALIS that we find that all teachers in all countries, on average, believe that the right way to teach is in a certain way with the teacher as a facilitator, the student as this active participant in the lesson; that's how, on average, all teachers believe teaching should be but when it comes to practices, we find that's not what they do; and we don't really know what the reason for that is.

Why teachers don't teach the way they believe they should may be explained by differing and inter-connecting factors which are policy and culturally related as well as embedded in the day-to-day pragmatic of schools and classrooms. Much has been written about the conventions and protocols of schools – the nature of classrooms, the physical orientation of the desks, movement from one class, one subject, one teacher to the next, a constant struggle against time and timetable and, as Mary Bousted described it, against the inexorable rise of data driven reform.

> Not only do teachers have to comply in a highly repressive system where we use data for all the wrong reasons – we're the most data-rich education system in the world – we make the least effective use of it, I think, judged on hard measures as defined by National Curriculum levels and by tests.

The latitude to divert from a prescribed curriculum, held in place by assessment pressures and, in many countries prescribed methodologies, conspire to frustrate teachers' initiative and creativity. Paradoxically, as Philippa Cordingley has argued, these measures tend to be welcomed because they attenuate both workload and risk.

Incentives, damning findings, shocking statistics

TALIS data have been welcomed in a number of different quarters and for a number of different reasons. As Michael Davidson related it, the Italian government has 'pounced on it' because of the endorsement by an external authority and the independence of the evidence. It is, as he says, 'a good opportunity for the minister to push public policies'. He also claimed there has been a positive response from teachers who, he says, welcome feedback and its more formalised form of appraisal, regarding these as helpful for them, or as potentially helpful for their professional development. Over fifty per cent of teachers in Italy have never had feedback and, given that teachers in Italy stay in these schools for a long time, 'that's a pretty damning kind of finding', he said. It is, unfortunately, not a singular case.

> The other shocking statistic that comes out of TALIS is, on average, across the 23 countries, is that 75 per cent of teachers say that they won't be rewarded in any way for improving the quality of their work. The same percentage holds for being more innovative in their teaching and that isn't just monetary reward, that's any kind of reward. That, for me, is a shocking statistic and, in some of the countries it's over 90 per cent. I don't think that in any country it's less than 50 per cent, so if you believe what teachers are telling us in TALIS, there's something missing in their working conditions that encourages them to raise their own standards or reach the standards that others may be setting for their education system.

This finding seems to have had an effect, at least in some countries. Speaking in Kuala Lumpur in January 2010, the education minister promised that Malaysia would be moving fast in introducing performance management and differential pay awards for effective teachers. Yet there is little evidence to support such a policy. She reflected the interest of some OECD members, and to a growing extent OECD itself, in promoting individual performance related pay for teachers. TALIS found that three quarters of 'the most effective teachers do not receive the most recognition' and that the 'school principal does not take steps to alter the monetary rewards of a persistently underperforming teacher' (OECD, 2009a: p. 18), a finding which Michael Davidson was deeply concerned about. In responding to this 'shocking statistic', TALIS then takes a leap of faith in concluding that:

> There are substantial opportunities for strengthening – in most cases creating – links between teacher appraisal and feedback and the rewards and recognition teachers receive.

The OECD's agreement with the Mexican government, *Improving School Education in Mexican Schools* (OECD, 2008) has provided it with just such an opportunity to explore those links. OECD's commissioned study triggered by the agreement, *Evaluating and Rewarding the Quality of Teachers' International Practices* (OECD, 2009), draws on TALIS data and seeks to make the case for introducing financial incentives. However, try as it might, it fails to provide the evidence for its case. Indeed Graham Holley's own reservations about any link between standards and performance related pay in a UK context seem to be mirrored internationally.

The gap between aspiration and lack of evidence is highlighted in the study (OECD, 2009). While it finds there is 'an upswing in interest in creating teacher incentives to attract talent into teaching [and] reward high-performing teachers' (p. 137) and argues for 'a well-designed evaluation and reward plan' (p. 239), the study admits it cannot identify comprehensive evidence to accompany these proposals. Indeed it says that:

> Despite the interest in using incentives to influence teachers, relatively little is known about the right types of incentives to influence performance or distribution (p. 137) . . . and . . . . at the very least, we know that performance measures, particularly those that focus on individual teachers, are likely to be noisy and will necessarily only reflect the material covered by test assessments.
>
> (p. 140)

Michael Davidson himself recognised the difficulties in exploiting the opportunities TALIS describes as being available to governments.

> Even if there is such evidence of individual pay in a few cases which shows that this can be the result of improvement, the difficulties in getting a performance measure that can be truly attributed to the teacher and not be divisive within the teacher group within a school; to get these two things in place is such a tall order that it makes sense to stand back from that.

Unlike the countries such as the United States, Chile, Mexico and England and Wales where performance related pay has been introduced, other countries have taken a different route. In Hong Kong, for example, building professional capacity rests on a more distributed and collegial practice. On the day of his retirement in 2009 from his role as deputy secretary for education and manpower in Hong Kong's Education Bureau, Chris Wardlaw singled out as a key reason for that country's success the commitment to sharing and networking of practice within and across schools.

> If I was going to pick out one thing, I think the collaboration amongst teachers in a whole series of ways is the most significant change. Probably since 2000 we've been emphasising professional collaboration and I think it's in terms of teachers going into each others' classes, supporting each other and lesson planning outside the class, looking at the feedback from assessment data, I think these are the things that have been quite significant if we're going to look now and then look back at what's different.

Collaborative lesson planning, peer observation and (borrowing from Japan) lesson study, have all shared the common aim of enhancing pedagogy through professional dialogue and through a discourse which extends beyond Hong Kong's geographical boundaries. Chris Wardlaw added:

> It's been a wonderfully outward looking system and I think it's tried to draw in best practice from other places, but I have to say in my own country in Australia, particularly in secondary schools, it's not natural to have teachers working with

each other like it is here, possibly at primary school level in Australia and the UK and other places there's been a lot more of that tradition but I do believe that Hong Kong teachers have taken up this in a much more proactive way.

Leadership: flying below the radar

Leadership is a concept that travels across national borders, but only in recent years has it had such a common international currency. A decade or so ago some languages didn't have a word for leadership thus without the resonances that the term carries in English. In German the word 'Fuhrer' was too potent a reminder that strong or charismatic leadership could lead to a nasty place. In Swiss primary schools there was no headteacher as classroom teachers shared management tasks and didn't see the need to be led by an authority figure. In the UK leadership was (and tends still to be) synonymous with the headteacher. The 'headmaster' has enjoyed almost mythical status in England, the stuff of comics, books and films with a long history of celebrated heads such as Arnold of Rugby, Sanderson of Oundle, Neill of Summerhill. And currently, Anthony Seldon, Master of Wellington College.

The heroic head in modern guise is the saviour of failing schools, many of those heads recipients of Queen's Honours. A similar high profile is given to principals in North America, Australia and New Zealand, countries which up until recently have accounted for something like 90 per cent of all publications on educational leadership. A review of academic publications by Phil Hallinger of the newly established Asia Pacific Centre for Leadership and Change at Hong Kong Institute of Education, finds that progressively journals are now carrying articles from other countries as leadership becomes a high profile topic for policy, research and professional development.

In the world of twenty-first century schooling, writes Hess (2003: 1), school leaders must be able to 'leverage accountability and revolutionary technology, devise performance-based evaluation systems, re-engineer outdated management structures, recruit and cultivate non-traditional staff, drive decisions with data, build professional cultures, and ensure that every child is served'. The underlying assumption is that school improvement can be accomplished by superheads. Fiona Millar questioned whether this is feasible in the current restless policy context.

> I think it's almost too much for one person to be the leadership person across such a vast range of policy initiatives which are being rolled-out all at the same time.

Leadership, a politician's obsession, said Philippa Cordingley, pointing to the establishment of a National College, is symbolic of the belief that importing the heroic, head, imbued with authority and charisma and equipped with a set of guiding principles and appropriate comptencies, will sort out wayward staff and raise student performance.

David Hargreaves had a slightly different take on the issues. Survival as a head in England, he says, means 'flying below the radar'. He referred to successful heads as subversive, following their own instincts.

They are not intimidated and oppressed by 'the centre' because with imaginative leaders and committed creative teachers they follow their best professional instincts. There is an extra-ordinary generation of school leaders who have bucked the trend, who don't say 'I'd love to do innovation but I can't afford to because of Ofsted or the league tables or whatever', and they've just got on innovating and doing exciting things and running very good schools and also schools that tend to do very well by conventional criteria because they're exciting places for teachers and kids to be in.

In few other countries is there the same degree of politicisation of school leadership, although OECD's recent report, *Improving School Leadership* has raised the policy stakes (Pont *et al.*, 2008).

Taking the politics out of education

You will never take the politics out of education, says Graham Holley, because political parties are tied into the five-year-cycle. This was explicitly acknowledged by Gillian Shephard who said, in retrospect, that if she had known at the time that the Tories were going to hold on to power so long she/they would have been more adventurous. It is in this respect that policy makers in Singapore frame their ambitions for educational change well beyond the immediate horizon, made possible, some would argue, by the fact that the governing party has to face a mere handful of opponents in parliament. In 1997, Prime Minster Goh Chok Tong declared that 'what is critical is that we fire in our students a passion for learning, instead of studying for the sake of getting good grades in their examinations', commenting on the fragility of assessed achievements. He described the future (more than a decade on) as one in which 'it is the *capacity to learn* that will define excellence in the future not simply what young people achieve in school'. It is a vision still to come to fruition but there is both a patience and an optimism that it can become reality.

Seven years on this was reiterated by Lee Hsien Long who, in the 2004 National Day Rally speech, said:

> We have got to teach less to our students so that they will learn more. Grades are important, don't forget to pass your exams, but grades are not the only thing in life and there are other things in life that we want to learn in schools.
>
> (Singapore Government Press Release, 22 Aug 2004)

Beyond the natural cycle of ministers

Graham Holley was adamant that for him and the agency he represents a ten-year vision, 'beyond the natural cycle of ministers', was necessary for any kind of valid and sustainable innovation.

> What it is the job of good agencies and good officials in the department to do is to construct – taking account where they know ministers want to go – a strategy which is permanently fixed on the horizon that has more than a five-year vision.

In the US education is a bi-partisan issue and less subject to the thesis and antithesis of British politics, although not exempt from ideological divides between Left and Right. Before they began looking to the East, policy makers and politicians in Britain were strongly influenced by what was happening in the US. Numerous delegations from England and Scotland borrowed policies and practices from their American counterparts. When in Britain fewer than ten per cent of students went on to higher education, many in the UK envied the ability of the US to take half of its student population beyond high school. The breadth of the curricular 'offer', the advantages of modularisation, credit and the United States' approach to vocational education was adopted. The UK embraced the US's drive for equity, diversity and multi-culturalism and created a school effectiveness movement in its image, rooted in a belief that with the appropriate tools and strategies it would be possible to close, or at least narrow, the gap between the highest and lowest achieving students, between the richest and poorest, the best and worst schools. Indeed since the 24 years since Coleman's Report on *Equality of Educational Opportunity* launched the school effects debate, and Rutter (1997) and Mortimore (1998) recast that debate in the UK, there has been an optimism abroad for a brave new educational world.

According to Andreas Schleicher it is vital, however, that optimism about education reform is translated by political parties into coherent policies in government. Agreeing that there should be more attempts by governments to achieve consensus on educational reform, Schleicher made it clear that:

> Consensus and coherence are the two very powerful forces for change . . . if your goals vary, how do you motivate anyone, be it the teacher of a class or the student, to take learning seriously? . . . If you're a teacher, you know today they're trying this and tomorrow there is something else . . . the lack of coherence in education policies, I think, is the biggest obstacle . . . (in) . . . the political climate.

Indeed, Schleicher points to the reluctance of governments taking part in PISA to commit to long-term strategic analysis.

> We try to develop what we call a PISA longitudinal study component . . . We had presented proposals to governments in 1994 . . . I don't think that, without longitudinal studies, we will ever sufficiently understand what is cause and what is effect . . . but . . . policy makers [are] often uninterested . . . in finding the answers to the questions they have in many years time.

In the UK, we are a long way from the consistency and coherence in policy-making called for by Schleicher in an international context. Indeed, there have been calls for the new government not to 'set its calendar as if election day is year zero'. (Progressive Education Network, 2010)

Optimism will not be maintained by attempting to re-invent schools within the same assumptions that have failed our children and teachers in the past. Nor will it achieved without a critical reappraisal of the curriculum diet and the modes of assessment which accompany it. The persisting gap between the advantaged and disadvantaged can only be achieved by governments having the courage, foresight and moral integrity to embark on something completely different; long-term, effective strategies based on coherence and consensus as to what is most worth pursuing in this, hopefully, brave new world.

9   There's nothing rational about decision-making

Alastair Campbell in his 2007 diary, *The Blair Years*, for example, devoted little attention to education despite the priority given by Blair to the issue. Michael Barber's account of education policy making in his book *Instruction to Deliver* is more detailed but inevitably is limited by his overall focus on the prime minister's Delivery Unit. The 2009 Cambridge Primary Review includes a short section on governance which concentrates on the specific issues of centralisation and decentralisation. The nearest thing to an insider's account of education decision-making in the Blair years is Peter Hyman's *1 Out of 10* (2005).

This chapter is intended to complement the relatively small amount of published material on how education policies are developed. It is certainly not an exhaustive analysis but it does reflect on the insights of a number of key actors. Their contributions lend a perspective which is vital to the development of evidence-informed policies which school communities can own and believe in.

Clear blue water

Mike Tomlinson's comment in his interview for this book that 'there's nothing rational about decision-making at all' is particularly relevant to the fate of his own report on the future of 14–19 qualifications. However, while the nature of policy formation, particularly in the last febrile 20 years, is more complex than that, his remark does highlight how central the intuitive nature of politics is to policy formation. Given the high profile of education and health in the Blair and Brown governments' public service reform programme, political considerations were always going to be uppermost, certainly in the minds of prime ministers and their secretaries of state. Or need they have been? Need education policy and decision-making be as irrational as Mike Tomlinson says?

To explore these questions, it is perhaps worth starting with Mike Tomlinson's account of the fate of his 14–19 report. Tomlinson himself had no doubt about the support he had achieved for the General Diploma structure which his report proposed.

> By the time the report was published we had for the first time every sector of the education and employment sector on board. . . . We almost had consensus, not that every detail was right, but [that] the blueprint was right.

His confidence was bolstered by the fact that David Milliband, who as minister was directly responsible for the report's publication, was in at the beginning of the Diploma as an idea.

> [Charles Clarke and David Milliband] wanted to look at possible reform across 14–19 and this of course harked back to a paper that David Milliband had produced earlier when he was part of the think-tank on the English Diploma.

In answer to the question, where did it all go wrong? Tomlinson told a fascinating story.

In order to achieve consensus around the report, Tomlinson had received permission from Milliband to show the leaders of the Opposition the draft report. 'Unusually', he said, ' we were allowed to send (the Final Report to) them in advance of it being presented'. He went on to recount that Milliband met the two Opposition education members to brief them. This openness backfired however.

> As we reported in Chapter 5 the availability of the report allowed Michael Howard to up the ante, to create apprehension that the gold standard of A levels was under threat. With an election looming Tony Blair felt he had to respond to the challenge, to defend the currency from devaluation. It was an off-the-cuff response that left his ministers wrong footed, at that very seminal moment when, elsewhere in the country, ministers were promising that the Tomlinson proposals would 'be implemented in full'. However rational, however well worked, and however carefully constructed the 14–19 Report may have been, the prime minister was, in a politically charged arena, pursuing his own rationale.

How had this come about? How did the government find itself in this contradictory situation? After all Blair's position was not new. As Tomlinson went on to say:

> Remember, he was clear in his own mind that the people who put him into power were Middle England and the last thing Middle England wanted to see was their beloved A levels abandoned.

Despite Blair's views, Tomlinson had thought he had achieved the difficult trick of convincing Blair that he had maintained the gold standard status of A levels within the Diploma. However, the advice being given to Blair was not as strong as Tomlinson expected it to be. Tomlinson noted that Number 10 policy advisors, including Andrew Adonis, were urging Blair to 'look at the educational politics of it as distinct from the educational importance of it'.

Something else happened which was probably more undermining than the combination of Michael Howard abusing a political confidence in the smoke of a general election or indeed Andrew Adonis urging caution. Richard Garner, Education Editor of *The Independent* newspaper, recalled a conversation with David Milliband about the Tomlinson Report.

> I remember David Milliband telling me that he went into Tony Blair's office to talk about the Tomlinson Report and the only question Blair asked was, 'Are A levels going to be safe?' He said that he had tried to . . . . answer saying that they were going to be safe but then he thought that he rambled on a bit longer which led Tony Blair to think perhaps they weren't safe as he and Milliband thought they were . . . and he said that Tony Blair had this picture of an election campaign in which the *Daily Mail* [saying], 'They are going to ruin A levels' . . . was the motivating factor.

Thus, according to Garner, the person who had been in at the beginning of the English Diploma had contributed to Blair's decision to block it.

One other factor sealed the fate of the Tomlinson Report. By the time of its publication, Charles Clarke, who had commissioned the report, had been replaced by Ruth Kelly. As Garner says, Kelly had no agency in the decision-making on the Report, leaving Milliband to represent its virtues directly to a suspicious prime minister.

There is an interesting historical contrast to be made here. By its own admission the Labour government saw 14–19 qualifications as a top priority for reform. Tomlinson himself saw it as the most exciting opportunity he'd had in his career. This was the opportunity to solve the oldest conundrum in education: how to achieve credibility for vocational education in its own right and how then to construct a framework which would allow students to accumulate credits in both vocational and academic education.

Kenneth Baker had, two decades earlier, an equally momentous task: that of creating a National Curriculum. He had argued then for a 'rounded education' against Thatcher's preference for a basics curriculum of English, maths and science. Against a prime minister as equally determined and powerful as Tony Blair, and perhaps with the advantage of being appointed as a secretary of state in a new government, Baker won.

Yet despite the enormous backing Tomlinson had achieved, far greater than Baker for his National Curriculum, Tomlinson lost. The reason for this may not be uniquely original but it is worth emphasising. What the Tomlinson Report lacked was not rationality in decision-making but ministerial belief. Leaders of political parties may be enthusiastic about creating clear blue water between themselves and their opponents but only if they are confident in their reforms, particularly in the run-up to a general election. It is also a truism, more obvious elsewhere in Whitehall than in education which has had so much prime ministerial interest devoted to it, that the fate of a public service rests on the quality, enthusiasm and confidence of its secretary of state and ministers. It even applies to initiatives endorsed by the prime minister and implemented by the government's Education Department.

Thus it was that the writing on the wall for the government's Literacy and Numeracy Strategies appeared long before the Brown government's decision to terminate them.

A deeper sharper focus

Michael Barber was dismayed by Charles Clarke's 2003 decision to introduce the *Excellence and Enjoyment* policy for primary schools – a policy which emphasised the broader creative possibilities in the curriculum – and a policy Barber (2008) described as a 'set-back'.

> What was needed in 2001–6 was a deeper, sharper focus . . . so it would get more refined, more targeted, and you'd be dealing with aspects of pedagogy at a more refined level . . . What actually happened was the focus got wider . . . I'm in favour of children enjoying schools, but you don't need a government policy for enjoyment . . . people got a holiday.

This frustration sharpened as a result of the publication of a House of Commons Education Select Committee Report in 2005 on early reading. By then Charles Clarke, an independent minded secretary of state who had established *Excellence and Enjoyment*, had been replaced by Ruth Kelly who left her schools minister, Stephen Twigg, to defend the Literacy Strategy to the Select Committee. The committee had been advised by a range of phonics specialists, supported by Chris Woodhead, ex HCMI, who himself had been appointed by Michael Howard as his education adviser for the general election. The committee's report was explosive, particularly as it was published prior to the general election. Its reception by the opposition and government demonstrated just how far the general election campaign had politicised the teaching of literacy.

Barber has recorded his concern at Stephen Twigg's performance in the Select Committee and on the Today programme for failing to defend the Literacy Strategy. Arguing that Twigg wasn't confident enough to assert that the strategies were right, Barber (2008) wrote, 'You start sliding when you feel you have to apologise for the main point of the policy'.

John Stannard, as ex director of the National Literacy Strategy, quoted by Barber in *The Learning Game*, goes much further in describing the impact of the Select Committee Report.

> The public message was abundantly clear. The NLS was trendy, out-dated, typical old-Labour thinking and opposed to phonics, while phonics was effective, traditional, rigorous and conservative . . . Kelly, seriously weakened by the Select Committee's attack, with a long agenda of other pressing worries and little understanding of the issues, was not prepared to defend or justify the Strategy. . . . The uncompromising effort to bring phonics to the forefront did little to build up the fragile confidence of teachers.
>
> (Stannard *et al.*, 2007)

Whatever the merits or demerits of the Tomlinson reforms and the NLS, they highlight just how much reforms which have apparently received cross-party consensus can disintegrate during a general election campaign.

Deliverology and Trust

There is nothing inherently right or wrong in strong leadership from a ministerial team. Strong leaders do not guarantee good policies just as policy making during general elections does not guarantee bad ones. The 'as good as it gets' objective is of course to have effective policies which are owned by schools.

Such an objective sounds ideal but it somewhat of a holy grail. A good policy for one group may be an undermining policy for another. Strong leadership can be responded to positively but it may also be seen as bullying or deskilling. The efficacy of the mix of policies also depends on who implements them.

Reforming governments depend on their civil service for implementing their policies. There is a great deal of evidence that the incoming Blair government did not trust its civil service to implement its public service reform programme. Michael Barber describes in detail the raison d'être of the prime minister's Delivery Unit in *Instruction to Deliver*. The term, 'deliverology', a term invented by a treasury official according to Barber, was born of Blair's frustration with not being able to implement his public service reform programme fast enough. As Barber says:

> The challenge for a government badgered by a prime minister with a 'mandate for reform' is to design an effective reform programme, prepare a strategy to take it forward and seek to motivate a huge, sceptical workforce to implement it.
>
> (Barber, 2008)

The education service experienced deliverology in its purest form between 1997 and 2002 with schools being set a range of targets by government, and with the DfEE/DfES ('the department') and Ofsted pressuring schools and local authorities to deliver them. From 2003 deliverology took on a different form with government seeking to co-opt public service unions, in health as well as education, into social partnerships to help delivery. The effects of deliverology on schools are rehearsed elsewhere in this book. What is less well known is its effect on those responsible for delivery.

The mechanism for delivering the government's education reforms in 1997 was the Standards and Effectiveness Unit (SEU). Its job was to focus on 'a small number of things and do them properly', as Barber put it. Its very existence represented an implied and strong distrust of the DfEE to deliver the government's programme. The SEU appeared to be the essence of New Labour – proactive, breaking with a time-serving civil service, getting the job done.

In fact, despite her opposition to the idea of government intervening in pedagogy, much of the rationale for the unit was drawn from David Blunkett's conversations with the outgoing secretary of state, Gillian Shephard, according to Conor Ryan, David Blunkett's special advisor at the time.

> One of the things that David realised . . . from discussions with Gillian Shephard, ideologically on education they were fairly similar . . . one of the things that Gillian said to David was the thing that most frustrated her was delivery in the

department . . . so David had decided and agreed with Michael Barber . . . that if Labour won there would be a Delivery Unit in the department and that Michael Barber would head it.

Its creation was opposed by Robin Butler, the then cabinet secretary, and as Ryan and Barber recall, Blair overruled him. The creation of an elite delivery unit not only discomforted the Civil Service, according to Conor Ryan, it angered the then chief inspector, Chris Woodhead.

> There was also what you might call a 'creative tension' between Ofsted and the unit because, the reason that Chris Woodhead left was because . . . Michael had a unit in the department and he was at one remove down in Holborn and he couldn't stand the fact there was a rival . . . advising the secretary of state.

Indeed Kevan Collins in the SEU described Ofsted as 'hostile', waiting to see the strategies fail, and 'taking a sort of detached position'. Nevertheless, despite the opposition of the cabinet secretary and the chief inspector, the SEU quickly bedded in. They were no match for Blair and Blunkett. The unit was assiduous about achieving its main targets. Conor Ryan tells an interesting story about achieving a target which had drawn support from schools, as well as government: the infant class size target. He paints a picture of hapless civil servants trying to get their heads around the New Labour pledge.

> DfES statisticians at one stage had produced a report on class sizes . . . in which there seemed to be several classes in the country which had over 40 in them and this was after a couple of years of it being illegal . . . I mean this was ridiculous . . . so, sheepishly, they came back a few days later and said, well actually, it seems that, at schools on the day of the census, there were a few classes sitting together watching a movie, or having a joint assembly, and these were being counted in the class size data.

The setting of the literacy and numeracy targets had 'no evidential base'. Although Michael Barber claimed that the department had looked at the data from 1995 and 1996 tests he frankly admitted they were 'educated guesses'. Judy Sebba, for seven years the DfEE's senior advisor (Research), concurred, questioning the rationale for targets.

> How can a target ever be evidence based? . . . You can say at the moment children make . . . one level or one-and-a half levels [of progress] in a year, therefore we'll set it at two . . . but what's the evidence base for challenging targets?

Sandy Adamson, a senior civil servant, was even less ambiguous as to the evidential base:

> It was the delivery mechanism that was the problem and the stupidity of targets, unobtainable targets, simply pulled from the air and then applied to every school

in the country. Twenty thousand primary schools and the majority of reaction was 'this is unachievable' and for a substantial minority it was never achieved.

The problem with the 'educated guess' was being less 'educated' than it ought to have been and understood internally at the department as purely a marker of progress. As it had not been based on an evaluation of whether primary schools had the capacity to meet the targets, it was to come back later to haunt Estelle Morris as secretary of state. Quizzed by the House of Commons Education Select Committee, she had to admit that the literacy and numeracy targets had not been achieved despite a previous guarantee she had made, an admission that contributed to her subsequent resignation.

Despite these developments, prior to the plateauing of pupil achievement in literacy and numeracy and the heated debate about why it had happened, the DfEE itself was convinced that it had both the machinery in place for demonstrable improvement and the broad support of teachers. Kevan Collins' shock at how passive teachers were and how quickly they took to the strategies, was an example of the department's reading of teachers' receptivity to government reforms.

In fact teachers' receptivity offered a temptation to the DfEE to exploit it and roll out a raft of other initiatives. As Kevan Collins said, the beguiling thing was that it 'could be done'.

> You actually can change the behaviour of a quarter of a million primary teachers without passing a piece of legislation and . . . that was beguiling because the question was, we can do that – and then you've got this insatiable appetite which was the perverse side of it.

Although this was the attitude of the SEU towards teachers, it was not confident about the rest of the department. One interviewee described the composition of the department in 1997 as consisting of:

> Either people who had a breath-taking ignorance or arrogance (or people who were) incredibly bright . . . [or] people who were bright but really didn't know how education worked . . . and actually [had] never been part of the education system . . . [so] when they went out to confront, or to meet, or to engage with the profession . . . [they] found themselves talking to an audience they just could not connect to.

In Sandy Adamson' equally descriptive words they were 'staggeringly ignorant contextually or systematically of the realities of school life'. It was, with this in mind, together with the ability to break the mould and to 'break out of all kinds of protocols and processes' that a non-profit making trust, CfBT Education Trust, was hired to run the strategies.

The effect of this distrust elevated the SEU to the position of appearing to be responsible for the only policies that mattered; thus downgrading other policies which in fact might have had equal or greater merit.

Richard Harrison's experience with the 2001 Professional Development Strategy is an example. The obsession with measurable progress also went, occasionally, to absurd lengths as Judy Sebba recalls, finding herself in a position in the SEU of being told to devise a test which would demonstrate improvement in children's learning, after three weeks of numeracy summer school:

> And I said you must be joking . . . We can show that we've learned a few, very . . . specific skills . . . but you cannot give children a pre and post test before and after a three week summer school.

In fact the SEU's supremacy was not sustainable. Michael Barber, with his close relationship to Blair and the Number Ten Policy Unit, moved on to the prime minister's Delivery Unit which gave Department officials the opportunity to dissolve the SEU. Other policies appeared, not least from Number Ten, which ironically undermined the SEU's original focus.

Kevan Collins described the collision when Blair became interested in, to use Barber's words, 'market incentives or market like incentives'.

> Standards, not structures was [a mantra] which created the space for us to work freely across the whole system . . . We were not interested in structures, we were interested in standards . . . It meant you could have audiences in rooms up and down the country from Cornwall to Newcastle, have a common language, a common script and a common . . . set of priorities that were universal.

Collins contrasted this with the move to the debate about how to introduce market incentives:

> We moved straight away from the universal language of teaching and learning and children's . . . and young people's outcomes and began to believe that the solution was in just creating certain types of schools . . . The absolute shining example of that was the academies debate . . . It fractured a working alliance between individuals and the endeavour . . . and it basically segmented the profession.

Kevan Collins' observation is fascinating and prompts a reflection. The arguments against a choice and diversity agenda for schools are strong but campaigns against them have focused on the damaging impact of privatisation and the opening up of a local democratic deficit. A more profound criticism, as Collins indicated, is that the shift from standards to structures shifted attention away from a collective discourse on school improvement to a fractured discourse on the virtues and sins of Academies and Trust Schools. Thus it was that the standards focus of the first Labour government began to dissolve: a situation that Estelle Morris now regrets:

It is standards not structures, and if ever we've gone wrong over the past 13 years, it was when we started to believe again that it was about structures not standards.

(Evidence to the House of Commons Children, Schools and Families Committee, 8 March 2010)

Parallel lines, bowdlerisation and institutional amnesia

Internally the department is not particularly well equipped to handle profound debates on standards versus structures and it certainly wasn't after the SEU had waned. Its focus was further complicated by the Children's Services agenda which meant that the department has had to juggle the competing claims of a wider welfare and well being role with maintaining a focus on standards.

Those who have direct dealings with the department have a clear impression of how it copes with juggling. Alasdair MacDonald likened the headteacher to a prism and the department as a set of parallel lines:

There were all these people beavering away, all on their own initiatives, they never spoke to one another, and they came out from the department as parallel lines, and there on the headteacher's desk you had a prism, and [you] had to make sense of it.

Indeed MacDonald puts his finger on a question at the heart of this book; the relationship of policy makers' conceptions and the experience of schools;

There's something about the department that seems to militate against good policy making getting from an idea to schools, something in . . . the department frequently doesn't facilitate that . . . but actually bureaucratises it.

MacDonald gives an example of an idea which has become bureaucratised. The idea of creating a 'critical friend' for headteachers – the School Improvement Partner – emerged from discussions he had with other heads.

There was an idea . . . I was willing to go there . . . but in between the department couldn't cope with something that was relatively open ended and which you couldn't initially measure, so it was bureaucratised.

'Bowdlerised, distorted and watered down' was the fate of dialogic teaching in the hands of the department, said Robin Alexander. As was also the case with assessment for learning, he added – 'Potentially powerful ideas are taken over and have the stuffing knocked out of them'.

One reason for the emasculation of powerful ideas may be attributed to the deliverology culture created by the Standards and Effectiveness Unit. The need to direct and control almost always expresses itself in bureaucratic procedures. Another reason could be that 'bright people' never get a chance to follow the effects of the implementation of the policies for which they are responsible. Indeed Jim Knight repeated the long established argument that civil servants should have generic skills and not build up specialist knowledge.

> The trick is to get round the fact that we keep people fresh by moving them around, to have proper engagement and other consultation so that before they are set in stone we have the chance to expose them to comment that includes people who've been around the system a long time.

Admitting that the department had to rely on 'stakeholders and the occasional senior official for its institutional memory', Knight simply said that this was 'a feature of government'. Others are more troubled by the department's lack of institutional memory. As Richard Harrison said:

> This is a common criticism of the department, that it has no institutional memory . . . the Treasury may be an exception . . . [but] you don't need to be more than two or three years beyond any initiative and have no one working in the area [with] any memory of it . . . Your standard civil servant might look back a couple of years to what had been there but it's all based on what's currently around . . . nobody looks back'

Conor Ryan found this mindset, or lack of it, a major problem.

> The big problem you've got is the lack of continuity . . . there's a curious thing that happens with all the policy people of the department . . . the ones who are really good quickly get moved on . . . so you lose that memory, so you get someone else who's on a learning curve and may or may not be any good at it . . . the ones who are plodding . . . stay there.

This two tier approach creates another problem according to Ryan. The plodders remain in silos.

> I would sometimes say to somebody . . . that's quite similar to what such and such is doing . . . [and they] . . . might actually be sitting at their desk a few yards away.

Conor Ryan is right. The lack of institutional memory in the department is a serious issue. Its importance as an issue was obscured temporarily by the SEU with the introduction of outside advisers such as Michael Barber and Judy Sebba. However, the absence of such a memory has even greater implications than a lack of political continuity. The most important of these is that few civil servants ever really get a chance to learn and understand the impact of policies on teachers in the classroom and whether such policies need modifying or changing.

This lack of memory also means that the department has no knowledge about the initiatives of previous governments and ministers. Ministers, therefore, become reliant on the historical knowledge of specific interest groups, a fact that Jim Knight confirms when he says that he was not short of people 'reminding us'. It also means that ministers rely on the serendipity of whether some civil servants have some historical knowledge; a fact confirmed by at least three interviewees for this book who named the same civil servant who did, in fact, have a sense of history.

Nevertheless, since 1997, parts of the department such as research have maintained some continuity of expertise. However, continuity in this area has brought its own problems, particularly for researchers commissioned to carry out evaluations on the effectiveness of particular initiatives. 'Why does the research commissioned only ever bring us bad news?', one exasperated minister is reported to have asked, raising the obvious question of whether the policies were informed by evidence in the first place.

Mary Bousted, as the general secretary of a union inside the Social Partnership, confirmed that, despite 'some profoundly good things' the Labour government made some profound mistakes.

> It has done some profoundly good things especially in the essentials, . . . where it's gone wrong is layer upon layer . . . of initiatives . . . centrally driven by bright young things in the DCSF who have got no idea about how policy plays out on the ground . . . they don't really think about impact . . . it's when you get a bright young thing coming in, naively presenting something which you just take one look at and you just think that it'll take some poor sod in school two days.

The SEU was, of course, intended to alter this culture and in its own terms it did deliver on its limited number of initiatives. It did not however change the culture, either in terms of growing deep expertise among civil servants or in terms of government 'doing a few things well' as Michael Barber put it.

Doing a few things well?

Doing a few things well may be beyond a reform minded government with its constant need to show that it hasn't run out of ideas. Nevertheless, there is no professional group more than teachers who aspire to government education policy 'doing a few things well'.

It is, after all, ministers whose own aspirations as well as those of their government which determine a reform programme. Other than Kenneth Baker, Conservative ministers rarely chose to make their mark in terms of education policy. Indeed it was more than ten years from Prime Minister Jim Callaghan's Great Debate to the Education Reform Act. During the mid-nineties, as Gillian Shephard confirmed in interview, a dying government meant that options for initiatives dried up. The Labour government of 1997 intended to sweep this sense of statis away and in its own terms has tried to maintain a public profile of reform through constant initiatives; a situation recognised by Estelle Morris, who said in evidence to the House of Commons CSF Committee, 'There have been too many initiatives, there is no doubt about it . . . we need a different way of managing change'. Yet on big strategic decisions, such as the Tomlinson Report on 14–19 education, it has found like all parties in power that the constraints, pressures and anxieties of government have kicked in.

One area where government anxieties and defensiveness express themselves is through the medium of its agencies. Since the Education Reform Act, governments have created agencies to advise them and carry out the practical details of education reform. Most prominent among them have been Agencies responsible for 'delivering' curriculum and assessment reform. The National Curriculum Council (NCC) and the School Examinations and Assessment Council (SEAC) and subsequently the School Curriculum and Assessment Authority (SCAA) were created by the Conservatives and the Qualifications and Curriculum Authority (QCA) and then the Qualifications and Curriculum Development Agency (QCDA) and Ofqual by Labour. They testify to the fact that both Parties in a government have felt the need for arms-length agencies to do their work, to sometimes save their bacon, and occasionally to carry the blame.

Under Sir Ron Dearing, SCAA saved the Conservative government from teachers who objected to teaching an overloaded National Curriculum and continued to boycott National Curriculum tests. The QCA had a more chequered history under Labour. It successfully introduced reforms in the secondary curriculum but took the blame for failure in examination reform and the implementation of National Curriculum tests.

Barry Sheerman, chair of the House of Commons Children, Schools and Families Select Committee, has succinctly described how convenient an agency like the QCA can be as a fall guy for hard pressed ministers:

> They would prefer a more compliant person as head of the QCA than a less compliant [one] . . . because they would like to get their own way . . . but it's not only getting their own way, it is quite convenient for ministers to say well, it wasn't the department . . . it was the independent organisation the QCA and their boss who got it wrong . . . that's very convenient in August when the world and his wife is blaming someone for cocking up the key stage test results. . . . the only way to counter that in my view is to make these organisations much more independent and as far as possible answer to . . . parliament through a select committee.

Certainly Ken Boston, the former chief executive of the QCA, would probably agree with the thrust of Barry Sheerman's solution to the Janus-faced position in which the government placed his authority. Giving evidence to the CSF Select Committee on 22 April 2009 he described the impact on ministers of the direction he chose for the QCA:

> One of the great sources of agitation [from ministers] has been the way in which I have played my role and allowed other senior people to play their roles . . . particularly . . . Mick Waters, the director of curriculum. The QCA was set up to be a constructive participant in education discussion . . . It has not been bound by a set of speeches that were basically constructed around government press releases of the day . . . It has never publically criticised government but has been prepared to shoot the breeze about other ways of doing things.

The reward for his role as constructive participant, Sheerman felt, was to be seen by the government as a 'troublesome priest'.

Mick Waters is more specific in his analysis of the ministers' attitudes to the QCA's work. He felt they were far too responsive to the effects of short-term lobbying. The sharp U turns he described which took place in the secondary curriculum review – 'lobbying temporarily focused on history and on cooking and then on science and sex' – illustrate the contradictions between civil servants' inherent conservatism and ministers' perceived need to 'go with the breeze'. Civil servants, according to Waters, think that

> The curriculum is what you comply with and, in any review, their mindset has been, 'hang on to the best and get rid of the rest'.

The question they do not ask, he said, is how you make the curriculum better for young people.

Despite tensions between the department, QCA and ministers, the review of the Secondary Curriculum went well. The reason was, Waters said, that during the review process itself ministers were 'out a lot' and were 'close to what was going on' and were also involved with teachers and their professional associations. In fact the picture he paints is of a review process in which the department's experienced junior ministers were actively engaged despite their secretary of state's evident empathy with his own civil servants' position on curriculum review. Indeed, Andrew Adonis comes in for particular praise for supporting the QCA's proposals for the new secondary curriculum.

However, civil servants' distrust of the QCA's perceived role as constructive participant gained the upper hand when the government decided to review the Primary Curriculum. Despite the QCA's successful stewardship of the secondary review, it was sidelined and the responsibility given to Jim Rose. QCA, relegated to the subsidiary role of managing the consultation, was barred from any proactive public engagement. QCA's relative independence, which had acted as a useful lightning rod between ministers and schools was not available to the government.

The result was that the government, following its principle of 'hang on to the best and get rid of the rest' came into direct conflict with the Cambridge Review of Primary Education. Led by Robin Alexander, and funded by the Esmee Fairbairn Foundation, it was the most significant review of primary education since the Plowden Report. It was determinedly independent and sought to ask 'the necessary questions without fear or favour' (Alexander, 2009).

The contrast between this approach and the Brown government's increasing inclination to listen to civil servants who say, 'don't discuss it, keep it off the agenda . . . it's better we don't talk about this' (as Mick Waters recalls) couldn't have been starker. Mick Waters is clear that the government's decision to initiate their own review of the primary curriculum was in fact triggered by Robin Alexander's decision to initiate the Cambridge Primary Review. Indeed, Waters didn't think that a review of the primary curriculum was even necessary.

You could have made the old curriculum work and [shown teachers] what it meant . . . [Nevertheless] the view was put about that because Robin was starting his study of primary education, we should have a curriculum review.

Waters was very critical of the government's approach to appointing 'externals' to conduct reviews rather than asking the agencies who 'had the voice of authority' to do the job. He said that the government diminished the agencies' authority. Instead the 'really clever thing', according to Waters;

> [W]ould have been to take what Robin and his team were producing and then come back with a big heap of questions . . . and dig deep into some of these really big issues . . . some brilliant points [were] raised in the Alexander Review . . . we could have engaged with the workforce, stakeholders, parents and talked about that in different ways and then said, 'So, Robin, the questions that arise are [these], what are we going to do about it?'.

Instead, the government refused to allow the QCA to provide a public forum in which Rose and Alexander could debate the future of the primary curriculum. Rose was prevented from publicly acknowledging the significance and depth of the Cambridge Review until a brief reference was allowed in his final report.

The arms length approach adopted by the department to the Cambridge Review triggered enormous resentment from Alexander. There were also many who were shocked by the department's refusal to engage with the Cambridge Review. They even included Matthew Taylor, the Royal Society of the Arts director and Blair's ex head of policy, who publicly criticised the department's stance.

> So extensive was the consultation exercise undertaken by the research team and advisory panel it was hard to imagine that anyone interested in primary education didn't have the chance to get their voice heard . . . but when the report was published last week it was subject to a concerted critique by ministers, shadow ministers and most parts of the press . . . not only that . . . its key recommendations were systematically misrepresented.
>
> (Matthew Taylor's blog, http://www.matthewtaylorsblog.com/
> (accessed 30 October 2009))

Taylor finished his blog with a downbeat note:

> Dreading the quality of debate about schools we will have to endure in the run-up to the general election.

Compared to the QCA and its previous iterations, the other Agencies such as the Training and Development Agency and the National College (previously the NCSL) have kept a comparatively low profile. They have had their bumpy passages but, by and large, they have delivered the government's agenda to its satisfaction. The QCA was different. Since 1997 two of its chief executives have been dismissed. One left after less than a year. Another left after disputing the government's decision to suspend the statutory requirements for the foundation subjects in order to introduce the Primary Literacy and Numeracy Strategies. Perhaps the QCA has been so troubled in its relationship with successive Labour governments because, as the Cambridge Primary Review said:

> The curriculum, and the debate it stimulates, are of the most profound importance to children and to the country in which the fruits of their learning are applied.
>
> (Alexander *et al.*, 2009)

Indeed, debates on the curriculum and its assessment are a proxy for national debates on the nature of society itself. How governments engage these debates is of profound importance not only for the content of the curriculum but for the concept of pluralism in a democratic society.

Goodbye Winston, two fingers to Churchill

Nowhere is pluralism more self-evident in all its rough and ready glory than in the press and media's relationship with governments. Much has been written about the Blair government's relationship with the press and media; its capacity for spin; and its later war of attrition with the Fourth Estate, particularly surrounding the Iraq War.

The history of modern governments in the media age illustrates an undoubted truism. The longer a political party remains in government the harder it finds to remain 'new', both in the eyes of the public and in the eyes of the press which mediates public perception. The idea of governments 'reinventing themselves', therefore, reflects their perceived need to remain new, not only in order to respond to the public's expectations but the media's. In the last twenty years, reinvention has come after changes in party leadership. In short, education has been reinvented with each successive government.

The Education Reform Act was the hallmark of the last Thatcher government and School Evaluation and Inspection were a dominant theme of the two Major governments. The 1997 Labour government focused on standards, with its trademark literacy and numeracy targets. The second two Blair governments concentrated on encouraging 'choice and diversity' in school provision. The Brown government devoted its energies to the Children Plan. A leitmotif which has run through all government policy over the last twenty years, however, has been curriculum, assessment and examination reform.

All governments tried, and go on trying, to give the public clear and understandable messages about their reforms. The medium for the message is the media, to adapt Marshall McLuhan's famous aphorism. Indeed as Barber admitted, the message and even the policy were tailored to the public's perceived need for reform which it understood. The national literacy and numeracy targets were a classic example of the need to 'demonstrate' that you could improve the system.

Many in the press and media have responded positively to the reported improvements in primary schools. Richard Garner, the Education Editor of *The Independent*, for example, believed that indeed 'We do have a higher level of performance in maths and English in primary schools'. But added a note of scepticism:

> Some of them actually believe that exams like GCSEs and A levels have got easier and that is the reason [for] the increased pass rate.

The Ratner effect

There is an interesting question to be explored about why the efficacy of public examination questions themselves have been the subject of so much media criticism. It could indeed be that examination standards over time have not remained the same. A more likely reason is that the government's public arguments for reform in secondary education have backfired. Jim Knight himself describes this problem as 'a bit of a rat' – citing Gerald Ratner, who destroyed public confidence in his own company's jewellery products by describing them as rubbish. Indeed, Knight explicitly identified the problem:

> How do you still sound impatient for improvement while not rubbishing what you've already done'?

While the 'Ratner effect' may not have impacted on primary schools, one outcome of Number 10's belief that 'comprehensive schools were a disaster', as Fiona Millar put it, may have fuelled the media's scepticism about comprehensive education. According to Garner, the 'Ratner effect' was not exclusive to the post-1997 Labour governments.

> I think (Labour) have fallen into the trap of governments of all time . . . the Conservatives, after however many years they were in office . . . were . . . hammering on about how the education system was in dire straits and they had to reform it . . . but any sensible person would think, you've been in charge for 15 or 16 years so therefore it's you that's not brought it up to where you think it should be . . . and Labour falls into the same trap . . . everybody's now thinking, well if there are problems, you've created them.

For long-serving parties in government the 'Ratner effect' combines with two other pressures; pressures which now afflict governments however long they have been in power. The first is '24 hour news', as Garner described it:

> We have to be one step ahead and we have to provide something that's more enticing than what you've seen on television and . . . radio . . . that's true of every aspect of the news coverage, education as well and . . . therefore there is more attendance to exaggeration and accenting the negative now, than there was say a decade ago.

The other effect is that some journalists, but not all, reflect their papers' attitudes. Garner admitted that:

Even I come under pressure to accentuate the bad and neglect the positive . . . it's more marked in papers like the *Daily Mail* . . . [where] I get the feeling they believe the 'mantra'.

Interestingly, Garner believes that the inclination of education correspondents to accentuate the bad and neglect the positive does not apply to teachers themselves:

I think the majority of education correspondents actually do realise that teachers have a hard life . . . where they part from that is . . . thinking sometimes that they are architects of their own downfall . . . particularly Key Stage 2 SATs.

While Garner and his colleagues believe that teachers are 'over-egging the pudding' on the testing issue, journalists tend to sympathise with some of the problems which teachers face, particularly in relation to deteriorating standards of behaviour.

[While] sometimes the sympathy doesn't come out in the copy . . . where the sympathy comes out for teachers is in dealing with behavioural problems and discipline.

There are many factors and attributes which contribute to a secretary of state's effectiveness. Previous experience in another department can be one of them as Shephard believes. A powerful special adviser is another, particularly if a secretary of state is new to government. Conor Ryan, David Blunkett's adviser was, according to Garner:

The most powerful special adviser that there has been in the department . . . as an ex-working journalist and press officer for various organisations, he knew how the media worked.

Indeed, Conor Ryan implicitly confirmed Garner's analysis.

A lot of civil servants would come to me before papers went to David to take a view on . . . what I thought David's view was going to be . . . I would say this is what I think the secretary of state will want to happen.

Ryan's 'sounding board' role in policy making perfectly complemented his relationship with the press, despite the fact that he was not part of the department's press office. As he said:

Most days I would spend about an hour a day on [the] media, the rest was dealing with policy, and about two or three in the afternoon, I would ring around the education correspondents individually and just check they were alright . . . this was quite helpful to the press office because you'd have some official holding up a quote and I had the authority to give the senior source quote which would give the department's view . . . and once a week I would have a strategy meeting with the press team.

The politics and perils of spinning and leaking

Ryan's description of his relationship with the department's press office and civil servants provides a fascinating vignette of how the interface between policy-making and the press operated in the first Labour government. It enabled the government to confidently spin its message. Garner recalled an early example – the launch of the Gifted and Talented Programme:

> It was spun to *The Sunday Times* as trying to woo the middle classes back into the state sector [but] at the general press briefing . . . [it was described] . . . as being something that improved the performance of deprived kids in working class areas.

Spin can of course go wrong. Giving sympathetic newspapers exclusives can cause resentment among other journalists as Garner recalled:

> I remember that one of the PricewaterhouseCoopers' reports on academies was 'leaked' to *The Times* . . . it said that . . . they were doing a wonderful job – all honey and flowers – and the report . . . wasn't that critical of academies . . . [but] because of the leak to *The Times* had been so over the top, I actually focused on the one negative conclusion which was that they were excluding badly behaved pupils . . . I'm sure if they hadn't leaked this straight to *The Times*, the piece [I wrote] for *The Independent* would have been a summary of what the report said.

It is not just bad news management which can create a story which boomerangs against a government. Some issues are so potent that they have all the explosive power of nitro-glycerine. Mick Waters' account of the launch of the secondary curriculum review showed how too clever news management can explode in the government's face.

> It was mischief in the press about Churchill . . . that unsettled some ministers . . . for all the endless proof reading, nobody in the QCA or the department picked up on the absence of the word 'Churchill'.
>
> In probably the first two weeks of Ed Balls arriving in office, the Secondary Review was . . . launched in Lords Cricket Ground . . . the *Evening Standard* carried a thing about the end of Churchill . . . that weekend the press was full of 'Goodbye Winston, two fingers to Churchill' and all that stuff.
>
> Ed Balls, like many of them, lives by the media . . . I can tell you why it got into the media . . . all week I kept telling them . . . on the Monday, the department briefed the press to say the Secondary Review was going to be about financial capability; on Tuesday it was about global sustainability; Wednesday, about cooking. The press just hate being told what to write so, by the end of the week, they go for anything.

It is an analysis which Richard Garner confirmed:

Unless there is something in the report which is sufficiently new and exciting, you can't produce the headline from writing about the report that is going to interest people . . . if your reaction is unfavourable that is where we get the headline . . . it is simply a question of news values . . . you have to produce something that looks sufficiently different to entice people to want to read it.

The department's response to 'two fingers to Churchill' was that it was the QCA's fault. As Mick Waters said somewhat ruefully:

I'm afraid the civil servants don't say, 'we got it wrong, we kept briefing the wrong thing', they say, 'the QCA never thought of it'.

Despite their turbulent relationship with the Fourth Estate, ministers continued to 'live by the media' up until the 2010 general election, a relationship likely to intensify rather than diminish in the future. Journalists, however, did not have a view that all ministers were the same. Estelle Morris, for example, was admired by Garner for being a 'genuine minister' doing 'her best for the education system'. Ed Balls was viewed as 'ruthlessly ambitious' but not above taking on tough issues such as 'tackling the faith schools . . . for putting pressure on parents to pay before offering places', says Garner. What is clear, however, is that ministers do not think enough about the impact of their policies on schools. 'Often, they think something looks quite enticing', adds Garner, but they can't see the alternative reaction that might emerge from it. His comment probably summarises the greatest problem of governments 'living by the media'; the unforeseen consequences of doing so can be both profound and unexpected.

Beyond the Ratner effect

The background to policy-making in government, certainly in the last decade-and-a-half, is summarised by the advice the prime minister received about the future of the Tomlinson Review; that he should look at the educational politics of it rather than its educational importance. Such a comment should not come as a surprise. Decision-making in any government has always been influenced by political considerations.

Nevertheless, since 1997, consideration of the educational politics of any policy has been much more prominent in the department's and ministers' collective minds than it was under previous governments. The demands of the 24 hour news cycle have fuelled the need for immediate political response. Such pressures have undoubtedly raised the political stakes but it is not only a voracious media which has been responsible for shaping government decisions. The government's education reform programme was and is reliant on the press and media promoting it.

Originally the relationship between the media and Labour policymaking was symbiotic. The government needed the media to promote its reform messages. The media needed the stories. However, Blair's urge to be more radical than the Conservatives fractured his government's focus on standards. The development of academies may have trumped the Conservatives' policy initiatives towards opening up the market but the government was not prepared to contemplate radical reform of the public examination system or maintain its early single-minded focus on standards. Also government confidence in its policy-making does not seem to have been helped either by a lack of collective historical knowledge and deep and continuing expertise in particular policy areas among civil servants.

The education reform agenda, so enthusiastically promoted when Labour came to power, demanded a continuing trajectory of success. Descriptions of school failure and low standards were necessary to provide the arguments for both radical reform and public agreement to increased school funding. The engine for further reform had necessarily to be based on demonstrating the need for further reform. However, over time, these arguments became a double-edged sword. As Jim Knight, so pithily summarised it, they became 'a bit of a rat'. The perceived need to feed the press and media with stories about reform has inevitably led journalists to ask whether the responsibility for failure rests with the very government which demands reform. In short, permanent imposed reform, like permanent revolution, is self-fulfilling and self-defeating.

Attempts by the Brown government to shift the reform agenda away from the Blair government's choice and diversity policies towards encouraging schools to act collectively have been inevitably shackled by anxieties that the opposition would attack this shift. It is perhaps ironic that the net product of a driving radical reform agenda should be that of caution.

Nevertheless, governments of the last 20 years can point to a range of achievements despite the buffeting of political pressures. Successive Labour governments have a range of achievements to their name; not least a record number of teachers and support staff in employment and substantial improvements in school building stock. The Conservatives can also point to the inheritance and continuation of much of its Education Reform Act architecture, particularly the National Curriculum and local management of schools.

There does, however, need to be a deep examination of Tomlinson's comment about the irrationality of policy making; despite the fact that some policies have enduring and tangible results. The educational importance of reform must trump its political importance. The examples in this chapter only too clearly demonstrate why. The political imperative will always win out when political parties seek to create clear blue water between themselves on education policy. Yet the deeply troubling thought is that the very nature of the parliamentary democratic process itself militates against sustained and effective educational reform based on consensus. A clue on how to resolve this conundrum is contained in the very consensus Tomlinson achieved for his report. Our final chapter explores what this might mean for the current coalition government and those that might follow.

10 And now for something completely different?

> It was the best of times, it was the worst of times, it was the age of wisdom, it was the age of foolishness, it was the epoch of belief, it was the epoch of incredulity, it was the season of Light, it was the season of Darkness, it was the spring of hope, it was the winter of despair, we had everything before us, we had nothing before us.
>
> (Dickens, *A Tale of Two Cities*, p. 1)

This book could be described as a tale of two parties. It is about success, failure and opportunities missed. 'If the Conservatives had known that they were going to be in for 18 years, the whole of the reforms would have been completely different', said Gillian Shephard. Her regret was at the lost opportunity to focus on teacher quality and, in Pauline Perry's words, to foreground a celebration of commitment, celebration of professionalism, and of what teachers do 'brilliantly'. 'What if?' – the ghost in the machine.

If New Labour had conceived of 13 years of power, would it have been less impatient to 'drive up' standards, an apt metaphor for what was described by a senior civil servant as 'Stalinist' in the government's unwillingness to brook dissent?

While the leitmotif of all general elections is inevitably 'Time for a Change', in the weeks leading up to the 2010 election there was a progressive wintering of discontent among the public with both main political parties and their leadership. The spring of hope that was in the air in 1997 had become only a distant memory.

The best of times

In 1997, the day after the election, Tim Brighouse addressed a hundred bleary eyed headteachers, most of whom had been up until the early hours celebrating; some having come straight from election partying to the opening session of the conference. Brighouse informed them of plans afoot to set up a taskforce in which he would be a key player. As he described it, in an interview for this book, Blunkett had said to him:

> 'I want you involved when the election is over'. 'I said in what way?' So he said 'what I'd really like you to do is give up your job and come and work for me

and he said, we'll set up a task force and you will run it and we'll change every-thing'.

While Tim Brighouse was not prepared to give up his job as CEO in Birmingham, he did agree to chairing the task force. It was, however, to be some time before that appointment was to come to fruition, and not quite as anticipated, as 'changing everything' was set about from the outset by pragmatism and compromise. As Tim Brighouse himself told it:

> They got swept up by a machine. I was real friends with these people and, well, it was like they had got on a boat in a fast moving stream and I stayed on the bank and, bit by bit, they got smaller and smaller in the distance and, you know, I kept waving from the bank.

Becoming swept up in the machine was to be a recurring theme. The compromise over the task force was hugely symbolic of how policy was to be shaped under what was then 'New' Labour. Tim Burghouse recounted a series of telephone calls from David Blunkett:

> The Standards Task Force, I want you to chair it and I said ok, that's fine and then he rang me up two days after the election and said, I'm terribly sorry but you can't chair it, I have to chair it, you can advise on it. I said ok. Then he rang me up and he said, I don't want you to take this (badly) but we would like two vice-chairs and the other one needs to be Chris Woodhead and I said I think that's one request too far.

In the event, Brighouse's generosity of spirit and commitment to the cause led him to accept the appointment, as joint chair with Her Majesty's Chief Inspector. It was a marriage made in political expediency. Brighouse, worked hard to consummate the relationship but could not bridge either the ideological distance or gulf in personal style. In one corner there was someone who was always open to another point of view, in the other there was someone for whom only one view counted – his own. In Judith Judd's words, 'Woodhead was a man who deals in certainties'. Comparing the two protagonists as representing the twin faces of government, she wrote:

> Teachers saw the former as their friend, the latter as their scourge. The two were meant to symbolise the twin policies of 'pressure and support' which ministers have placed at the centre of their campaign to raise standards.

> (Judd, 1999)

These tensions, while portrayed in two hugely contrasting personalities, say some-thing significant about a government, uneasy with its own radical promise, bring-ing every issue to the touchstone of the *Daily Mail* reader. This juxtaposition of conviction and ambivalence was to remain a constant theme. The bold assertion seemed always to be accompanied by its handmaid – a timidity which attended many attempts to do something completely different; a timidity exemplified most power-fully by Blair's dumping of the Tomlinson report in 2004. 'The biggest failure over this period of the Labour government', as Charles Clarke was to say to the Government Select Committee in March 2010.

New Labour was, from the outset, a government careful never to allow the Opposition to steal a march or alienate middle England. The public and private stance over Chris Woodhead's reappointment, exemplified by the letters below, demonstrate the tensions caused by the need to be seen to be tough and uncompromising.

Sanctuary Buildings
Great Smith St.
SW1P 3BT   18th September 1998

Dear Chris,
I am pleased to offer you a further term of office as HMCI, extending your current term by a further four years. I have greatly appreciated the valuable work that you and Ofsted have done over the past four years and look forward to your continuing support as we drive forward the standards agenda.

With all good wishes
David Blunkett

Fast forward one year.

> Mr Blair has come under pressure to replace Mr Woodhead from David Blunkett, secretary of state for education, who is conducting a private war with the chief inspector.
>
> (*The Independent*, 10th October 1999)

Decisions made in the first four years of government laid the groundwork for what was to come in the next decade. The Task Force on Standards, sitting uncomfortably between the polarities of its two vice-chairs, played a central role in the fashioning of policy under a newly elected government. As a policy sounding board, it reveals much about the nature of political decision-making and consequently about whose voices were heard, and not heard in the policy process.

A chain of voices

Our original title for this book, *Architects, Critics and Prophets*, was dropped in order to avoid librarians misplacing it on the architecture shelves or among Film, Theatre Criticism or Religion sections. Its intention, however, was to highlight the nature of those differing voices, their interplay, the harmonies and discords, those most persua-sive in pushing government in one direction or another and as a consequence which impact most powerfully on the lives of children.

What can we learn from the creation of a policy advisory forum such as the task force? Whose voices did it wish to hear and what combination of people did it assemble around the table? What role for architects, critics and prophets?

The task force was chaired by David Blunkett, supported by a ministerial team of Estelle Morris, Stephen Byers, Charles Clarke and Jacqui Smith (although not all simultaneously), together with an assorted collection of apparatchiks, architects, a few prophets and, only by default, one or two critics. The favourite among the architects was Lord Puttnam, one of whose first acts was to create Oscars for teachers and to help make staffrooms professional places less redolent of shoddy caricatures beloved of films and TV series. Among the prophets was Stephen Heppell who, in 1997, foretold the death of pencils, which he prophesied, by the millennium, would be replaced by hand held computers, equally accessible and likely to be just as cheap. At Blunkett's right hand was Michael Barber who, in his testimony for this book, could claim to be architect, critic and prophet as well. To which another of our witnesses adds, 'ideologically dogmatic and ruthlessly pragmatic'.

And then there were the critics. They were subject to a complete intolerance of criticism of any kind. This lack of tolerance was exemplified in an angry missive sent by David Blunkett to three of his 'ambassadors': Tim Brighouse, Sir David Winkley and John MacBeath, all of whom had the temerity to attend a satirical presentation in Birmingham entitled 'Gradgrind's Children'.

Sanctuary Buildings,
Great Smith Street,
SW1P 3BT   22nd May 1998

Dear John

Gradgrind's Children
I am writing on Friday afternoon having just seen a highly misleading flyer which bills your involvement with the above event on the 31st of May.

I assume the promotion is intended to be satirical. I'm afraid I don't find it amusing. If it is supposed to influence Government thinking, then it has not. It has simply made me angry – and I have to say disappointed that you should lend your name to such an event.

Yours Sincerely

David Blunkett

Sandy Adamson, at the time, the senior civil servant in charge of administering the task force, describes it as 'well meaning floating alongside, or abutting, a whole structure of policy making and delivering'. He asked rhetorically:

> These people you have invited, do you want them there because you genuinely want objective advice? But the points you [John MacBeath] and others, made fell

largely on deaf ears because they had decided what they were going to do anyway. It quickly became a largely ceremonial occasion, reflected clearly in the attitudes of the participants, particularly those from the frontline.

The notion of 'voice'– who is speaking and who is listening – is a central theme of this book. It is a story of policy, how it gets made, by whom, with whom and in whose interests. Through the witnesses called to testify, it raises questions about the extent to which schools can be meaningfully re-invented and how they can make a difference in the lives of children and those who teach them.

The reforming architects whom we interviewed drew attention to the boldness of design, while the critics focused on what it means for people to inhabit those structures and live with the consequences of inherently flawed blueprints. A case in point were the widely diverging views on the impact and success, or otherwise, of the Literacy and Numeracy Strategies. Designed to drive up standards, the architects of the Strategies described them as unapologetically top-down. For example, Michael Barber argued that in order to demonstrate immediate returns, it was necessary to raise the stakes to establish quick wins and demonstrate to the Treasury and the public at large that New Labour would be intolerant of low standards. National targets, 'plucked from the air', as Sandy Adamson described them, were from the architects' perspective, to be the signal drivers of the improvement process.

While 'capacity building' was an implicit goal within the current policy rhetoric, it was juxtaposed with a desultory view of teachers which worked against efforts by government agencies or quangos to try and restore teacher morale and return to them respect for professional judgment. The critics are not alone in reserving judgment as to the success of that wishful intent. There were rueful admissions from minsters in both main political parties that this was a patent failure of policy. There is a fairly wide body of opinion among our witnesses that restoring the professional self-confidence will, for a government of any colour, be a significant challenge; one to be addressed with imagination and a strong grasp of history.

Reinventing schools

> It could be all glass and marble, sir, but it's still a bloody school.

These words, taken from the 1963 Newsom Report and quoted in our Preface, suggest that reinventing schools may be futile unless they are cast in a radically different mould. In 2001, the OECD's *Schooling for Tomorrow* programme proposed six possible scenarios for the future, setting these within a time span of five to fifteen years. These were:

1. Robust bureaucratic systems.
2. Extending the market model.
3. Schools as core social centres.
4. Schools as focused learning organisations.
5. Learner networks and the learning society.
6. The meltdown scenario.

As defined by OECD, the first of the six scenarios is characterised by a focus on the curriculum, usually in the form of a common curriculum and common assessment system aimed at reinforcing standards. Final certificates provide the passport to economic/social life – increasingly necessary, but insufficient. As a scenario, it exists together with continuing inequalities and alongside policy endeavours to combat failure. In the words of the OECD it is, 'built on the continuation of powerfully bureaucratic systems, strong pressures towards uniformity, and resistance to radical change'.

The Labour government's own version of *Schools for the 21st Century* (DCSF, 2008) would find in such description a fairly neat fit. It would be instantly recognisable by the boy in the Newsom report. Yet a 'robust bureaucratic system' may only be a partial description of our current school system which would also be recognisable by the second scenario of an 'extending market model'. Indeed, England's education system would also have aspirations to the third, fourth and fifth scenarios – schools as core social centres, as learning organisations networked with other schools and with centres of learning and socialisation.

In the first of these six scenarios, curriculum and assessment define the nature of schooling. Every political party shares an aspiration for a more egalitarian system. All seek to reduce the gap between haves and have nots. All pursue the objective of raising standards across the board. All aspire to create more equitable routes to higher education and to the economy. No major party would find exceptional Michael Gove's comment that:

> The critical question for me is are we giving our young people the same degree of opportunity that other countries which are comparably wealthy do in theirs?

However, as we noted in a previous chapter, the curriculum is a canvas on which political parties paint their aspirations for society. Yet the language of the curriculum as an 'offer' and the curriculum as an 'entitlement', recurring themes in the previous chapters, sit uncomfortably alongside a curriculum which has effects that are discriminatory and divisive – in Peter Mortimore's words, a system in which 'we make children feel failures from an early age'.

In fact, as our interviews demonstrate, a form of consensus existed between the Conservative Party and the Liberal Democrats at least on education policy in the months prior to the 2010 general election. While during the days after the election there was much speculation about the potential inability of the Conservative and Liberal Democrats Parties to merge their policies, our interviews with Michael Gove and David Laws belied that assumption. That the two parties had fundamental ideological differences is not substantiated by interviews with the two then shadow ministers. If anything, both demonstrated a common weariness with centrally-driven reform. It was David Laws who said in interview that:

> We don't think that you get that [big difference in standards] by having somebody in central government trying to drive improvement for 22,500 schools.

And it was Michael Gove who invoked Tony Blair to make a similar point:

My aim is to carry on with the broad trajectory of change that Blair was on . . . I would argue that Blair . . . had become more convinced of the need for greater professional autonomy than he was in the first few years of his premiership.

Indeed the zeitgeist of greater professional freedom spilled over into the Coalition Agreement post the 2010 general election, which coupled an aspiration to tackle education inequality with all schools having greater freedom over the curriculum.

Whether the coalition in government will go as far as the OECD in its analysis of how freedom in the curriculum and equity should relate to each other is a moot point.

For OECD's Andreas Schleicher, the question is not 'how to protect an established body of knowledge' but how to:

[B]roaden the range of competencies that we use as criteria to define success, how to balance the need for people to act autonomously and to work with socially heterogeneous groups, fostering the capacity and motivation to keep learning.

Motivation to keep on learning may, of course, be undermined by the nature of assessment that accompanies the curriculum. Dylan Wiliam claimed that from the moment they assumed power the Labour government perpetuated a number of fundamental errors; one that entitlement should be age, rather than achievement related; two, to base tests on attainment targets which were defined around subject content in the programmes of study rather than cognitive skills and, three, to misunderstand the nature of standards. Taken together these, he claimed, 'led government to drive policy in directions that are simply not supported by the evidence'. Peter Mortimore concurred:

We know from the Education Select Committee's report that there are serious problems with high stakes testing. The Select Committee says it all – there is little I need to add. The paper submitted to the Committee by three statisticians argues that 30% of the grades are wrong. All this pressure on the system; all this angst amongst pupils and their families and 30% of the grades are wrong! Sadly, but not altogether surprisingly, a few teachers are pressured into doing the wrong thing by massaging the data, or worse.

Nonetheless, governments have persisted in doing what experts have for decades counselled against, and many teachers know to their cost, and that is making assessment serve two masters; of making it serve both formative and accountability purposes. As Peter Mortimore (2009) wrote:

Teachers are encouraged to focus on those students who may help lift the school's rankings. Those who are likely to be borderline candidates in tests are often given the most help. Students with special needs are less likely to be welcomed in schools as they may use more resources – and do less well in the tests

– thus pulling down the school's scores. Our impatient government insists on starting schooling much earlier than in most other countries and thus confronts children with early failure - from which it is very hard to recover.

Assessment *is* for learning, as Scottish policy has it. There the government worked closely with Dylan Wiliam to inform policy development. As we reported in Chapter 6, in England, Judy Sebba warned Paul Black that 'I can't sell this to my guys in the department until you have got evidence that it improves test scores'.

Comparing the stance of the then Labour government with what was happening elsewhere, Mary James said in interview, 'Wales sought to put clear educational water between itself and England', putting money into a development programme on assessment for learning and thinking skills, while Northern Ireland also has created a different system.

> So it's England that has resisted fundamental change and hardened its approach through policy initiatives called *Making Good Progress*, *Assessing Pupil Progress* and the single level test notion. This has been very much pushed by some civil servants, notably the chief adviser on school standards . . . despite the fact that people like Gordon Stobart said this is fundamentally flawed in terms of technical validity and reliability.

Mary James, who has been an adviser to the Welsh Ministry and a member of the Assessment Reform Group since 1992, compared the 'hard measurement' people with the 'softer' approach of the ARG group, coincidently (or perhaps highly significantly) led by a number of women (Eva Baker, Lauren Resnick, Wynne Harlen, Caroline Gipps, Patricia Broadfoot, Sue Swaffield). Their perspective was one that was essentially concerned with the potentially adverse impact on children of measurement ill-conceived.

> The group at one point was described as 'new romantics' by some 'hard measurement' people. I suppose we have been seen as representing something on the softer edge. This may be legitimate but I think our real drive was a need to refocus, less on the instruments, more on the impacts of these experiences on those who were being subjected to them.

Yet despite the strength of the evidence regarding the backwash effects of the current testing regime, government representatives of all persuasions continue to put their faith in summative paper and pencil tests for fulfilling a variety of purposes. In March 2010, four former secretaries of state for education, Conservative and Labour, appeared before a Government Select Committee at which cross-party harmony broke out in robust defence of testing.

MR CLARKE: I am completely with Ken Baker and David Blunkett on this . . . I do not agree with the charge that teaching to the test is destroying the quality of education in schools, and I do not agree that there are too many tests.

BARONESS MORRIS: I am absolutely in favour of testing. If we went away from testing at key points in the education system, we would do a huge disservice to children. That is my fundamental belief.

PAUL HOLMES [MEMBER OF THE PANEL]: So you all think that Ofsted is surely wrong in its report on teaching to the test and the way it distorts schools? Four secretaries of state all think that Ofsted got it completely wrong?

The evidence then is clear. It may not have appealed to policy makers, but without fundamentally rethinking curriculum and assessment and above all the current system of public accountability, schoolchildren will continue to be at the receiving end of high stakes testing and schools will continue to be reinvented in their own image.

Both Michael Gove and David Laws went some way to recognising this in their pre-election interviews, that their reformist views 'weren't always welcomed by professionals' – Laws arguing strongly for an Independent Standards Authority and Gove acknowledging the rigidity of accountability measures. It should not have been surprising that the door to reform swung open with the coalition government's agreement to simplify the regulation of standards to reform league tables and to review Key Stage 2 tests. We believe that the opportunity for a fundamental rethinking now lies within the grasp of schools and policy makers together.

The worst of times?

The sixth OECD scenario – meltdown – is predicated on a new world of growing up in which schools are no longer the only, or even main, educational providers. It is a world in which information and 'intelligence' (in at least one sense of that world) reside more in the ether than in the classroom, less contained, less linear, more characterised by lateral exchange than vertical transmission. What is the 'real' world and what is the 'virtual' world become less easy to distinguish. The meltdown scenario is also premised on a teacher exodus, described as due to 'low teacher morale and buoyant opportunities in more attractive graduate jobs', 'a fortress mentality' and the increasingly unattractive nature of the job in a pressured policy climate. While evidence from the four successive National Union of Teachers' commissioned studies (summarised in Galton and MacBeath, 2008) brought vividly to the fore the potential of that sixth scenario, a fairly dramatic reversal of the teacher shortfall during the 2009 economic recession has at least postponed the realisation of that pessimistic forecast.

What then are the implications for something completely different?

A question of pedagogy

For many our witnesses such as Paul Black, Robin Alexander, and Mary James it comes back in the end to a question of pedagogy. It is a view with places centre stage the agency, initiative and creativity of teachers which successive policies of both political parties have done so much to undermine.

In many situations, particularly those in which high stakes testing play an important role, teachers often behave as if they could do the learning for the learner, with disastrous consequences.

(Black and Wiliam, 2009: 22)

Outlining a coherent theory of assessment, Paul Black and Dylan Wiliam argue for three key spheres of pedagogy of which assessment is an integral part – the internal world of each student, the inter-subjective relationship of teacher-student and student-student, and the teacher's agenda. The teacher brings to his/her interaction with students not a single pre-determined outcome or government mandated target but 'intentions' conceived within a 'horizon of possibilities' within which formative feedback works in both directions – teacher to student and student to teacher.

The Black and Wiliam perspective is one which understands the social world of the classroom, always seeking a 'a more fine-grained understanding of classroom discourse'. It relies on a quite different comprehension of 'standards' from the narrow definition which has slipped so easily and insidiously into what Giroux calls the 'grand narrative'. He wrote a number of years ago:

There is no grand narrative that can speak for us all. Teachers must take responsibility for the knowledge they organise, produce, mediate and translate into practice. If not there is a danger that they come to be seen as simply the technical intervening medium through which knowledge is transmitted to students, erasing themselves in an uncritical reproduction of received wisdom.

(Giroux, 1992: 45)

The implications are in this case again clear. It means giving back to teachers their vital role in classroom assessment, mediating and translating, critical to received wisdom - teaching as an intellectually subversive activity. Ted Wragg once posed the question 'How many assessments do teachers make in the course of a day?' and gave the answer based on his own observation of teachers at work – 'over a thousand'. Those minute by minute assessments tend to be implicit and intuitive but almost always prompted by a learning intentions. It is what teachers do. They can, by their own admission, do it better and are professionally inclined to do it better if the thrust of policy is to enhance the way in which a thousand assessment decisions are taken. This will not happen, as the Primary Review puts it, until there is an 'uncoupling of assessment for accountability from assessment for learning'. Nor will it happen in any meaningful way without an assessment system which takes account of the breadth of students' learning. As the Cambridge Primary Review (2009: 31) said, there is a need for summative assessment which is 'broader, more innovative, and conducted under entirely different conditions than the current system'.

What to do with Ofsted

Given the issues raised in Chapter 7 about inspection and the continued failure to provide an effective and independent form of school review, what to do with Ofsted, has to be high on any government agenda. Liberal Democrat education spokesperson, David Laws, formerly was not entirely confident, either of its independence or the robustness of its data sources.

> The only thing I'm worried about Ofsted is that I have a bit of a sense that it has become, to quite a large extent suffused with the sort of culture and objectives entirely of the government and has got knotted up in the government's objectives and the government's need to improve performance and to show data is improvement that I kind of feel its independence has been rather compromised . . . I think there's a bit of a risk that Ofsted may simply come to measure what government says is important, which may be one particular part of the school system and therefore that Ofsted has got a bit too close to the government and politicians.

Concerns also exist about the ability of some Ofsted inspection teams to understand the principles associated with certain initiatives. Mary James in Chapter 6 points to the failure to understand the ideas associated with Assessment for Learning. Mike Tomlinson hints at this problem during his interview, recalling the days when HMI carried out school inspections:

> Everybody says the same. I've never been in an environment, even where we were delivering difficult messages where the empathy, understanding and respect for our judgments wasn't there. That rapidly disappeared with the new inspection regime.

The inherent problem, argued Carol Fitzgibbon (1998) is a situation where various consortia bid to carry out school inspections, and HMI do not themselves visit schools but use these reports to provide governments with an overall view as to the success or otherwise of their reforms. So it provides its critics with the ammunition to point to the variability in approach of different inspection teams. More crucially, it can be argued that consortia, whose income is derived through inspections, may have a tendency to report in ways that endorse the assumptions inherent in government policy of what works and what does not.

The above quote from David Laws makes it clear that he recognised the problem of Ofsted becoming too 'knotted up' with the government's performance objectives and lacking an independent voice. There is an irony in this as protracted battles had been fought between the Government Select Committee and HMCI Woodhead, who continually asserted Ofsted's independence and refused to acknowledge any accountability, except to the Queen.

David Laws' solution to this problem is to create an independent Education Standards Authority which would 'take Ofsted as one of the things under its umbrella'. Only time will tell whether the coalition government's commitment to 'simplifying the regulation of standards' opens up the possibility of a fundamental review of the way in which schools are evaluated.

The future role of Local Authorities

Mrs Thatcher's pet hate was Local Education Authorities. She was determined to clip their wings and through the financial inducements associated with the Grant Maintained Scheme to encourage schools to remove themselves completely from LEA control. Successive governments have continued to reduce Local Authorities' ability to influence what happens in schools while continuing to hold them accountable for weaknesses. Local Management of Schools ultimately gave headteachers and governors the final say over the deployment of resources, choice of professional development partners and the hiring and firing of teachers. Control of the curriculum was centralised. The Local Authority can offer advice, arrange for professional development if contracted to do so by a sufficient number of schools, but the school ultimately decides whether to avail themselves of these services.

LEAs, it is can be argued, contributed to their own demise. Pauline Perry's account of the failure of some authorities at the time to know anything about the time allocated to each subject during a school week (quoted in Chapter 2) was undoubtedly a serious failing and symptomatic of many lax attitudes towards ensuring that all children were getting 'a fair deal'. Elsewhere, to cite another example, Leicestershire the authority's officers were called advisers, not inspectors, and could only visit schools at the invitation of the headteacher. There was however, one important role that LEAs of the time undertook: they acted as a communication bridge between the teacher in the classroom and the politicians and officials in central government who were responsible for the various interventions and reforms.

Researchers who have studied the innovation process in schools have argued that neither 'top down' or 'bottom up' strategies for promoting change will work unless there is an organisation in the middle dedicated to informing policy makers of the anxieties and problems of implementation faced at school level while at the same time informing schools of the political, social and economic factors that require policy makers to rethink the educational system (Geijsel, Van Den Berg and Sleegers,1999).

In England, acting as the 'communication bridge' should have continued to be a key role of Local Authority inspectors and advisers. One has only to look at the current titles of those working as local inspectors compared to a previous era to see how these roles have changed. Whereas a person might have been previously listed as an English or mathematics inspector they are now designated School Improvement Partners or Community Learning and Skills Development Advisers. One consequence may well be that vital advice on pedagogy and subject knowledge will be lost to schools.

Contrary to the general perception of past Conservative Party attitudes to local authorities, at the time of interview neither Michael Gove nor David Laws considered that the role of local authorities should be scaled back. Both were in agreement about the future role of local authorities. According to Michael Gove:

> Some local authorities . . . want to play a more active role in delivery . . . One of the things I'm most interested in is identifying what it is that we can say or do for local authorities in order to allow them to do that . . . Letting me know what, in Lincolnshire or in Kent, would be an appropriate strategy for school improvement in the next five years.

David Laws took a similar position. Local authorities should:

> have the responsibility for being the first tier of performance management over the school and for driving school improvement.

However, within two weeks of government Gove was, on the right hand, talking of freeing schools from local authority control while with the left writing to LAs to reaffirm his commitment to working with them 'to ensure local authorities continue to play a full strategic part in securing the improvement we all want to see'. (Letter to local authorities of 27th May 2010)

The role of local authorities in the 'vertical relationship' between schools and government is a critical agenda item for all political parties. Rather than basing policy on half full glass of the worst performing Local Authorities there is much to be gained by the learning from the exemplary LAs who have been the lynchpin in making schools better places for children, and their teachers. Framing a positive school improvement role for local authorities, with their aspirations and those of schools at the centre of the debate, would be a step towards regenerating the latent capacity of all schools to work together.

There is a strong argument for the new government to re-examine the education functions of local authorities to refocus them in order to provide practical support in building their relationship with their communities. This requires an imaginative recasting. A democratic relationship between schools and their wider communities needs to be restored, not for its own sake, but to restore to schools a sense of corporate self-efficacy which is the bedrock of 'going the extra mile'.

Schooling for tomorrow?

If curriculum and assessment inexorably shape the experience of school, what is the latitude for children to have a different experience of learning and who holds the key to making schools a place fit for all children? In theory, and in professional aspiration, curriculum and assessment are liberating impulses. Their purpose is to ensure an equal entitlement to skills and knowledge. In practice they tend to be a constraining influence.

Drawing on the OECD six scenarios the French commentator Jean Michel Saussois suggests a two dimensional matrix, a dynamic model in which we can locate the push and pull factors, those which pull schools back to the bureaucratic model and those which push towards schools as social centres, learning organisations and learning networks.

The horizontal axis is a continuum on which to locate schools as closed or open systems. As policy pushes schools towards closed systems, they become more competitive with one another. They lay greater emphasis on internal structures, management of limited time and resource, and allocation of time to curricular and assessment priorities. Teachers are more inclined to be managed through standard operating procedures and are expected to transmit codified knowledge efficiently. Students, for their part, are managed through a constancy of 'flow' from measure to measure,

Figure 10.1 Reinventing schools, Reforming Teaching

grade to grade. Tight integration, co-ordination, and control ensure compliance and stability.

The vertical axis, the north and south poles, represent a continuum from schools as social centres, concerned with equity, social cohesion and collaboration, to, at the opposite pole, schools individualistically oriented, geared to their 'clients' – consumers who exercise choice for individual benefit and to the benefit of one's children.

These idealised schemata are helpful in shedding light on how visions of *Schools for the Future* have to try and resolve the ambiguities and tensions as policy moves along both the values dimension (north to south) and the delivery dimension (east to west). The more they move down the values line the less the authority of societal and consensual values; the more they move from west to east along the delivery axis the greater the competition between public and private, and the 'bog standard' comprehensive school and the academy. Many of government reforms have been conceived from honourable motives. While the economic imperative has been a key driver for most initiatives, another key driver has been grounded in the morality of securing equality of opportunity. Primarily, but not exclusively, the idea of equity of entitlement to high quality education has been a driver for Labour-government policy and is a strong theme in the coalition government.

There have been, of course, common characteristics to this reform process. It has been both imposed and prescriptive. The voices of school communities and teachers have tended to have only a marginal influence on the creation of new policies. The mechanism for driving school reform has been through the use of hard-edged accountability measures with the carrot represented by individualised financial incentives. While school based innovation has had an influence on policy making, it has taken place through the medium of governments cherry-picking individual innovations and converting them into policy. Indeed over the last ten years, cherry-picking by governments has gone global with aspects of whole education systems being used to form policy. Another common characteristic of government during this current reform period is that, for the most part, the development of teachers themselves, particularly their professional learning and the strengthening of self-efficacy has been a low priority. Consequently a characteristic of outstanding education systems, a teaching profession confident in its own knowledge and judgements, is still a long way from being fully realised.

This book has attempted to explore the interweaving, complex and sometimes contradictory motives of government reform programmes. It would be tempting to ask rhetorically whether education reform has been as good as it gets or has simply been sound and fury signifying nothing. That, however, would be a mistake. The dynamics of England's parliamentary democracy are so central to reform that any holier than thou analysis which solely criticises is, in the end, a waste of time. It is far more important that analysis leads to practical and positive recommendations. Such recommendations recognise also that if the optimistic ideal of school improvement is to be maintained then the realities of a robust and combative pluralistic society have to be taken into account.

As our chapter on decision-making showed, the serendipity of public perception and the needs of ministers skew the logical stream of rationality. A recent speech by the department's director general for schools, John Coles, sought to come to terms with the realities of educational policy making (Coles, 2010). He described three overlapping circles of equal importance in developing policies: 'political objectives', 'the evidence base' and the 'delivery reality'. Recognising the political legitimacy of policies and their delivery reality was vital to their success. When asked about whether any policies could maintain a continuum across governments of different political complexions, he said that the maintenance of democracy had to be more important than individual policies. It was the duty of the civil service to make sure that new ministers were aware of the evidence base of what did and didn't work.

In taking this view, Coles echoes Graham Holley's comment that, 'You'll never take the five year cycle out of education'. They both believe however that, again to quote Holley:

> It is the job of . . . good officials . . . to construct, taking into account where they know ministers want to go, a strategy which is permanently fixed on the horizon that has more than a five year vision.

As Andreas Schleicher's comments in Chapter 4 show, Holley's yearning for consistency while acknowledging the political realities is not a recipe for a quiet life. The implication of Schleicher's view that 'consensus and coherence are the two very powerful forces for change' and that 'the lack of coherence in education policies is one of the biggest obstacles' are profound. To co-opt one of Michael Barber's classifications, no country's education system can be outstanding without consensus and coherence. Schleicher himself is very clear that the nature of such coherence has to be based on a set of national values for education achieved through a national consensus. It would be possible to conclude pessimistically that the vagaries of irrationality inherent in England's parliamentary democracy will forever militate against the achievement of national values vital for a world class education system. On the surface that pessimism would seem to have been compounded by the first actions of the coalition government in removing the DCSF's branding and title and casting doubt over all the education policies and guidance of the previous Brown government. Indeed on its first day the coalition government placed the following statement on the new Education Department's website.

> A new UK government took office on 11 May 2010. As a result the content of this site may not reflect current government policy. All statutory guidance and legislation published on this site continues to reflect the current legal position, unless indicated otherwise . . . Thanks to everyone for all your interest in the DfE. Policy teams are now working on the new department's policies to be confirmed in due course.

Apart from the obvious subliminal message that the old ways of doing things continued to operate – with government and its civil servants handing down policies to school communities – the other effect was to give the impression that the entire English education service was temporarily rudderless. There could not have been a more extreme demonstration of how not to create coherence, consistency and continuity.

However, the twin pillars of parliamentary democracy and coherence in policy making are not innately antithetical. It should not be left solely to senior civil servants to seek a vision beyond the natural life of a parliamentary term while juggling the political preferences of their masters. It should be an expectation of all democratically elected governments and opposition parties that they should lay the basis for continuity and coherence..

Some have argued that this vision can be achieved by the 'depoliticisation' of schooling (Ball, TES, 2 April 2010). They imply that coherence and consensus, rather than being dynamic and developing concepts, can be agreed by neutral and disinterested parties. In fact, such debate will never go away and certainly could never be confined to a mythological depoliticised arena. Instead, the fundamental arguments should be about how that debate can be reframed so that the voices of schools and local communities can contribute to the formulation of government policy. We believe that it is a realistic aspiration to expect coherence and consensus to be established within a set of national values. We believe it is the responsibility of government and parliamentary parties, together with school communities, and anyone with a stake in education, to seek to achieve them.

It is vital also that the department creates for itself a culture of in-depth expertise amongst its civil servants instead of seeing such a culture as an impediment to career advance. The default position for the department should be to ask itself, when asked to implement any initiative promoted by ministers and their advisers, what similar initiatives had preceded it and whether they had succeeded or failed? Integral to this approach would be the department's research base whose role should be to not only evaluate current initiatives but to review research on broad themes relating to previous policies. In short, its purpose would be to evaluate what worked and what could work.

Giving teaching back to the teachers

A continuum of policies would not be enough however. Such an approach may ease schools' sense of initiative overload but if the policies are imposed they are hardly likely to be embedded. Lorna Earle's warning about the consequences of teachers' lack of ownership of the strategies is one possible explanation of why the halting of the government's multi-million pound professional development investment was barely noticed by the teaching profession. A comment, by Michael Barber, on why the ending of strategies went unremarked at first sight appears to contradict Earle's recommendation, but in fact, it complements it.

> I think it is because, in the last three/four years, the strategies have had little edge and teachers have neither loved them nor hated them. Or, put another way, they became marginal.

Whereas in the first phase, 1997–2000, some loved them, some hated them, but everyone knew them and very many respected them. Moreover, they knew they were a top priority for government.

Government initiatives may work, but they will not last unless teachers believe they can develop them themselves. Numerous reasons are advanced for the marginalisation and ultimate demise of the strategies and whether they were loved or hated depended in part, as we have argued, on the endorsement or otherwise of the headteacher or other influential voices. Whether they were 'brilliant' in conception or flawed from the outset is now more a matter of history and longstanding differences of opinion on pedagogy which will, possibly forever, remain unresolved. The following footnote from Bethan Marshall of King's College is worth noting, less as a retrospective addition to the debate but as reminder of the importance of the authentic voice.

> Dewey has a great phrase, 'It makes all the difference in the world between having something to say and having to say something' and too often now children have to say something rather than having something to say.

There is an inherent danger, lying in wait in every curricular prescription of children's learned behaviour, a dutiful adherence to form and formula; perhaps an endemic flaw in the very nature of schooling rather than in any particular strategic intervention. As Bethan Marshall comments:

> Children tend to say that there is an exercise and this is what you must do and then they tend to write down what the rubrics of the exercise are rather writing what they actually mean and what they want to say.

Any attempt at changing teachers' practice, however apparently brilliant in conception, has to take account of the fact that imposed change may have positive (or indeed negative) effects but that those effects are generally unlikely to last very long beyond the life of the policy. In such a situation, if there is no deep resonance with teachers' beliefs, the simplest course of action will be a token gesture, 'bolting on' to existing practice without the emotional attachment of 'sticky knowledge'. Imposition may not simply fail to stick but have its own inhibiting effect on teachers' innovation and creativity, as our chapters on accountability and community cohesion show in particular. Government policy-making is most likely to be effective when it is shaped by the principle that a government's role should be to provide the conditions for change rather than trying to legislate the behaviour.

When asked by the Select Committee about the ending of government investment in the programme then Secretary of State Ed Balls responded:

> Twelve years on we are in a more mature place than a national field force giving advice to schools . . . .The National Strategies have had their day, but those days have gone.

Whether the strategies had had their day or the political motive had more to do with the cutting of £200 million from CPD is a moot point, but serves as a further reminder of the processes and politics of re-invention.

What then should happen next? Which policies are likely to influence schooling for tomorrow? What will aid 'transformation' as Saussois describes it?

First, governments need to recognise that to effect this transformation their relationship to schools must be a balanced one in which schools recognise the drivers of policy and governments exhibit greater sensitivity to the pressures facing teachers. Our analysis shows that in the past this lack of balance has led to distortions in the curriculum and to what is taught and amongst many schools to a culture of timidity and caution rather than intellectual adventure and risk-taking. This has been accompanied by an excessive 'long hours' culture whose driver has often been fear of punitive accountability rather than enthusiasm for the job.

Second, there needs to be a recognition by government that schools are at the centre of their communities and that their impact on communities, and their communities' impact on them, is a symbiotic relationship. In many schools located outside London there are children whose parents attended the same schools and were taught by the same teachers. This gives rise to a relationship that can only be defined locally by schools themselves and by local democratic structures. The current top-down approach, accompanied by Ofsted's regulatory model is not an encouragement but an inhibitor to the crucial role schools can play in their communities. The *Every Child Matters* agenda serves as an example. It has evolved into a complex bureaucratic machinery which is miring schools in excessive accountability, particularly in relation to safeguarding, and is distracting local authorities from their core purpose of supporting schools. In their interviews, both Michael Gove and David Laws expressed concerns about the implications of the children's services model, as did a previous secretary of state, Estelle Morris. Michael Gove, for example, said:

> My worry is that the role of Local Authority director of Children's Services is vast. Not just in terms of the proportion of the local authority budget . . . but also . . . [responsibility] . . . for Children's Services, whether it's both crisis management or deep, structural social problems . . . and there is also the whole school improvement agenda.

David Laws said something similar:

I am quite worried . . . [about] . . . attempts to turn schools into multi-disciplinary delivery units [which] . . . are in danger of overloading schools and refocusing them away from the major priorities and tasks . . . and it worries me when I see that the inspection regime is getting fixated on safeguarding.

Those worries not only cross all parties but, as our evidence shows, they are shared by many school communities. Any new government has to ask itself whether the current Children's Services model can continue in its present form.

Our evidence also suggests that if young people without the advantages of a culturally and socially rich home background are to successfully make their way in the world, then there will have to be some imaginative rethinking as to how that disadvantage, re-created from generation to generation, will be addressed. Sufficient funding is of course vital to schools' generative and regenerative role but targeted funding has so far failed to recognise the profound influence of social class on pupil self-efficacy as well as their well being and achievement. Exemplary initiatives such as the Children's University and Playing for Success need continuing support and investment but need to be seen less as compensatory mechanisms than complementary and collaborative ways of enhancing curriculum and assessment.

Hong Kong's recent changes to its secondary school curriculum offers an example of what can be done. Schools are now required to allocate 15 per cent of the allocated curriculum to what is termed, 'Other Learning Experiences'. These require students to take modules in five areas; moral and civic education, aesthetic development, physical development, career related experiences and community service. As such it is a bold move, one designed to counterbalance the intensity of focus on the academic curriculum while at the same time reducing the number of required subjects. The coalition agreement promises a somewhat different path with new Technical Academies proposed, as had been argued for by Kenneth Baker, with an implicit focus on developing separate vocational and international academic qualifications. The argument for a fundamental and integrated 14–19 qualification remains.

Learning beyond the formal curriculum

Building the social, cultural and educational capital which vouchsafe success for all relies on the kind of radical departure attested to by a group of 48 primary and secondary schools in England who work under the umbrella of *Learning to Lead*. These were schools who dared to open the Pandora's Box of learning beyond the curriculum and testing so as to grow young people's self confidence, self belief and self efficacy. In the foreword to the report, enthusiastically launched by Barry Sheerman MP in March 2010, he wrote:

The scheme has last such a lasting impression on me that I have become the ambassador for Learning to Lead and constantly extol its virtues when I am in education settings. Whether it is a system, programme, or a social level, I have seen how it empowers students and staff to transform their learning culture. I believe it should be at the heart of every school in the country.

(Frost and MacBeath, 2010, Foreword)

A visitor, equally impressed by the empowerment of young people through Learning to Lead was Michelle Obama who visited the pioneering school of the movement, the Blue School, in 2009. Founded on the belief that students have an incipient capacity for leadership, that they have natural desire to learn, and an ability to make a difference to their schools and communities, these are schools that have got hold of a big idea, that are able, in David Hargreaves' words to 'fly below the radar'.

> I felt like someone had catapulted me eight years into the future and shown me what meaningful education could be like.
>
> (Deputy headteacher)

These schools testify to the need for a flexible and supportive curriculum, the evidence for which is now overwhelming. A national framework curriculum which sets out common entitlements for all children and young people and which explicitly expects school communities to develop their curricula in response to their children's needs, including their educational capital, as these 48 schools show, is a pre-requisite for the successful entry of young people into the adult world.

It follows, therefore, that an accountability system for schools has to be located in the concept that school improvement must be owned by school communities themselves if it is to be embedded. Ofsted in its various attempts to reinvent itself remains patently unfit for purpose. Its rigidities and requirements are harnessed to a punitive model of imposed penalties for government-defined failure.

Crashing jumbos

School effectiveness and school improvement has been a potent influence on governments' thinking and on their approach to evaluating schools and school improvement ever since Michael Rutter and Peter Mortimore were able to show that 'schools make a difference'. It would be a surprising finding were it not otherwise, but the 'proof' rested on what was then known a 'school effects' paradigm resting on quantitative analyses of attainment and an attempt to control the annoying variables such as parents, prior learning and peer group influence.

The Holy Grail, as seen by some within the effectiveness camp was schools as HROs or High Reliability Organisations (Stringfield, 1995). This vision inspired, apparently, by watching successive aircraft land on the runway in almost the same spot was a model for schools if we could only get the science right. Famously, David Reynolds (one time chair of the Numeracy Task Force) told a bemused, and not altogether receptive, NUT audience, 'you are crashing jumbos every day'.

While not everyone within the effectiveness 'movement' was equally convinced of the HRO analogy, the influence of the quantification methodology was powerful, furnishing governments with comparative data, Ofsted with indicators, parents with league tables and the Department with a School Improvement Unit under the Conservatives, and a School Effectiveness Unit under Labour. With increasing sophistication in playing the numbers it gave us value-added which, unfortunately, had little to do with values. It is perhaps the saddest legacy of effectiveness research that its claim was to be 'value free', that its rationale was founded on measurement of inputs and outputs, or 'outcomes' – a term which now dominates and distorts the educational discourse and drives its handmaiden- accountability. The mechanistic language of outcomes lies uncomfortably with its strange bedfellow – 'vision', a characteristic generally associated with saints or the deranged.

There is, nonetheless, an urgent need for a new way of seeing improvement and reframing accountability, 'not as a final judgment' as Earle and Katz argue, but

> [A]s part of the toolkit for understanding current performance and formulating plans for reasonable action. . . . not as a static numerical accounting but as a conversation, using data to stimulate discussion, challenge ideas, rethink directions, and monitor progress, providing an ongoing image of their school as it changes, progresses, stalls, regroups, and moves forward again.
>
> (Earl and Katz, 2006: 13)

For a new government, how schools are 'measured', how improvement is 'measured' and how schools tell their story needs some bold and creative dismantling of the formulaic approaches to self evaluation, the prescriptive and undifferentiated role of the School Improvement Partner (the SEF and the SIP) and a radical revisiting of what Oftsed is for and what it achieves.

Accompanying Ofsted's accountability mechanism is its handmaiden, public examination and assessment results used as a proxy to evaluate institutional effectiveness. As our chapter on assessment shows, using such results as a high stakes school evaluation model has not only misled parents and the wider public about the effectiveness of schools, it has muddied and poisoned the nature of pupil assessment itself. Indeed, from the evidence we have received, the high stakes nature of the use of public examination results to evaluate schools has had a seriously damaging effect on examination standards.

For institutional accountability to be effective it has to create the conditions for change and improvement which lasts. The new government must therefore initiate a fundamental and independent review of the way in which schools are evaluated. Such a review must be accompanied by an independent review of the assessment of the National Curriculum, the principle purpose of which would be to disentangle it from institutional evaluation and refocus it on enhancing children's learning.

And what of teachers themselves? They and their support staff colleagues are members of powerful communities whose job it is to encourage children's optimism for the future as well as an enthusiasm for learning. The Cambridge Primary Review's evidence is that this is not empty rhetoric. That primary school children see their schools as beacons of hope is a testament to teachers and support staff. It is extraordinary, therefore, that no government since the early seventies has focused on enhancing, as a top priority, the professional development of teachers. There are, in our accounts, regretful retrospective testimonies from policy makers in both major parties that they did not do enough to support professional development and enhance the quality of teaching and teacher morale.

Management consultants such as PricewaterhouseCoopers and KPMG invest enormous amounts in the continuing training of their employees, believing rightly that it is the knowledge and skills of their employees which represent their companies' value. No such attitude as yet permeates government strategy for teacher learning. There is no reference to a strategy for the teaching profession within the Coalition Agreement. Indeed, the default position is that when economic times get tough, it is teachers' professional development which is the first to be cut. We believe this attitude has to change.

In this book we have sought to explore the relationship between teachers, their school communities and government. The Labour government's enthusiasm for education was entirely justified as key international evidence shows. Our argument is that, in recognising this self evident truth, education deserves better than being buffeted by the vagaries of decision-making which neither benefit the re-invention of schools nor the reform of teaching.

Democratic debate and focus on education are vital in that they signify an underlying recognition of the importance of education. It has to continue but the virtues of a pluralist society need also to be built on. Recognising areas of agreement as well as identifying differences should be the hallmark of future educational policy development. The teaching profession, school communities, parliamentary opposition parties and government itself, all have the capacity to develop coherent, consistent and long lasting common policies which work. For us there can be no other option.

And now? A postscript

Our book was written over a period of nearly a year in which we were continuously overtaken by events and a desire to rewrite history. The need to update our narrative was at its most acute in the days and weeks running to a general election, the outcomes of which could not have been predicted but have added a certain poignancy to the testimonies of some of our interviewees. A post election postscript allowed us to respond to decisions made by the coalition government three weeks into its political life. The impact of those decisions on the re-invention of schools and the reforming of teaching may prove to be as far reaching as they are unpredictable.

In this context the 2010 Academies Act represents a seismic change. The establishment of academies as state-funded schools will not now require local authority approval. In similar form, this represents a revisiting of the previous Conservative government's promotion of grant maintained schools.

The semiotics of the Academies Bill are fascinating. An accompanying Department for Education contained the following statements:

- The bill implements longstanding policy set out in the Conservative Party Manifesto on expanding the academy sector to include outstanding schools and give them greater freedom.
- There has been no consultation on the provisions of this bill, although the plans have been welcomed by expanding schools.

It is worth reflecting on these statements. The Academies bill is drawn from, and cited specifically as a Conservative Party Manifesto commitment and not as part of the Coalition Agreement. Justification for introducing the bill without consultation was made plain in Conservative Party manifesto and is not a product of an educational coalition.

Irrespective of the semiotics, it seems to us that the action and methodology of the new government in fast-tracking the bill parallels the 'roll out strategy' of the Labour government in 1997 with which we began this book. Seeking quick wins with 'low hanging fruits' reforms bypassed the courtesy of consultation and was a portent of troubles to come. Plus ça change? Perhaps. The continuation and acceleration of policy on academies initiative, entirely politically and ideologically driven without reference to the evidence, may still prove the government's undoing. As Simon Jenkins reminded the government (*The Guardian*, 27 May, 2010), while academies cost three times the amount of a local school, a 'steady trickle' of reports have shown no academy effect and indeed offer 'staggeringly bad value for money'.

Any comment that we might make at the time of writing on the bill is bound to have been superseded by legislative and political developments after this book's publication. It is worth considering, however, the strategic implications of the bill in relation to our own witnesses and to the evidence. A number of witnesses come to mind with the onset of a radical bill heralding major structural change. The first is Michael Gove who said that 'whenever you have a new government, people start off with zeal, enthusiasm and idealism'. In contrast, Mike Tomlinson's assertion that there is 'nothing rational about decision-making' and Andreas Schleicher's view that 'consensus and coherence are two very powerful forces for change', sit either side of Michael Gove's enthusiasm both as warnings and imprecations.

Perhaps even more pertinent is Andreas Schleicher's rhetorical question, which we believe any new enthusiastic and reforming government has to ask itself:

> If your goals vary, how do you motivate anyone, albeit the teacher of a class or the student, to take learning seriously ... if you're a teacher, you know today that they're trying this and tomorrow there is something else?

It is worth bearing in mind, however, Michael Gove's first message as secretary of state for education (internal communication, 12 May 2010) where he argued that he wanted to offer:

> All schools a chance to enjoy academy-style freedom so that heads and teachers across the country can be liberated.

It is a powerful rhetoric but one that begs the question – 'freedom' for whom and for what purpose? 'Liberation' from what and at what price? In previous chapters we referred to a weariness with centrally imposed initiatives expressed by both Michael Gove and David Laws in their pre-election interviews. Perhaps we should not be surprised that the first act of the new government should be to capitalise on that weariness by introducing structural reforms which the dominant partner of the coalition had historically treasured.

Despite the assertion in the Act's Impact Assessment 'that academies have been shown to raise standards more quickly than other types of school', we have are unable to find any evidence, either nationally or internationally, that structural reform of itself leads to an automatic rise in achievement against standards. Rather, our analysis of structural reform during the Labour years suggests that it tended to pre-occupy and slow down coherent and consensual change. Good examples of this were the stasis caused by the reorganisation of local authorities following the Children Act 2003, and concern that the Labour government's focus on standards dissipated once Blair had become pre-occupied with structural reform.

The legislation is also confused in its objectives. Bizarrely, academy status is both awarded to 'outstanding' schools which request it and required of failing schools as a punishment. It also appears to contradict the Coalition Agreement's commitment to:

> promote radical devolution of power and greater financial autonomy to local government and community groups.

Our analysis of the initiative is that, in fact, the academies programme undermines local community power and removes from local communities the power to hold their schools accountable. In fact, as Simon Jenkins noted:

> whatever is wrong with English schools . . . it is not governance… people seem to prefer them run through some sort of local democracy.

Despite this preference, we believe that the direction of travel of the coalition government's academies programme is towards a centrally run and centrally controlled school system with the levels of freedom enjoyed by schools now determined solely by the government.

It is unclear at the time of writing whether, in government, Michael Gove has now changed his mind in relation to earlier speculations about a future school improvement and quality assurance role for local authorities. Perhaps such comments demonstrated a confusion about the future of local authorities. Whether or not this is the case, his comments were surely right. School improvement and quality assurance should be the role of local authorities. Local authorities do not represent a collective ogre of imposition. The fact that the vast majority of schools have not opted out is testament to that. Indeed at their best, they can act as a protection for teacher entitlements as Judy Sebba so presciently identified in her interview for this book.

We believe that the coalition government has yet to take a strategic view about the relationship of schools to their communities. The policy borrowing from Sweden of the so-called 'free schools' is not, suggests Mats Ekholm (previously minster for education in that country), one he would commend. These schools, he says, have tended to be used by religious groups 'who want to isolate their children from the evils of normal society' and tend to be sited 'where the largest number of conservative voters live'. Fifteen years on from their creation and on the basis of numerous Swedish studies his considered verdict – 'much ado about nothing'.[1]

And we still await a strategy for the future of the teaching profession. Given its self-evident weariness with imposition, it would surely have been far better for the government to have initiated a genuine and thorough consultation about the future relationship of schools to their communities, including the role of local authorities. It was not, after all, local authorities who introduced excessive bureaucracy and imposition yet were in their own turn named and shamed for their lack of compliance to governmental dictate.

Whether consultation with teachers would have led to fundamental changes to the local authority/school paradigm is open to speculation but such an approach would have at least attempted the first principle of coherence; that of including in consultation all those who are expected to implement reform.

A deep concern remains. Neither the Coalition Agreement nor the government's intended Education Bills for the 2010/2011 parliamentary session heralded any strategy for the teaching profession. Like all those concerned with education, we share an anxiety about the potential impact of any future financial cuts and believe firmly that continuing investment in education is absolutely vital for boosting the country's knowledge economy. Yet, the default position, over time, seems to have been that programmes for the development of teachers are the first to be cut. The silence of the coalition government on the future of the teaching profession, in fact, heralds an opportunity. Manifesto commitments have not been made. Legislation is not already set in stone. We hope, therefore, that our book may persuade this and future governments to focus on what matters most to the achievement of an outstanding education system; a confident and positive teaching profession, at the edge of its game in terms of its learning and engaged as equals in the development of future reforms. The future for young people, and the nation, depends on it.

Notes

4 In the end, teachers are on their own

1 For readers who might be, like one of three authors, out of touch with rugby metaphors, there is apparently a reluctance among the rugger fraternity to catch a pass that, with an incredible hulk bearing down on him, has every possibility of landing him in hospital.

5 Inventing and reinventing the curriculum

1 *Creativity: Find it, Promote it. A 3-Year* QCA Project online. Available: www.ncaction.org.uk (accessed: 15 September 2008).

7 Promoting and delivering value for money?

1 Kupiainen, S. Hautamäki, J. and Karjalainen, T. (2009) *The Finnish Education System and PISA*, Ministry of Education.

8 Going global

1 UNICEF (2007) *An Overview of Child Well Being in Rich Countries: Report Card 7*, Geneva.
2 In Rhode Island, Newark, New Jersey and Seattle for example, described in MacBeath (2006) *School Inspection and Self Evaluation,* London: Routledge, pp. 183–93.

Postscript

1 Personal communication, May 2010.

Interviewees

Sandy Adamson Senior Civil Servant formerly in the DFEE, now Education Consultant at Serco

Professor Robin Alexander, Faculty of Education, University of Cambridge and Director of the Primary Review

Sir William Atkinson, Headteacher, Phoenix High School, Hammersmith and Fulham

Kenneth Baker, Peer and Former Secretary of State for the Department for Education and Science

Sir Michael Barber, Global Education Consultant, McKinsey Foundation, and former Head of the Prime Ministers Delivery Unit

Keith Bartley, Chief Executive of the General Teaching Council (England)

Professor David Berliner, Regents Professor of Education, Arizona State University

Paul Black, Emeritus Professor of Science Education, King's College, London

Mary Bousted, General Secretary, Association of Teachers and Lecturers

Sir Tim Brighouse, Formerly Director of Birmingham Education Authority and Director London Challenge

Kevan Collins, Former Director of Children's Services, Tower Hamlets, now Chief Executive of Tower Hamlets Local Authority

Philippa Cordingley, Chief Executive of CUREE

Michael Davidson, Senior Policy Analyst for the Organisation for Economic Co-operation and Development

Richard Garner, Education Editor of the Independent and the Independent on Sunday newspapers

Michael Gove, Shadow Secretary of State for Children, Schools and Families

Professor David Hargreaves, Former Director, QCA, Special Schools And Academies Trust, Emeritus Fellow, Wolfson College, University of Cambridge

Richard Harrison, Retired Civil Servant from the DfES/DCSF

Graham Holley, Chief Executive at the Training and Development Agency

Mary James, Professor and Associate Director of Research, Faculty of Education, University of Cambridge

Jim Knight, Peer and Former Minister of State for Schools

David Laws, Liberal Democrats Spokesperson for Education

John Lloyd, Former National Development Officer for the Amalgamated Electricians and Engineers Union

Alasdair MacDonald, Head Teacher, Morpeth Secondary School, Tower Hamlets

Bethan Marshall, Senior Lecturer, King's College, London

Fiona Millar, Journalist and Author, former Adviser to the Prime Minister

Estelle Morris, Peer and former Secretary of State at the DfES

Professor Peter Mortimore, Former Director of the Institute of Education, University of London

Pauline Perry, Peer and former Her Majesty's Chief Inspector

David Puttnam, Peer and Chairman, Board of Trustees, Futurelab

Conor Ryan, Former Education Adviser to David Blunkett and to the Prime Minister

Professor Karen Seashore, Rodney Wallace Professor at the University of Minnesota

Judy Sebba, Formerly Senior Advisor Research, Standards and Effectiveness Unit, Department for Education and Employment, now Senior Lecturer at the University of Sussex

Barry Sheerman, MP and former Chair of the House of Commons Children's Services and Families Select Committee

Gillian Shephard, Peer and Former Secretary of State at the DfES

Andreas Schleicher, Head of the Indicators and Analysis Division (Directorate of Education), OECD

Sir Mike Tomlinson, Former HMCI and Chief Advisor for London Schools, Department for Children, Schools and Families

Mick Waters, Former Director of the Curriculum at the Qualifications and Curriculum Authority and Chair of the Curriculum Foundation

Geoff Whitty, Director of the Institute of Education, University of London

Bibliography

Academies Bill (2010). Introduced in the House of Lords. 26 May. http://www.publications. parliament.uk/pa/Idhansrd/text/100526–0001.htm (accessed: 15 June 2010).

Advisory Council on Education in Scotland (1947.) *Secondary Education: A report of the Advisory Council on Education in Scotland,* (Cmd.; 7005) Edinburgh: Her Majesty's Stationery Office. (Hamilton Report).

Alexander, R. (1997) *Policy and Practice in Primary Education: Local initiative, national agenda*, 2nd edn., London: Routledge.

—— (2000) *Culture and Pedagogy: International Comparisons of Primary Education*, Oxford: Blackwell.

—— (2004) 'Still no pedagogy? Principle, pragmatism and compliance in primary education,' *Cambridge Journal of Education,* 34 (1): 7–33.

—— (2009) Children, their world, their education: Towards a New Primary Curriculum: A report from the Cambridge Primary Review. Part I: Past and present, Cambridge: University of Cambridge, Faculty of Education (Interim reports). Final report and recommendations of the Cambridge Primary Review, London: Routledge

—— (ed.) (2010) *Children, their World, their Education: Final report and recommendations of the Cambridge Primary Review,* London: Routledge.

Alexander, R.J. and Flutter, J. (2009) *Towards a New Primary Curriculum: A report from the Cambridge Primary Revew. Part I: Past and present,* 17, Cambridge: University of Cambridge, Faculty of Education (Interim reports). Online. Available: http://www.primaryreview.org. uk/Downloads/Curriculum_report/CPR_Curric_rep_Pt1_Past_Present.pdf (accessed: 28 May 2010); Reproduced with amendments as: Curriculum: past and present, in R. Alexander (ed.) (2010) *Children, their world, their education: final report and recommendations of the Cambridge Primary Review,* London: Routledge: 202–236.

Ascham, R. (1888) *The Schoolmaster*, London: Cassell. (Cassell's national library; 137. Originally published in 1570 under the title, *The Scholemaster*).

Auld, R. (1976) *The William Tyndale Junior and Infant Schools: A report of the public Inquiry conducted by Mr Robin Auld, QC into the teaching, organisation and management of the William Tyndale Junior and Infant Schools, Islington, London N.1*, London: Inner London Education Authority (ILEA).

Baker, K. (1993) *The Turbulent Years, My Life in Politics,* London: Faber and Faber.

Ball, S. (2010) Battle lines drawn in fight to remove politics from education, London, *Times Educational Supplement,* April 2, Online. Available: http://www.tes.co.uk/article. aspx?storycode=6040351 (accessed: 20 May 2010).

Bangs, J. (2006) 'Social partnership: the wider context', *Forum: for promoting 3–19 comprehensive education,* 48, (2): 207, Online. Available: http://www.wwwords.co.uk/pdf/validate.asp?j=f

orum&vol=48&issue=2&year=2006&article=11_bangs__forum_48_2_web (accessed: 27 May 2010).

Barber, M. (1996) *The Learning Game, Arguments for an Education Revolution*, London: Victor Gollanz.

—— (1998) The Dark Side of the Moon: Imagining an End to Failure in Urban Education, in L. Stoll and K. Myers (eds.) *No Quick Fixes: Perspectives on Schools in Difficulty.* London: Falmer Press, pp. 17–33. (The TES-Greenwich Lecture 1995, Woolwich Town Hall, London, 11 May 1995)

—— (2007) *Instruction to Deliver: Tony Blair, the Public Services and the Challenge of Achieving Targets*, London: Politico's Publishing.

Bassey, M. (1978) *Nine Hundred Primary School Teachers*, Slough: NFER Publishing.

Bayley, R. (1998) Not another blooming sunflower, in S. Dainton (ed.) *Take Care, Mr Blunkett*, London: Association of Teachers and Lecturers (ATL).

Beard, R. (19989) *National Literacy Strategy: A review of the research and other evidence*. Sudbury: Department for Education and Employment.

Bennett, N. (1975) *Teaching Styles and Pupil Progress*, London: Open Books.

—— (1987) The Search for the Effective Primary School Teacher, in S. Delamont (ed.) *The Primary School Teacher*, Lewes, Sussex: Falmer Press, pp. 45–61.

—— (1988) The effective primary school teacher: The search for a theory of pedagogy, *Teaching and Teacher Education*, 4 (1): 19–30.

Bennett, N., Andreae, J., Hegarty, P. and Wade, B. (1980) *Open Plan Schools: Teaching, curriculum, design*, Slough: NFER for the Schools Council.

Bentley, T. (1998) *Learning Beyond the Classroom: Education for a changing world*, London: Routledge.

Berliner, D. (2006) Our impoverished view of Educational Reform, *Teachers College Record*, 108 (2): 949–995.

Bernstein, B. (1970) Education cannot compensate for society, *New Society*, 15 (387), 26 February: 344–347 (Reproduced in: Reproduced in B. R. Cosin, I.R. Dale, G.M. Esland, D.F. Swift (eds.) for the Schooling and Society Course at the Open University. *School and Society: A sociological reader*. London: Routledge & Kegan Paul in association with the Open University Press, 1971: 61–66. Also reproduced in B. R. Cosin, I.R. Dale, G.M. Esland, D. Mackinnon and D.F. Swift (eds.) for the Schooling and Society Course at the Open University. *School and Society: A Sociological Reader*. 2nd ed. for the Schooling and Society Course at the Open University. London: Routledge & Kegan Paul in association with the Open University Press, 1977: 64–69.

Black, P. and Wiliam, D. (2009) Developing a Theory of Formative Assessment, *Educational Assessment, Evaluation and Accountability*, 21 (1): 5–31.

Blatchford, P., Bassett, P., Brown, P., Koutsoubou, M., Martin, C., Russell, A., Webster, R. and Rubie-Davis, C. (2009) *Deployment and Impact of Support Staff in Schools: The impact of support staff in schools (results from strand 2, wave 2)*, London: Department for Children, Schools and Families. (Research report; DCSF-RR148). Online. Available: http://www.dcsf.gov.uk/research/data/uploadfiles/DCSF-RR148.pdf (accessed: 3 June 2010).

Boothroyd, H.S. (1923) *A History of the Inspectorate: being a short account of the origin and development of the inspecting services of the Board of Education*, London: Board of Education Inspectors' Association.

Bramall, S.N. and White, J. (2000) *Why Learn Maths?*, London: Institute of Education, University of London. (Bedford Way Papers; 13).

Brighouse, T. (1997) Leading and Managing Primary Schools: The changing world of the Local Education Authority, in C. Cullingford (ed.) *The Politics of Primary Education*, Buckingham: Open University Press, pp. 101–113.

Bright, M. (2000) Traumatised teachers hit back. Our report on the teacher who killed herself after an aggressive Ofsted inspection has prompted a flood of similar accounts, *The Observer*, 23 April: 10. Online. Available: http://www.guardian.co.uk/uk/2000/apr/23/education. ofsted (accessed: 4 June 2010).

Brophy, J.E. (2004) *Motivating Students to Learn,* 2nd edn. Mahwah, N.J.: Lawrence Erlbaum.

Brown, M., Askew, M., Baker, D., Denvir, H. and Millett, A. (1998) Is the National Numeracy Strategy research based? *British Journal of Educational Studies,* 46 (4): 362–385.

Bruner, J. and Haste, H. (eds.) (1987) *Making Sense: The child's construction of the world,* London: Methuen.

Cambridge Primary Review (2007) Community Soundings: Interim Report, University of Cambridge

Burgess, H. (2010) Primary workforce management and reform, in R. Alexander, R. (ed.) *The Cambridge Primary Review Research Surveys,* London: Routledge.

Campbell, J. (1993) A dream at conception: A nightmare at delivery, in R. J. Campbell, (ed.) *Breath and Balance in the Primary Curriculum*, London: Falmer Press, pp. 17–30.

—— (1998) Broader thinking about the Primary Curriculum, in S. Dainton and Association of Teachers and Lecturers (eds.) *Take Care Mr Blunkett: Powerful voices in the new curriculum debate*, London, Association of Teachers and Lecturers (ATL), pp. 96–101.

Carter, B., Stevenson, H. and Passy, R. (2010) *Industrial Relations in Education: Transforming the school workplace*, London: Routledge.

Castells, M. (2000) *The Rise of the Network Society: The information age: economy, society and culture*, 2nd edn. Oxford: Blackwell.

Central Advisory Council for Education (England) (1967) *Children and their Primary Schools,* A Report of the Central Advisory Council for Education (England). Vol. 1, The Report. London, Her Majesty's Stationary Office (HMSO) (Also known as: Plowden Report). Online. Available: http://www.educationengland.org.uk/documents/plowden/ (accessed: 7 June 2010).

Chowdry, H., Crawford, C. and Goodman, A. (2009) *Drivers and Barriers to Educational Success: Evidence from the longitudinal study of young people in England*, London: Department for Children, Schools and Families, (Research Report – DCSF-RR102). Online. Available: http://www. dcsf.gov.uk/research/data/uploadfiles/DCSF-RR102.pdf (accessed: 7 June 2010).

Coleman, J.S. (1966) *Equality of Educational Opportunity,* Washington, D.C.: U.S. Office of Education. Online. Available: http://www.eric.ed.gov/ERICDocs/data/ericdocs2sql/ content_storage_01/0000019b/80/33/42/82.pdf (accessed: 4 June 2010).

Conservative Party. Public Services Improvement Policy Group, (2007) *Restoring Pride in our Public Services: Submission to the Shadow Cabinet,* London: Conservative Party. (Chairman: Stephen Dorrell). Online. Available: http://www.conservatives.com/pdf/psipg-report.pdf (accessed: 7 June 2010).

Cordingley, P. and Bell, M. (2007) *Transferring Learning and Taking Innovation to Scale,* London: Innovation Unit. Online. Available: http://www.innovation-unit.co.uk/images/stories/ files/pdf/transferring_learning.pdf (accessed: 7 June 2010).

Cordingley, P., Bell, M., Rundell, B. and Evans, D. (2003) *The Impact of Collaborative CPD on Classroom Teaching and Learning: How does collaborative Continuing Professional Development (CPD) for teachers of the 5–16 age range affect teaching and learning?*, London: University of London, Institute of Education, Social Science Research Institute, EPPI Centre. Online. Available. http:// eppi.ioe.ac.uk/cms/LinkClick.aspx?fileticket=lvR%2bp8KX%2bRM%3d&tabid=132&mi d=758&language=en-US (accessed: 27 May 2010).

Coles, J. (2010) Making Policy Happen: Improving practice in the DCSF, Paper presented at the The DCSF Research Conference 2010, *The Use of Evidence in Policy Development and Delivery*, QEII Conference Centre, London, February 9.

Crichton, J. (2005) *School Drop-Out and its Consequences: The disadvantaged, the disaffected, the disappeared,* Zagreb: Network of Education Policy Centres. Online. Avaialble: http://www.edu-policy.net/images/old/57_johanna_crighton_do.pdf (accessed: 4 June 2010).

Cuban, L. and Tyack, D. (1995) *Tinkering towards Utopia: A century of public school reform,* Cambridge, Mass.: Harvard University Press.

Dainton, S. (1998) 'Introduction', in Association of Teachers and Lecturers (ed.) *Take Care Mr Blunkett: Powerful voices in the new curriculum debate,* London, Association of Teachers and Lecturers (ATL), pp. 13–20.

Department for Children, Schools and Families (DCSF) (2007) *The Children's Plan: Building Brighter Futures.* London: The Stationery Office. (Cm 7280). Online. Available at: http://publications.dcsf.gov.uk/eOrderingDownload/The_Childrens_Plan.pdf (accessed: 25 May 2010).

—— (2008) *21st Century Schools: A World Class Education for Every Child,* London, Department for Children, Schools and Families. Online. Available: http://publications.dcsf.gov.uk/eOrderingDownload/DCSF-01044–2008.pdf. (accessed: 25 May 2010)

——(2009) *Report of the Expert Group on Assessment,* London: DCSF. Online. Available: http://publications.dcsf.gov.uk/eOrderingDownload/Expert-Group-Report.pdf (accessed: 8 June 2010).

Department for Education Academies Bill. Memorandum for the House of Lords Committee on Delegated Powers and Regulatory Reform from the Department for Education. http://www.education.gov.uk/~/media/files/lacuna/academiesbillprrcmemo.ashx (accessed: 15 June 2011).

Department for Education and Employment (1998) *Teachers: Meeting the Challenge of Change,* London: The Stationery Office. Cm; 4164.

Department for Education and Skills (2003) *Excellence and Enjoyment: a strategy for primary schools,* London: DfES. Online. Available: http://nationalstrategies.standards.dcsf.gov.uk/node/88755 (accessed: 4 June 2010).

Dewey, J. (1916) *Democracy and Education: An introduction to the philosophy of education,* New York: Macmillian.

DfEE (Department for Education and Employment) (1999) Teachers: meeting the challenge of change (Government Green Paper) London: Her Majesty's stationary Office (HMSO).

DfES (Department for Education and Skills) (2003) *Excellence and Enjoyment: A strategy for primary schools,* London: DfES.

Dickens, C. (1970) *A Tale of Two Cities,* Harmondsworth: Penguin Books.

Dweck, C. S. (1986). Motivational processes affecting learning, *American Psychologist.* 41 (10): 1040–1048.

Earl, L. and Katz, S. (2006). *Leading in a Data Rich World: Harnessing data for school improvement.* Thousand Oaks, Calif.: Corwin Press.

Earl, L., Watson, N., Levin, B., Leithwood, K., Fullan, M. and Torrance, N. (2003) *Watching and Learning 3: Final Report of the External Evaluation of England's Implementation of the National Literacy and Numeracy Strategies,* (London), Department for Education and Skills. Online. Available: http://www.dcsf.gov.uk/research/data/uploadfiles/DfES-WatchLearn%20Main.pdf (accessed: 7 June 2010).

Fitzgibbon, C. (1998) Ofsted Methods Fail to Impress, London, *Times Educational Supplement,* 28 September.

Frost, D. and MacBeath, J. (2010) *Learning to Lead: An evaluation, Leadership for Learning.* University of Cambridge Faculty of Education, Online, Available: http://www.learningtolead.org.uk/pdfs/LtoLfinal_report.pdf (accessed: 20 May 2010).

Galton, M. (1989) *Teaching in the Primary School,* London: David Fulton.

—— (2006) *Learning and Teaching in the Primary School*, London: Sage Publications.

Galton, M. and Fogelman, K (1988) The Use of Discretionary Time in the Primary School, *Research Papers in Education*, 13 (2): 119–39.

Galton, M. (1987) An ORACLE Chronicle: A decade of classroom research, in S. Delamont (ed.) *The Primary School Teacher,* Lewes, Sussex: Falmer Press, pp. 21–44.

Galton, M. and MacBeath, J. (2002) *A Life in Teaching: The impact of change on primary teachers' work lives: A report commissioned by the National Union of Teachers concerning the workloads in primary schools,* London: National Union of Teachers. Online. Available: http://www.educ.cam.ac.uk/people/staff/galton/NUTreport.pdf (accessed: 4 June 2010).

—— (2008) *Teachers Under Pressure*, London: Sage in association with the National Union of Teachers (NUT).

Galton, M. and Pell, T. (2010) Study on small class teaching, in *Primary Schools in Hong Kong: Final Report*, Hong Kong: Education Bureau; Cambridge: University of Cambridge. Online. Available: http://www.edb.gov.hk/FileManager/EN/Content_4232/Final%20Report%20of%20Study%20on%20SCT_(Dec2009).pdf (accessed: 4 June 2010).

Galton, M., Simon, B. and Croll, P. (1980) *Inside the Primary Classroom*, London: Routledge & Kegan Paul.

Geijsel, F., Van Den Berg, R. and Sleegers, P. (1999) The innovative capacity of schools in primary education: a qualitative study, *International Journal of Qualitative Studies in Education*, 1366–5898, 12 (2): 175–191.

Giroux, H. A. (1992; 2nd edn 2005) *Border Crossings: Cultural workers and the politics of education* London: Routledge.

Gibbons, M., Limoges, C., Nowotny, H., Schwartzman, S., Scott, P. and Trow, M. (1994) *The New Production of Knowledge: The dynamics of science in contemporary societies,* London; Thousand Oaks, Calif.: Sage.

Goldstein, H. (1993) Improving assessment: A response to the BERA Policy Task Group Report on assessment, *Curriculum Journal*, 4 (1): 121–123.

Gove, M. (2010) Michael Gove: 'We will End the Political Controls of A Levels', speech delivered at Advisory Committee for Mathematics Education (ACME) Conference, Mathematical Needs – Implications for 5–19 Mathematics Education, Royal Society, London, 2 March 2010. Online. Available: http://www.conservatives.com/News/Speeches/2010/03/Michael_Gove_We_will_end_the_political_control_of_A_levels.aspx (accessed: 28 May 2010).

Graham, D. and Tytler, D. (1993) *A Lesson for us all: The making of the National Curriculum,* London: Routledge.

Hagell, A. (2009) *Time trends in parenting and outcomes for young people*, London: Nuffield Foundation. (Changing Adolescence Programme briefing paper). Online. Available: http://www.nuffieldfoundation.org/fileLibrary/pdf/Nuffield_CAP_web_final.pdf (accessed: 4 June 2010).

Hammersley, M. (1997) Educational Research and Teaching: A Response to David Hargreaves' TTA Lecture. *British Educational Research Journal*, 23 (2) April, 141–161.

Hampden-Turner, C. and Trompenaars, F. (1993) *The Seven Cultures of Capitalism: Value systems for creating wealth in the United States, Japan, Germany, France, Britain, Sweden and the Netherlands,* New York: Currency/Doubleday.

Hannath, S. (2000) 'Hope for a new humane reign', *The Times Educational Supplement*. 10 November: 18n (letter). Online. Available: http://www.tes.co.uk/article.aspx?storycode=340520 (accessed: 4 June 2010).

Hardman, F., Smith, F. and Wall, K. (2003) Interactive whole class teaching in the National Literacy Strategy, *Cambridge Journal of Education*, 33 (2): 197–215.

Hargreaves, D. H. (1967) *Social Relations in a Secondary School,* London: Routledge & Kegan Paul.

—— (1996) *Teaching as a Research-Based Profession: Possibilities and prospects*, London: Teacher Training Agency.

—— (1997) In defence of research for evidenced-based teaching: A rejoinder to Martyn Hammersley. *British Educational Research Journal*, 23 (4): 405–419.

—— (1999) The knowledge creating school, *British Journal of Educational Studies,* 47 (2): 122–144.

Hargreaves, L., Cunningham, M., Everton, T., Hansen, A., Hopper, B., McIntyre, D., Oliver, C., Pell, T., Rouse, M. and Turner, P. (2007) *The Status of Teachers and the Teaching Profession: Views from Inside and Outside the Profession,* Evidence Base of the Final Report of the Teacher Status Project. London: Department for Education and Skills. (Research Report; RR 831B). Online. Available: http://www.dcsf.gov.uk/research/data/uploadfiles/RR831B%20r.pdf (accessed: 4 June 2010).

Hargreaves, L., Moyles, J., Merry, R., Patterson, F., Pell, A. and Esarte-Sarries, V. (2003) How do primary school teachers define and implement interactive teaching in the National Literacy Strategy in England?, *Research Papers in Education,* 18 (3): 217–236.

Harlen, W. and James, M. (1997) Assessment and Learning: Differences and relationships between formative and summative assessment, *Assessment in Education*, 4 (3): 365–379.

Harris, J. R. (1998; rev edn. 2009) *The Nurture Assumption: Why children turn out the way they do,* New York: Free Press.

Hess, F. (2003) *A License to Lead? A New Leadership Agenda for America's Schools.* Wahington, DC: Progressive Policy Institute (21st Century Schools Project). Online. Available: http://www. ppionline.org/documents/New_Leadership_0103.pdf (accessed: 4 June 2010).

Hillage, J., Pearson, R., Anderson, A. and Tamkin, P. (1998) *Excellence in Research on Schools,* Sudbury: Department for Education and Employment. (Research Report; 74) Online. Available: http://www.dcsf.gov.uk/research/data/uploadfiles/RR74.pdf (accessed: 25 May 2010).

Hogan, D. and Gopinathan, S. (2008) Knowledge management, sustainable innovation and pre-service education in Singapore, Special Issue, *Teachers & Teaching.* 14 (4): 369–384.

House of Commons. Health Committee. Department of Health and Home Office (2003) *The Victoria Climbié Inquiry: Report of an inquiry by Lord Laming,* London: The Stationery Office. (Cm; 5730). Online. Available: http://publications.everychildmatters.gov.uk/eOrdering-Download/CM-5730PDF.pdf (accessed: 4 June 2010).

House of Commons. Children, Schools and Families Committee (2008) *The Department for Children, Schools and Families and The Children's Plan: Second Report of Session 2007–08: Report, Together with Formal Minutes, Oral and Written Evidence.* London: The Stationery Office. (HC 213) Online. Available http://www.publications.parliament.uk/pa/cm200708/cmselect/cmchilsch/213/213.pdf (accessed: 25 May 2010).

House of Commons. Children, Schools and Families Committee (2010a) *From Baker to Balls: The foundations of the education system: Ninth report of session 2009–10: Report Together With Formal Minutes and Oral Evidence.* London: The Stationery Office. (HC 422, Ev .16) Online. Available http://www.publications.parliament.uk/pa/cm200910/cmselect/cmchilsch/422/422.pdf (accessed: 25 May 2010).

House of Commons. Children, Schools and Families Committee (2010b) *School Accountability: first report of session 2009–10. Vol. I Report, together with formal minutes,* London: The Stationery Office. (HC 88–I). Online. Available: http://www.publications.parliament.uk/pa/cm200910/cmselect/cmchilsch/88/88i.pdf (accessed: 28 May 2010).

House of Commons. Childrens, Schools and Families Committee (2010c) *Training of Teachers: fourth report of session 2009–10. Vol.II Oral and written evidence,* London: The Stationery Office. (HC 277–II). Online. Available: http://www.publications.parliament.uk/pa/cm200910/cmselect/cmchilsch/275/275ii.pdf (accessed: 28 May 2010).

House of Commons. Education and Skills Committee. (2007) *The Work of Ofsted: Sixth report of session 2006–07: report together with formal minutes, oral and written evidence*, London: The stationery Office (HC 165). Online. Available: http://www.publications.parliament.uk/pa/cm200607/cmselect/cmeduski/165/165.pdf (accessed: 28 May 2010).

House of Commons. Health Committee (2003) *The Victorial Climbieè Inquiry Report: Sixth report of session 2002–03: Report with formal minutes together with oral evidence,* London: The Stationery Office. (HC 570). Online: Available: http://www.publications.parliament.uk/pa/cm200203/cmselect/cmhealth/570/570.pdf (accessed: 4 June 2010).

Howson, G. (2002) What mathematics for all? in S. N. Bramall and J. White (2000) *Why Learn Maths?*, Bedford Way Papers, London: Institute of Education.

Hutchings, M., Seeds, K., Coleman, N., Harding, C. Mansaray, A., Maylor, U., Minty, S., and Pickering, E. (2009) *Aspects of School Workforce Remodelling: Strategies used and impact on workload and standards*, London: Department for Children, Schools and Families. (Research Report – DCSF-RR153). Online. Available: http://www.dcsf.gov.uk/research/data/uploadfiles/DCSF-RR153.pdf (accessed: 4 June 2010).

Hyman, P. (2005) 1 *out of 10: From Downing Street vision to classroom reality*, London: Vintage.

Impact Assessment (IA) (2010) The Academies Bill, The Department for Education. 26 May. http://www.education.gov.uk/~/medial/files/lacuna/academiesbillimpactassessment.ashx (accessed: 15 June 2010)

Jackson, B. and Marsden, D. (1962) *Education and the Working Class: Some general themes raised by a study of 88 working-class children in a northern industrial city*, London: Routledge & Kegan Paul.

Jackson, P.W. (1968) *Life in Classrooms*, New York: Holt, Rinehart & Winston. (Re-issued with new introduction: New York; London: Teachers College, Columbia University, 1990).

Jencks, C. S., Smith, M., Ackland, H., Bane, M. J., Cohen, D., Gintis, H., Heyns, B. and Micholson, S. (1973) *Inequality: A reassessment of the effect of family and schooling in America*, New York: Basic Books.

Johnson, S. and Bell, J. (1985) Evaluating and predicting survey efficiency using generalisability theory, *Journal of Educational Measurement*, 22 (2): 107–119.

Judd, J. (1999) Education adviser resigns after rows, *The Independent*, 18 March: 5. Online. Available: http://www.independent.co.uk/news/education-adviser-resigns-after-rows-1081297.html (accessed: 4 June 2010).

Kincheloe, J. and Hayes, K. (eds.) (2006) Metropedagogy: Power, justice and the urban classroom, *Bold Visions in Educational Research*, vol. 3. Rotterdam: Sense Publishers.

Kliebard, H. (1986) *The Struggle for the American Curriculum, 1893–1958,* London: Routledge & Kegan Paul.

Kupiainen, S., Hautamäki, J. and Karjalainen, T. (2009) *The Finnish Education System and PISA*, Helsinki: Ministry of Education. Online. Available: http://www.minedu.fi/export/sites/default/OPM/Julkaisut/2009/liitteet/opm46.pdf (accessed: 4 June 2010).

Lamb, B. (2009) *Lamb Inquiry: Special Educational Needs and Parental Confidence: Report to the Secretary of State on the Lamb Inquiry Review of SEN and Disability Information.* London: Department for Children, Schools and Families. Online. Available at: http://www.dcsf.gov.uk/lambinquiry/downloads/8553-lamb-inquiry.pdf (accessed: 25 May 2010).

Lamb, B. (2009) *Inspection, Accountability and School Improvement: Report of the Lamb Inquiry to the Secretary of State,* London: Department for Children, Schools and Family. Online. Available: http://www.dcsf.gov.uk/lambinquiry/downloads/LAMB%20INQUIRY%20Inspection%20FINAL.pdf (accessed: 28 May 2010).

Lawleor, S. (1998) *The Correct Core: Simple curricula for English, maths and science*, London: Centre for Policy Studies. (Policy Study; 93). Online. Available: http://www.cps.org.uk/cps_catalog/CPS_assets/448_ProductPreviewFile.pdf (accessed: 4 June 2010).

Lawton, D. (1975) *Class, Culture and the Curriculum*, London: Routledge & Kegan Paul.

Layard, R., Dunn, J. and The Panel of The Good Childhood Inquiry (2009) *A Good Childhood: Searching for values in a competitive age*. London: Penguin.

Learmonth, J. (2000) *Inspection: what's in it for schools?*, London: RoutledgeFalmer.

Leeuw, F. (2001) *Reciprocity and the Evaluation of Educational Quality: Assumptions and reality checks*. Keynote paper for the European Union Congress, Karlstat, Sweden, April 2–4. Reproduced as: Reciprocity and educational evaluations by European inspectorates: assumptions and reality checks. *Quality in Higher Education*, 8 (2): 137–149.

Levin, B. (2005) *Governing Education*. Toronto: University of Toronto Press.

Linn, R.L., Baker, E.L. and Dunbar, S.B. (1991) Complex performance-based assessment: Expectations and validation criteria, *Educational Researcher*, 20 (8): 15–21.

MacBeath, J. (2006) *School Inspection and Self Evaluation: Working with the new relationship*. London: Routledge.

MacBeath, J., Boyd, B. and Rand, J. (1956) *Schools Speak for Themselves: Towards a framework for self-evaluation*, London: National Union of Teachers. Online. Available: http://www.teachers. org.uk/files/active/0/schools.pdf (accessed: 4 June 2010).

MacBeath, J. (1999) *Schools Must Speak for Themselves: The case for school self-evaluation*, London: Routledge; National Union of Teachers.

MacBeath, J., Gray, J., Cullen, J., Frost, D., Steward, S., and Swaffield, S. (2006) *Schools on the Edge: Responding to challenging circumstances*, London: Paul Chapman Publishing

Mansell, W. (2007) *Education by Numbers: The Tyranny of Testing*, London: Politico's Publishing

Marsden, D. and Jackson, B. (1962) *Education and the Working Class*, London: Routledge & Kegan Paul.

McIntyre, D. (2005) Bridging the gap between research and practice, *Cambridge Journal of Education*, 35 (3): 357–382

Milne, J. (2007) Return of the Gala Queen. *Times Educational Supplement*, no.4747, 27 July, p. 14. Online. Available: http://www.tes.co.uk/article.aspx?storycode=2414501 (accessed: 25 May 2010).

Mongon, D. and Chapman, C. (2008) *Successful Leadership for Promoting the Achievement of White Working Class Pupils: Report*. Nottingham: National College for School Leadership. (Research project jointly sponsored by the National Union of Teachers and National College for School Leadership). Online. Available at: http://www.nationalcollege.org.uk/docinfo?i d=17405&filename=successful-leadership-for-promoting-full-report.pdf (accessed: 25 May 2010).

Morris, H. (1925) *The Village College. Being a Memorandum on the Provision of Educations and Social Facilities for the Countryside, with Special Reference to Cambridgeshire*, Cambridge: Cambridge University Press.

Mortimore, P., Lewis, D., Stoll, L., Sammons, P. and Ecob, R. (1998) *School Matters: The junior years,* London; Wells, Som.: Open Books.

National Foundation for Educational Research (NFER) (2007). *Evaluation of the Impact of Section 5 Inspections*, Slough: NFER.

National Union of Teachers (NUT) (1990) *A Strategy for the Curriculum*, London: National Union of Teachers.

Organisation for Economic Co-operation and Development (OECD) (2007) *Child Well Being in Rich Countries,* Paris: OECD.

—— (2009a) *Evaluating and Rewarding the Quality of Teachers' International Practices*, Paris: OECD.

—— (2009b) *Doing Better for Children*, Paris: OECD.

Ofsted (1996) *The Annual Report of Her Majesty's Chief Inspector of Schools: Standards and quality in education 1994–95*, London: Her Majesty's Stationary Office. Online. Available: http://

www.ofsted.gov.uk/Ofsted-home/Publications-and-research/Browse-all-by/Annual-Report/1992–95/Annual-Report-of-Her-Majesty-s-Chief-Inspector-of-Schools-standards-and-quality-in-education-1994–95 (accessed: 4 June 2010).

——(1999a) *Handbook for Inspecting Schools: Primary and nursery schools: With guidance on self-evaluation*, London: The Stationery Office.

——(1999b) *Handbook for Inspecting Schools: Secondary schools: With guidance on self-evaluation*, London: The Stationery Office.

——(1999c) *Handbook for Inspecting Schools: Special schools and pupil referral units: With guidance on self-evaluation*, London: The Stationery Office.

——(2002) *The Curriculum in Successful Primary Schools*. London: Ofsted. Online. Available: http://www.ofsted.gov.uk/Ofsted-home/Publications-and-research/Browse-all-by/Education/Key-stages-and-transition/Key-Stage-1/The-curriculum-in-successful-primary-schools (accessed: 9 June 2010).

—— (2006) *Creative Partnerships: Initiative and Impact,* London: Office for Standards in Education. Online. Available: http://www.ofsted.gov.uk/Ofsted-home/Publications-and-research/Browse-all-by/Education/Leadership/Management/Creative-Partnerships-initiative-and-impact (accessed: 4 June 2010).

—— (2009a) *New Inspection System to Improve Outcomes for Pupils*, London: Ofsted. (Ref no.: NR – 2009–32, 12 June). Online. Available: http://www.ofsted.gov.uk/Ofsted-home/News/Press-and-media/2009/June/New-inspection-system-to-improve-outcomes-for-pupils (accessed: 28 May 2010).

—— (2009b) *Twenty Outstanding Primary Schools: Excelling against the odds*, London: Ofsted. Online. Available: http://www.ofsted.gov.uk/Ofsted-home/Publications-and-research/Browse-all-by/Documents-by-type/Thematic-reports/Twenty-outstanding-primary-schools-Excelling-against-the-odds (accessed: 4 June 2010).

Organisation for Co-operatioan and Development (2006) *Green at Fifteen? How fifteen year olds perform in environmental and geoscience*, Paris: OECD

Pinker, S (1999) *Words and Rules. The ingredients of language,* New York: HarperCollins Basic Books; London: Weidenfeld & Nicholson.

Plowden Report, The (1967) *Children and their Primary Schools,* A Report of the Central Advisory Council for Education (England). Vol 1, The Reports London: Her Majesty's Stationary Office.

Pont, B., Nusche, D. and Moorman, H. (2008) *Improving School Leadership. Vol. 1: Policy and Practice,* Paris: Organisation for Economic Co-Operation and Development.

Qualifications and Curriculum Authority (2003) *Creativity: Find it, promote it,* London: QCA.

Qualifications and Curriculum Authority (2004) *Creativity: Find it, promote it: Promoting pupils' creative thinking and behaviour across the curriculum at Key Stages 1, 2 and 3: Practical materials for schools,* London: QCA. Online. Available: https://orderline.qcda.gov.uk/gempdf/1847211003. PDF (accessed: 8 June 2010).

Qualifications and Curriculum Authority (2005) *Creativity: Find it, promote it,* London: QCA. (Video pack).

Rasch, G. (1966) An item analysis which takes individual differences into account, *British Journal of Mathematical and Statistical Psychology*, 19 (1): 49–57.

Reynolds, D. (1995) The Effective School: An Inaugural Lecture. *Evaluation and Research in Education*, 9 (2): 57–75.

Reynolds, D. and Farrell, S. (1996) *Worlds Apart? A review of international surveys of educational achievement involving England,* London: Ofsted.

Richards, C. (1997) *Primary Educational Standards and Ofsted: Towards a more authentic conversation,*

Coventry: Centre for Research in Elementary and Primary Education (CREPE), University of Warwick. (CREPE Occasional Papers).

Riley, K. (1998) *Whose School is it Anyway?*, London: Falmer Press

Rutter, M., Maughan, B., Mortimore, P., Ouston, T. (1979) *Fifteen Thousand Hours: Secondary schools and their effects on children,* London; Wells, Som.: Open Books.

Ryan, C. (2009) In a crisis, you still can't reach a social worker, *The Independent,* 25 June, p. 4. Online. Available at: http://www.independent.co.uk/news/education/schools/conor-ryan-in-a-crisis-you--still-cant-reach-a-social-worker-1716788.html (accessed: 25 May 2010).

Sammons, P., Sylva, K., Melhuish, E., Siraj-Blatchford, I., Taggert, B., Barreau, S. and Grabbe, Y. (2008) *Influences in Children's Development and Progress in Key Stage 2,* London: Department for Children, Schools and Families. (Effective Pre-school and Primary 3–11 Project (EPPE 3–11)) (Research Report DCSF-RR028). Online. Available: http://www.dfes.gov.uk/research/data/uploadfiles/DCSF-RR028.pdf (accessed: 28 May 2010).

Scheerens, J. and Bosker, R. (1997) *The Foundations of Educational Effectiveness,* Oxford: Pergamon.

Simon, B. (1981) Why no pedagogy in England? In B. Simon and W. Taylor (eds.) *Education in the Eighties: The central issues,* London: Batsford, pp. 124–145.

—— (1994) *The State of Educational Change: Essays in the history of education and pedagogy*, London: Lawrence & Wishart.

Smith, M. (2006) The First Term of the New Inspection Arrangements. Speech delivered, Lowry Centre, Manchester, 25 January. Online. Available: http://www.ofsted.gov.uk/layout/set/print/Ofsted-home/Publications-and-research/Browse-all-by/Education/Leadership/Governance/Speech-by-Maurice-Smith-HMCI-the-first-term-of-the-new-inspection-arrangements (accessed: 7 June 2010).

Smith, R. (2000) About space, in P. Dhillon and P. Standish (eds.) *Lyotard: just education*, London: Routledge, 125–139.

Smithers, R. (2000) Fear forcing teachers to quit, *The Guardian,* 2 August: p. 7. Online: Available: http://www.guardian.co.uk/uk/2000/aug/02/education.schools1 (accessed: 4 June 2010).

Stannard, J. and Huxford, L. (2007) *The Literacy Game: The Story of the National Literacy Strategy*, London: Routledge.

Stobart, G. (2001) How Can Educational Assessment Improve Learning? Paper presented at the International Association for Educational Assessment 27th Annual Conference, *The Future and Challenges of educational Assessment in the 21st Century,* Rio de Janeiro, Brazil, 6–11 May.

Stringfield S. (1995) Attempting to enhance students learning through innovative programs: The case for schools evolving into High Reliability Organisations, *School Effectiveness & School Improvement,* 6 (1): 67–96

Sutherland, Lord Inquiry (2008) *The Sunderland Inquiry: An Independent Inquiry into the delivery of national Curriculum tests in 2008: A Report to Ofqual and the Secretary of State for Children, Schools and Families,* London: The Stationery Office. Online. Available: http://www.official-documents.gov.uk/document/hc0809/hc00/0062/0062.pdf (accessed: 4 June 2010).

Swaffield, S. (2009) Support and challenge for headteachers, University of Cambridge, Unpublished PhD work in progress.

Swaffield, S. and MacBeath, J. (2005) School self evaluation and the role of the critical friend, *Cambridge Journal of Education,* 35 (2): 239–252.

Sylva, K., Melhuish, E., Sammons, P., Siraj-Blatchford, I. and Taggart, B. (eds.) (2010) *Early Childhood Matters: Evidence from the Effective Pre-school and Primary Education Project,* London: Routledge.

The Coalition; our programme for government. Cabinet Office. 22 Whitehall, London SW1 2AH. May 2010. http://www.cabinetoffice.gov.uk/(accessed: 15 June 2010).

Training and Development Agency (2009) *Strategy for the Professional Development of the Children's Workforce in Schools 2009–12*, London: TDA. Online. Available: http://www.tda.gov. uk/upload/resources/pdf/p/professional%20development%20strategy_2009–12.pdf (accessed: 4 June 2010).

Tomlinson, J. (1992) Retrospect on Ruskin: Prospect on the nineties, in M. Williams., R. Dougherty and F. Banks (eds.) *Continuing the Education Debate*, London: Cassell, pp. 43–53.

Tomlinson, S. (2005) *Education in a Post-welfare Society*, 2nd ed., Maidenhead: Open University Press.

Tooley, J. and Darby, D. (1998) *Educational Research: A Critique: A Survey of Published Educational Research*. London: Office for Standards in Education. (Tooley Report). Online. Available: http://www.ofsted.gov.uk/Ofsted-home/Publications-and-research/Browse-all-by/ Education/Leadership/Governance/Educational-research-a-critique-the-Tooley-report (accessed: 25 May 2010).

Tymms, P. and Merrell, C. (2007) *Standards and Quality in English Primary Schools Over Time*, Cambridge: University of Cambridge, Faculty of Education. (Primary Review Research Survey 4/1). Online. Available: http://www.primaryreview.org.uk/Downloads/Int_ Reps/2.Standards_quality_assessment/Primary_Review_Tymms_Merrell_4–1_briefing_ Standards_Quality_-_National_evidence_071102.pdf (accessed: 27 May 2010).

UNICEF. Innocenti Research Centre (2007) *Child Poverty in Perspective: An overview of child well being in rich countries. A comprehensive assessment and well-being of children and adolescents in economically advanced nations*, Florence: UNICEF Innocenti Research Centre. (Inncoenti Report Card; 7) Online. Available: http://www.unicef-irc.org/publications/pdf/rc7_eng.pdf (accessed: 7 June 2010).

Watkins, P. (1993) Book review: A lesson for us all, *Headlines: Journal of the Secondary Heads' Association* (SHA), 11: 65–66.

Webb, R. and Vulliamy, G. (1996) *Roles and Responsibilities in the Primary School: Changing demands, changing practices*, Buckingham: Open University Press.

—— (2007) Changing Classroom Practice at Key Stage 2: the Impact of New Labour's national strategies, *Oxford Review of Education*, 33 (5): 561–580.

White, J. (ed.) (2004) *Rethinking the Curriculum: Values, aims and purposes*. London: RoutledgeFalmer.

—— (2005) *The Curriculum and the Child: The selected works of John White*, London: Routledge. (World Library of Educationalists Series).

Whitty, G. (2009) Evaluating Blair's educational legacy? Some comments on the special issue of Oxford Review of Education, *Oxford Review of Education*, 35 (2): 267–280.

Whitty, G. (2006) Education(al) research and education policy making: Is conflict inevitable? *British Educational Research Journal*, 32 (2): 159–176.

Wiliam, D. (2001) *Level Best? Levels of attainment in national curriculum assessment*, London: Association of Teachers and Lecturers. Online. Available: http://arrts.gtcni.org.uk/gtcni/ bitstream/2428/56215/1/Level%20best.pdf (accessed: 4 June 2010); http://www.aaia.org. uk/pdf/2001DYLANPAPER4.PDF (accessed: 4 June 2010).

Wilkin, A., Kinder, K., White, R., Atkinson, M. and Doherty, P. (2003) *Towards the Development of Extended Schools*. Nottingham: Department for Education and Skills. (Research Report; 408) Online. Available at: http://www.dcsf.gov.uk/research/data/uploadfiles/RR408.pdf (accessed: 25 May 2010).

Willis, P. (1977) *Learning to Labour: How working class kids get working class jobs*, Farnborough, Hants: Saxon House.

Woodhead, C. (2002) *Class War: The state of British education*, London: Little, Brown.

Yair, G. (2000) Educational battlefields in America: The tug of war over students' engagement with instruction, *Sociology of Education*, 73 (4): 247–269.

Younge, G. (2000). The day of reckoning: nothing strikes fear into a teachers' heart like the news that the inspectors are coming: last month all 12 teachers at a south London primary threw in the towel after receiving a bad resport, *The Guardian*, 3 July: p. 2. Online. Available: http://www.guardian.co.uk/education/2000/jul/03/schools.comment (accessed: 4 June 2010).

Index